CECIL COUNTY, MARYLAND MARRIAGE LICENSES
1777 - 1840

The Captain Jeremiah Baker Chapter
Daughters of the American Revolution

CECIL COUNTY COURT HOUSE, ELKTON, MARYLAND

CECIL COUNTY, MARYLAND MARRIAGE LICENSES

1777 - 1840

Copied by
The Captain Jeremiah Baker Chapter
Daughters of the American Revolution

Originally published by
The Captain Jeremiah Baker Chapter
Daughters of the American Revolution
Elkton, Maryland, 1928

Reprinted by
Genealogical Publishing Co., Inc.
Baltimore, Maryland, 1974, 1976

Library of Congress Catalog Card Number 73-16489

Reprinted for Clearfield Company by
Genealogical Publishing Company
Baltimore, Maryland, 2015

ISBN 978-0-8063-0596-7

This Book is dedicated with deepest appreciation
of her aid and counsel,
To the Memory of Its First Regent,
MRS. CORDELIA ANNA SIMMONS
By
The Captain Jeremiah Baker Chapter
Daughters of the American Revolution

		MAN		WOMAN	MINISTER
1777					
July	23	William Hewston	to	Isabel Crookshanks	William Thomson
"	29	James Steel	to	Elizabeth Mahaffey	William Thomson
"	30	Nathan Phillips	to	Elizabeth Kankey	William Thomson
Aug.	5	Jacob Pettit	to	Ann Green	William Thomson
"	5	John McCutchon	to	Elizabeth Hathorn	William Thomson
"	15	Francis Ross	to	Mary Andrews	William Thomson
"	21	Samuel Morris	to	Mary Walmsley	William Thomson
Sept.	22	Isaac Grear	to	Martha McCracken	William Thomson
"	24	William Hugg	to	Mary Flintham	William Thomson
Oct.	8	John Sheperd	to	Mary Hudson	William Thomson
Nov.	4	Archibald Boggs	to	Sarah Sutton	William Thomson
"	16	James Thackery	to	Ann Hart	William Thomson
"	18	John Cunningham	to	Elizabeth Caldwell	William Thomson
"	20	John Crouch	to	Sarah Hull	William Thomson
"	20	Adam Ross	to	Jane Chambers	William Thomson
"	20	John Hill	to	Sarah Naley	William Thomson
Dec.	8	Jessey Comegyes	to	Mary Everyt	William Barrell
"	8	William Booth	to	Rosannah Dougherty	William Thomson
"	22	William Drake Penington	to	Mary Hutchison	William Barroll
"	28	Garratt Kirk	to	Sarah Wingate	William Barroll
1778					
Jan.	4	Fergus Clements	to	Elizabeth Grier	William Thomson
"	5	Gilbert Nowland	to	Esther Hollings	William Barroll
"	14	James Trew	to	Grace McKnight	William Thomson
"	22	Rhubin Bateman	to	Rebecca Gears	William Barroll
"	23	William Thomas	to	Mary Ball	William Thomson
"	25	John Stoops	to	Susannah Ward	William Barroll
"	26	Jesse Porter	to	Rachel Cann	William Barroll
Feb.	2	Peter Hukill	to	Mary Eliason	William Thomson
"	5	John Roberts	to	Ann Severson	William Barroll
"	12	Henry Hollingsworth	to	Jane Evans	William Thomson
"	13	Jacob Wood	to	Honour Kidney	William Thomson
"	17	John Knight	to	Prudence Reynolds	William Thomson
"	17	Spencer Beedle	to	Sarah Pearce	William Barroll
"	17	John Watts	to	Elizabeth Hattery	William Thomson
"	18	James Perry	to	Martha Gladen	William Thomson
"	21	William Brown	to	Mary Bowen	William Thomson
"	26	Henry Bulteal	to	Ann Anderson	William Thomson
"	27	John Andrewson	to	Jane Patterson	William Thomson
"	28	William Stoops	to	Rachel Ford	William Thomson
"	28	Denis Dempsey	to	Ann Ellice	William Thomson
Mar.	3	George Cother	to	Margaret McCluar	William Thomson
"	6	James Conner	to	Ann Johnson	William Thomson
"	10	John Layhua	to	Hannah Walker	William Thomson
"	17	Richard Hayes	to	Susannah Vansant	William Barroll
"	21	Elisha Johnson	to	Ann Baker	William Thomson
"	28	John McCloud	to	Ann Vanlear	William Thomson
"	30	Robert Hopkins	to	Fanny Crewil	William Thomson
"	31	Robert Cather	to	Hannah White	William Thomson
Apr.	5	John Craig	to	Mary Bryan	William Thomson
"	7	Samuel Bond	to	Elizabeth McVea	William Thomson
"	9	William Sproutt	to	Sarah Yorkson	William Barroll
"	18	Valentine Carpenter	to	Mary Barneby	William Thomson
"	22	John Watt	to	Elizabeth Colvin	William Thomson
"	30	Iliander Campball	to	Ann Simpers	William Thomson
"	30	James Criswell	to	Elizabeth Dean	William Thomson
May	3	George Simpers	to	Sarah Arrance	William Thomson
"	11	Robert Hawood	to	Sarah Maltwood	William Thomson
"	12	Charles McKinley	to	Catherine Smith	William Thomson
"	14	Samuel Crockett	to	Elizabeth Jackson	William Thomson

		MAN		WOMAN	MINISTER
"	16	Robert Biles	to	Elenear McArrin	William Thomson
"	16	John Roberts	to	Ann Wroth	William Thomson
"	19	James Wroth	to	Ann Severson	William Thomson
"	19	Thomas Horn	to	Ann Shepard	William Thomson
"	20	Archable McIntier	to	Ann Simmins	William Thomson
"	24	John Boyed	to	Mary McBurney	William Thomson
June	8	John Bolding	to	Mary Love	William Thomson
"	9	James McBride	to	Mary Pew	William Thomson
"	13	William Miller	to	Rebecca Bradford	William Thomson
"	16	Joseph Moss	to	Jemima Penington	William Thomson
"	23	Walter Taler	to	Ann Caughum	William Thomson
July	14	James Andrews	to	Martha Blake	William Thomson
"	28	Richard Lewis	to	Ann Arrants	William Thomson
Aug.	3	John Miller	to	Margaret McCray	William Thomson
"	5	James Baylay	to	Jane Harkness	William Thomson
"	5	Benjamin Severson	to	Ann Wroth	William Thomson
Aug.	6	Samuel Bayard	to	Ann Lawrence	William Thomson
"	9	John Ryan	to	Pricilla Carr	William Thomson
"	11	Alexander Dougherty	to	Jane McCan	William Thomson
"	11	Michael Smith	to	Rebecca Brooks	William Thomson
"	11	Joseph Lark	to	Sarah Reynolds	William Thomson
"	12	William Cook	to	Hannah Hasa	William Thomson
"	13	Alexander Work	to	Elizabeth Johnson	Willian Thomson
"	20	Phillip Kennedy	to	Martha Guthery	William Thomson
"	24	William Young	to	Ann Brown	William Thomson
Sept.	7	James McTwilley	to	Isabella McCon	William Thomson
"	10	John Reynolds	to	Rachel Cowgale	William Thomson
"	11	Thomas Hanson	to	Susannah Foster	William Thomson
"	30	Samuel Kilpatrick	to	Rebecca Campbell	William Thomson
Oct.	1	Richard Sandobersey	to	Feby Hariss	William Thomson
"	8	Hackrey McGowne	to	Ann Pettit	William Thomson
Oct.	11	Jehu Brown	to	Sarah Garter	William Thomson
"	23	William Veazey	to	Mary Louttit	Thompson
"	27	Lewin Perry	to	Debrah Barnett	Thompson

A LIST MADE TO THE 1ST NOVEMBER, 1778

Oct.	29	John McToy	to	Mary Banebridge	Thompson
Nov.	1	Thomas Kenb	to	Ann Ralston	Thompson
"	2	Solomon Blake	to	Mary Dougherty	Thompson
Nov.	7	S. James Kidman	to	Margaret Leright	Thompson
"	10	William Jones	to	Sarah Lynch	Thompspn
"	15	Wm. Gibson	to	Mary Mitchell	Thompson
"	18	Samuel Coulter	to	Sarah Foster	Thompson
"	21	Richard Thomas	to	Mary Read	Thomson
"	24	Thomas Ferguson	to	Sarah Oldham	Thomson
Dec.	2	John Sulvan	to	Margaret Kirk	Thomson
"	7	John Kirk	to	Ann Parsley	Thomson
"	9	Daniel Gonce	to	Mary Lowery	Thomson
"	21	James Barckley	to	Margaret Finley	Thomson
"	23	Alexander McMun	to	Agnes Jake	Thomson
"	30	George Lasly	to	Amelia Johnson	Thomson
	1779				
Jan.	2	Tesey Manley	to	Rachel George	Thomson
"	3	Edward Parsley	to	Rebecca Walmsley	Thompson
"	4	John Etherington	to	Sarah Ware	Thomson
Feb.	1	Morrico Jobe	to	Lidya Bond	Thomson
"	10	William Ward	to	Rachel Ricketts	Thomson
"	13	Isaac Hooper	to	Jane Crage	Thomson
"	14	Francis Curtis, Esq.	to	Elizabeth Forester	Thompson
"	16	Thomas Stephens	to	Susannah Gynson	Thompson
"	23	John Cromwell	to	Ann Johnson	Thompson

		MAN		WOMAN	MINISTER
Mar.	7	Isaac Hylan	to	Mary Johnson	Thompson
"	8	John George	to	Frances Clark	Thompson
"	8	James Spear	to	Mary Marquiss	Thompson
"	8	Amos Evans	to	Sarah Wood	Thompson
"	11	Seward White	to	Grace Brady	Thomson
"	13	Lewis Price	to	Mary Roberts	Thomson
"	16	Richard Bowen	to	Tammy Ricketts	Thomson
"	27	Samuel Beaty	to	Ann Bryan	Thomson
"	29	Robert Knox	to	Lidia Williams	Thompson
Apr.	1	John Meray	to	Sarah Wakefield	Thomson
"	1	Herman Arrants	to	Francina Price	Thomson
"	2	Jacob Vanhorn	to	Mary Mansfield	Thomson
"	3	Thomas Bird	to	Sarah Beedle	Thomson
"	6	William Edge	to	Catharine Connor	Thomson
"	12	William Work	to	Ann Meeck	Thomson
"	17	John Benjamin	to	Elizabeth Winchester	Thomson
"	27	Christopher Irvine	to	Mary Rudolph	Thompson
May	2	Stephen Rich	to	Jane Blackburn	Thompson
"	8	William Brown	to	Rebecca Hendrickson	Thomson
"	16	James McCullough	to	Jane Green	Thomson
"	16	John Fisher	to	Ann Robinot	Thomson
"	17	John Wood	to	Elizabeth Watson	Thomson
"	30	Wm. Pearce	to	Sarah Lynch	Thomson
June	9	John Corcoa	to	Jane Kincaid	Thomson
"	27	Thomas Gallaher	to	Bridget McBride	Thomson
July	10	George Harvey Campbell	to	Mary Roberts	Thompson
"	10	Robert Hart	to	Ann Hyland	Thompson
"	10	Morrie Moloney	to	Margaret Riely	Thompson
					NOT PAID
"	17	William Whittam	to	Angusta Heawking	Thompson
"	24	Maland Ely	to	Mary Sittor	Thompson
Aug.	1	Curtis Metcalf	to	Charity Sidwell	Thompson
"	3	Robert Wallace	to	Mary Chambers	Thompson
"	4	William Graw	to	Mary Knight	Thompson
"	18	James Reik	to	Hannah Horner	Thompson
"	27	Geo. M. Forester	to	Temperance Redgrave	Thompson
"	28	Thomas Gorrole	to	Hannah Crawford	Thompson
Sept.	8	John Holihan	to	Jane Campbell	Thompson
"		John Marquis, Jr.	to	Eleanor Meak	Thompson
"		James Mercer	to	Ann Othoson	Thompson
"	20	Ephraim Too (Lee)?	to	Susannah Walmsley	Thomson
"	21	James Campbell	to	Mary Morrice Tiledon	Thompson
Oct.	13	Robert Gilchrist	to	Elizabeth Maxwell	Thompson
"	29	George Neal	to	Jane Elliott	Thompson
Nov.	1	Thomas Coulson, Jr.	to	Ann Stump	Thompson
"	9	Robert Nesbit	to	Eleanor Lyon	Thompson
"	17	Thomas Ramsey	to	Elizabeth Aiken	Thompson
"	20	Robert Morrow	to	Jane Worth	Thompson
"	21	Elias Jeneas	to	Mary Donaley	Thomson
Dec.	22	Richard Barrinton	to	Catharine McGarvey	Thomson
"	29	Thomas Trimble	to	Jane Holland	Thompson
"	29	Joseph Carroll	to	Mary Hughes	Thompson
"	30	William Mackey	to	Mary Mackey	Thompson
1780					
Mar.	4	Francis Foster	to	Rebecca McConnell	Thompson
"	8	John Mackey	to	Jane Mackey	Thompson
"	8	Thomas Russell	to	Mary Wilkinson	Thompson
"	18	Brice McKeney	to	Jane Marton	Thompson
"	14	Wm. Bateman	to	Sarah Pearce	Thompson
"	17	John Pennington	to	Catherine Money	Thompson

	MAN		WOMAN	MINISTER
" 20	John Ore	to	Kezior Touchstone	Thompson
" 22	Wm. Field	to	Elizabeth Wood	Thompson
" 22	Andrew Crow	to	Susannah Laurenceson	Thompson
" 22	Stephen Phillips	to	Mary Baker	Thompson
"	Luke Teague	to	Rachel Kinsey	Thompson
Jan. 18	Edward Burris	to	Eleanor McMullan	Thompson
			OR ANY OTHER AUTHORITY	
" 20	Vachel Horry	to	Elizabeth Cosden	Thompson
" 21	James Nowland	to	Ann Hood	Thompson
" 23	Wm. Sears	to	Anna Couden	Thompson
" 29	Ralph Whitaker	to	Mary Shields	Thompson
Feb. 12	James Hukill	to	Millicent Manly	Thompson
" 16	John McKeown	to	Mary Winchester	Thompson
"	Philip Anto Hendrick	to	Elizabeth Lackland	Thompson
May 24	George Walsh	to	Ann Cameron	Thomson
" 31	William Patterson	to	Jane Callender	Thomson
June 8	Timothy Cummins	to	Rachel Pennington	Thomson
" 11	James North (Worth?)	to	Diana Platt	Thomson
" 11	Jesse Pierce (Price?)	to	Eleanor Ryan	Thomson
" 13	Benjamin Sappington	to	Rebecca Boothe	Thomson
" 20	John Phillips	to	Margaret McCallor	Thomson
July 6	Benjamin Walmsley	to	Rachel Money	Thomson
" 11	Nathaniel Piner	to	Hannah Bing	Thomson
" 11	William Hall	to	Catherine A. Walmsley	Thomson
" 26	James Crangle	to	Mary Jane Jay	Thomson
Aug. 6	Jesse Hukill	to	Sarah Miller	Thomson
" 10	Henry Miller, Jr.	to	Sarah Knox	Thomson
" 13	Thomas Mofill?	to	Margaret Atchison	Thomson
" 16	Robert Walmsley	to	Temperance Brewer	Thomson
" 23	George Greiner	to	Sarah Chick	Thomson
" 23	John Matherman	to	Catherine Satterly (Lafferty?)	Thomson
Sept. 2	Robert Rowland	to	Esther McCoy	Thomson
Oct. 11	Jeremiah Collings	to	Elizabeth Miller	Thomson
" 18	Alexander Boys	to	Margaret Robertson	Thomson
" 30	James Foster	to	Catherine Boyce	Thomson
" 31	Garrett Vansant	to	Edy Newlin	Thomson
Dec. 2	William Pearce	to	Amelia Taler	Thomson
" 6	Robert Armstrong	to	Elizabeth Wallace	Thomson
" 10	Samuel Ladd	to	Hester Walker?	Thomson
" 18	Stephen Sutton	to	Mary Patterson	Thomson
" 20	James Baxley	to	Sarah White	Thomson
" 29	William Dawson	to	Elizabeth Graves	Thomson
1781				
Jan. 1	James Davis	to	Sophia? Davis	Thomson
" 31	John Cooper	to	Ann Kankey	Thomson
Feb. 11	Sidney George	to	Ann Barrol	Thomson
" 13	Andrew Price	to	Sarah Cammell	Thomson
" 14	Robert Hamelton	to	Jane Jack	Thomson
" 19	Robert Young	to	Rebecca Taylor	Thomson
" 24	Noble Veasey	to	Elizabeth Biddle	Thomson
" 26	Wm. Arrants	to	Susannah Latham	Thomson
Mch. 11	Robert McCauley	to	Sina Baker	Thomson
" 24	Thomas Brookes Veasey	to	Mary Thompson	Thomson
Apr. 2	William Lusby	to	Camilia Roberts	Thomson
" 17	Anthony Pennington	to	Marthy Ryland	Thomson
" 20	Benjamin Bayard	to	Rachel Lawrence	Thomson
" 22	Michael Cosgrove	to	Ann Cammil	Thomson
" 24	Thomas Hoyt	to	Catherine Nowland	Thomson
May 19	Elisha Rogers	to	Rebecca Ferguson	Thomson
" 26	George Crage	to	Elizabeth Taylor	Thomson

	MAN		WOMAN	MINISTER
July 3	James Patterson	to	Rebecca Creswell	Thomson
" 25	Thomas Taylor	to	Deborah Leffler	Thomson
" 30	Jacob Jennings	to	Rebecca McCauley	Thomson
" 30	Ezekiel Veasey	to	Elizabeth Veasey	Thomson
" 31	Vincent Lockerman	to	Mary Chew Knight	Thomson
Aug. 1	William Stewart	to	Deborah Miller	Thomson
" 12	Joseph Pennington	to	Elizabeth Crouch	Thomson
" 18	James Crouch	to	Mary Jones	Thomson
" 23	John Sterrett	to	Sarah Finley	Thomson
" 22	William Killan?	to	Jane Miller	Thomson
" 29	Isaac Turner	to	Tabitha Chick	Thomson
Sept. 17	Robert Gibson	to	Martha Craig	Thomson
Oct. 7	James Daugherty	to	Mary Glasgow	Thomson
" 12	William Veasey	to	Sarah Lewis	Thomson
" 22	Ephram Gearvis	to	Elizabeth Huckin	Thomson
" 24	John Carr	to	Ann Caldwell	Thomson
Nov. 11	John Robinson	to	Ann Cather	Thomson
" 23	John Griffee	to	Ann Cammell	Thomson
Dec. 1	James Fagan	to	Catherine McCain	Thomson
" 19	Richard Hall	to	Sarah Corlett	Thomson
" 20	Peter Devine	to	Margaret Meale Neale?	Thomson
" 25	William Thackery	to	Mary Murser?	Thomson
" 26	John McClay	to	Rachel Groves	Thomson
1782				
Jan. 6	Jackson Lauferty	to	Eleanor Kid	Thomson
" 8	James McCollom	to	Margaret Reed	Thomson
" 17	Samuel McCullan	to	Margaret Brickton	Thomson
Feb. 20	John Ward	to	Elizabeth Pennington	Thomson
Mar. 1	William Parker?	to	Elizabeth Savin	Thomson
" 24	Nicholas Parizot	to	Sarah York	Thomson
Apr. 5	Everet Everson	to	Susanna Ward	Thomson
" 16	Noble Price	to	Catherine Walmsley	Thomson
" 20	Phillip Stoopes	to	Sarah Lland?	Thomson
" 23	Jacob Simpers	to	Milicent Mills	Thomson
" 31	Stephen Hair	to	Ann Bazil	Thomson
May 11	John Martin	to	Elizabeth Can	Thomson
" 21	David Wallace	to	Eleanor Alexander	Thomson
June 5	Morgan John Roberts	to	Sarah Ryland	Thomson
July 18	Alexander Livingston	to	Mary O'Brien	Thomson
Aug. 10	Thomas Empson	to	Letitia Simmons	Thomson
Oct. 1	Abner White	to	Margaret Johnson	Thomson
Nov. 11	William Brison	to	Mary Reynolds	Thomson
" 12	Henry Pennington	to	Sarah Hastings	Thomson
" 20	John Hamilton, Jr.	to	Francis Davis (Hughes)	Thomson
Dec. 5	Aaron Latham	to	Sarah Bryson	Thomson
" 18	William Humphrey	to	Elizabeth Cosden?	Thomson
" 24	William Comagys	to	Elizabeth Worthington Etherington	Thomson
" 31	Joackin Brackley	to	Martha Hagar	Thomson
1783				
Jan. 20	John Thomas Ricketts	to	Mary Barr	Thomson
Feb. 3	James Newill	to	Martha Wright	Thomson
" 20	Harry Glasford	to	Ann Reed	Thomson
" 28	Samuel Barrett	to	Catherine Barrett	Thomson
Mar. 24	Thomas Crouch	to	Mary Simpers	Thomson
Apr. 5	William Linton	to	Elizabeth Creswell	Thomson
" 15	John Lasley	to	Kazia Price	Thomson
" 16	John Crouch	to	Mary Hart	Thomson
" 21	William Terry	to	Elizabeth Johnson	Thomson
May 6	James Little	to	Mary Reynolds	Thomson
" 22	James Barnes	to	Rozanna Johnson	Thomson

MAN			WOMAN	MINISTER
"	26	Robert Lewite	to Rebecca Childon	Thomson
June	17	Nicholas Phillips	to Lydia Arnott	Thomson
"	25	Noble Boulden	to Mary Lowry	Thomson
July	25	John Allen	to Mary Allen	Thomson
Aug.	6	James Orick	to Hannah Slycer	Thomson
"	10	Abraham Cazier	to Elizabeth Crockett	Thomson
"	26	John Dennis	to Arramantha Harvey?	Thomson
Sept.	8	Robert Roberts	to Rebecca Aires	Thomson
Nov.	26	Harry Pearce	to Elizabeth Slytor	Thomson
"	28	William Beaston	to Elizabeth McDowell	Thomson
Dec.	2	John Theason	to Ann Comegys	Thomson
"	2	Robert Lyon	to Susannah Hall	Thomson
"	7	Robert Glasgow	to Elizabeth Kilpatrick	Thomson
Nov.	26	Henry Pearce	to Sarah Sluyter	Thompson
"	28	William Beaston	to Elizabeth McDowell	Thompson
Dec.	2	Joseph Reason	to Ann Comegys	Thompson
"	2	Robert Lyon	to Susannah Hall	Thompson
"	7	Robert Glasgow	to Elizabeth Kilpatrick	Thompson
1784				
Jan.	13	Nathaniel McCleland	to Elizabeth Wheatley	Thompson
"	14	Isaac Money	to Rachel Husley	Thompson
"	18	Richard Robinet	to Elizabeth Loyd	Thompson
Feb.	12	John Lee	to Naomi Cord	Thompson
"	14	William Richardson	to Ann Copper?	Thompson
"	19	John Davis	to Elizabeth Stogden	Thompson
Mar.	3	William Grimes	to Ann Norris	Thompson
"	7	John Bristow	to Rachel Thackery	Thompson
"	30	Andrew Beedle	to Mary Bouldin	Thompson
Apr.	4	John Lynch	to Margaret McClane	Thompson
"	11	Richard Biggs	to Sarah Price	Thompson
May	5	John Bailey	to Ann Hitchcock	Thompson
"	5	Augustine Beedle	to Mary Noble	Thompson
"	5	John Carr	to Sarah Nugent	Thompson
"	5	James Kirk	to Rachel Morgan	Thompson
"	15	William Jones	to Sarah Moore	Thompson
"	15	Thomas Cooper	to Rebecca Kankey	Thompson
"	18	Richard Bond, Jr.	to Mary Brumfield	Thompson
"	19	Abraham Broom	to Elizabeth Rumsey	Thompson
"	24	Robert Ewing	to Isabella Lissey	Thompson
"	25	Robert Barr	to Agnes Ferguson	Thompson
"	26	John Jackson	to Mary Ewing	Thompson
"	31	Phillip Bennett	to Amelia Brown	Thompson
June	3	James Mackey	to Catherine Mackey	Thompson
"	5	John Pennington	to Rebecca Price	Thompson
"	11	James Evans, Jr.	to Catherine Porter	Thompson
"	19	John Smith	to Rebecca Connelly	Thompson
"	29	John Chappell	to Mary Sappington	Thompson
July	3	Nathan Smith	to Ann Chew	Thompson
"	9	Bartholomew Lyons	to Mary Hawley	Thompson
"	15	Gideon Clark	to Hannah Hynson	Thompson
Aug.	4	James Roach	to Mary Barr (Widow)	Thompson
"	9	Hugh Mahaffey	to Mary Duff	Thompson
"	26	Edward Mitchell	to Ann Haley	Thompson
Oct.	9	James Mackey	to Sarah Wallace	Thompson
"	9	Amos Ewing	to Deborah Coulson	Thompson
"	13	Alexander Simpson	to Margaret Wilson	Thompson
"	18	William Foster	to Sarah Hill	Thompson
"	30	Samuel Marquiss	to Rachel Touchstone	Thompson
Nov.	19	William Ward	to Ann Veazey	Thompson
Dec.	1	Bartholomew Etherington	to Sarah Beedle	Thompson
"	1	Benjamin Hugg	to Rebecca Pearce	Thompson

MAN			WOMAN	MINISTER
" 7	Thomas Beedle	to	Rebecca Beedle	Thompson
" 5	Moses Patterson	to	Lydia Haines	Thompson
" 14	Dr. John H. Montgomery	to	Mary Currer	Thompson
" 22	Elijah Cole	to	Sarah Bouldin	Thompson
" 23	Thomas Bevans	to	Rachel Savin	Thompson
1785				
Jan. 8	William Leather	to	Jane Hill	Thompson
" 12	John C. Sutton	to	Iby? Murphy	Thompson
" 18	Stephen Owens	to	Elizabeth Harwood	Thompson
" 25	Nicholas Milburn	to	Jane Moody	Thompson
Feb. 17	Greenbury Dawkings	to	Rebecca Taggart	Thompson
Mar. 24	William Lowry	to	Sarah Aldridge	Thompson
" 27	John Craig	to	Rebecca Manley	Thompson
Apr. 6	Thomas Connor	to	Rebecca Sterrett	Thompson
" 2	Thomas Simpson	to	Sarah Scott	Thompson
" 27	Edward Savin	to	Elizabeth Mercer	Thompson
May 17	Thomas Pearce	to	Sarah Bayard	Thompson
" 25	George Reese	to	Ann Ryland	Thompson
" 31	James Bell	to	Jane Bell	Thompson
June 2	Isaac Rutter	to	Rachel Cavender	Thompson
" 21	Benjamin Cox	to	Millicent Etherington	Thompson
" 30	Lewis Johannah	to	Jane Nollow	Thompson
July 13	Elijah Lowry	to	Ann Savin	Thompson
" 13	John Sears	to	Mary Dutton	Thompson
" 20	Robert Calvert	to	Susannah Young	Thompson
Aug. 24	Samuel Beedle	to	Rebecca Sappington	Thompson
" 25	Jeremiah Lackland	to	Lydia Johnson	Thompson
Sept. 16	Joshua Meekins	to	Hannah Price	Thompson
Oct. 22	Benjamin Sappington	to	Elizabeth Wroth	Thompson
" 26	James Bouldin	to	Rebecca Thompson	Thompson
Nov. 30	James Cowardin	to	Rebecca Etherington	Thompson
" 30	Thomas Jones	to	Elizabeth Knight	Thompson
Dec. 26	William Howell	to	Ann Palmer	Wilmer
1786				
Jan. 3	William Wiely	to	Mary Harwood	Wilmer
" 9	Richard Hodgson	to	Sarah Ellis	Wilmer
" 9	Peregrine Hynson	to	Rebecca Ellis	Wilmer
" 9	Archibald Williams	to	Susannah Brookins	Wilmer
" 16	Benjamin Silvester	to	Eleanor Wallace	McCreary
" 18	Edward Price	to	Rebecca Etherington	McCreary
" 24	William Kinney	to	Mary McMillen	Monrow
" 28	Joseph Dickey	to	Rachel Collins	Monrow
Feb. 6	William Shields	to	Ann McCauley	Monrow
" 21	Andrew McClain	to	Margaret Anderson	Monrow
" 28	Robert Williams	to	Mary Kirkpatrick	G. Directions
Mar. 8	Lewis Roberts	to	Elizabeth Goodwin	G. Directions
" 8	Thomas Lisby	to	Araminta Roberts	G. Directions
" 15	John Stump	to	Hannah Stump	Wilmer
1785				
Nov. 30	John McCoy	to	Elizabeth Arbuckle	Latta
1786				
Mar. 15	William Hutchman	to	Ann Gillespie	Wilmer
" 21	Robert Smith	to	Ann McCrea	G. Directions
" 22	Samuel Neigley	to	Rebecca Pennington	G. Directions
" 22	John Ward	to	Sarah Walmsley	G. Directions
" 24	Isaac Belme	to	Ann Lambert	G. Directions
" 27	Seth Ruley	to	Eleanor Parsley	G. Directions
" 27	Charles Oar	to	Jane Lyon	Monrow
" 27	Samuel Keingsly	to	Barbara Miller	Monrow
" 28	David Marquiss	to	Lydia McNeal	G. Directions

	MAN		WOMAN	MINISTER
Apr. 2	Henry Pearce	to	Rebecca Clark	G. Directions
" 19	Spencer Etherington	to	Araminta Miller	G. Directions
" 25	Adam Wallace	to	Fanny Henderson	Smith
May 3	William Farris	to	Arenia Bravard	Creary
" 3	Allen Wiely	to	Mary Wood	Creary
" 10	Robert Campble	to	Elizabeth Brumfield	Burton
June 19	Anthony Smith	to	Mary Battey	G. Directions
Dec. 14	Hezekiah Ford	to	Sarah Lawrensen	Smith
" 21	Wilson Waters	to	Jean Montgomery	Monrow
Jan. 13	Robert Veazey Lewis	to	Mary Cunningham	Monrow
" 16	Edward Alexander	to	Susannah McCauley	Monrow
" 24	William Mauldin	to	Margery Hyland	Monrow
" 27	Noble (Harmon) Hamm?	to	Ann Hart	Monrow
" 27	Samuel Aldridge	to	Amelia Hyland	Monrow
June 23	William Beaston	to	Hester Price	G. Directions
July 11	Abraham Cazier	to	Mary Currier	Monrow
" 19	Jonathan Bowen	to	Mary Hall	Wilmer
Aug. 14	Edward Crouch	to	Elizabeth Latham	Wilmer
" 24	Robert Creswell	to	Mary Hartshorne	G. Directions
Sept. 2	Thomas Price	to	Margaret Smith	G. Directions
Oct. 6	Andrew Wilson	to	Ann McCoy	Monrow
" 20	Thomas McDowell	to	Rebecca McDowell	Monrow
" 24	Samuel Gilmore	to	Ann Ferguson	Lewis
" 31	George Rhea	to	Margaret Hill	Wilson
Nov. 9	Samuel Campbell	to	Sarah Coulter	Wilson
" 25	John Scott	to	Mary Bouching	Monrow
Dec. 20	Joshua George	to	Elizabeth B. Thompson	Wilmer
" 21	Abner Kirk	to	Sarah Chambers.	Monrow
1787				
Jan. 25	James Bevins	to	Catherine Price	Wilmer
" 25	James Bevins	to	Mary Bevins	Wilmer
" 27	James Craig	to	Gertrude Eliason	Wilson
Feb. 2	John Lynch	to	Mary Wilson	Wilmer
" 5	Alexander Nesbitt	to	Elizabeth Love	Wilmer
" 19	Jonathan Nesbitt	to	Elizabeth Ryan	Monrow
Mar. 12	John Finley	to	Margaret Rowland	Wilmer
" 21	Ephraim Price	to	Amey Simpers	Wilmer
Apr. 30	John McVey	to	Mary Shields	Wilmer
May 21	Felix Kirk	to	Susanna Robinson	Wilmer
" 24	Francis Brumfield	to	Elizabeth Creswell	Wilmer
" 26	Isaac Redgraves	to	Henrietta Cox	Wilmer
June 12	William McDonald	to	Sarah Shepherd	Coudon
" 14	Samuel Cowden	to	Jane Caurothers	Coudon
" 26	Moses Taylor	to	Hannah Lee	Coudon
July 18	William Loag	to	Elizabeth Gerish	Wilmer
" 19	Samuel McGill	to	Mary Palmer	Wilmer
" 26	Nathan Ireland	to	Sarah Price?	Wilmer
Sept. 17	Pasmore Meve Moore?	to	Eleanor McCullough	Coudon
" 26	Samuel Pippen	to	Letitia Wilson	Coudon
Oct. 3	Benjamin Severson	to	Elizabeth Pennington	Wilmer
" 9	Robert McCormick	to	Sarah Beazley	Coudon
" 16	Richard Simpers	to	Rose Christfield	Wilmer
" 13	Robert Ratliff?	to	Mary Kirk	Coudon
" 29	Nathaniel Dawson	to	Ann Beaston	Coudon
Nov. 12	Samuel Bristow	to	Mary Irwin	Coudon
" 12	John Ginna	to	Hannah Reynolds	Coudon
" 12	Robert Walmsley, Jr.	to	Margaret Gooding	Wilmer
Jan. 14	William Jefferys	to	Mary Miller	Wilmer
" 16	Thomas P. Sappington	to	Hester Reyland	Wilmer
Nov. 17	John Williams	to	Sarah Boyd	Coudon
" 24	John Callender	to	Elizabeth Swink	Coudon

MAN		WOMAN	MINISTER
Dec. 7 John Caruthers	to	Elizabeth Beard	Coudon
" 20 John Fulton	to	Rachel Love	Coudon
" 25 Elijah Rogers	to	Elizabeth Ferguson	Coudon
1788			
Feb. 7 James Batton	to	Mary Conway	Coudon
Mar. 8 Elijah Kirk	to	Mary Allen	Coudon
" 25 John Campbell	to	Hannah Piner	Coudon
Apr. 1 James McGinnas	to	Ann Forden	Coudon
" 10 Andrew Wilson	to	Sarah Miller	Coudon
" 15 John Hartshorne	to	Agnes Miller	Coudon
June 7 Hugh Boyd	to	Jane Steel	Coudon
Aug. 11 John Nowland	to	Lydia Welden	Coudon
Oct. 1 John Russell	to	Jean Guy	Coudon
Nov. 3 David Patton	to	Eleanor Guy	Coudon
" 12 Solomon Eagon	to	Mary Blackburn	Coudon
" 12 William Winchester	to	Jane Logan	Coudon
1789			
Feb. 6 Andrew Hall	to	Rose McHaffey	Coudon
" 25 James Stevenson?	to	Abigal Wilson	Coudon
Mar. 3 James Douglas	to	Mary Woodrow	Coudon
June 29 Alexander Gibony	to	Elizabeth McNeely	Coudon
July 16 Patrick Ewing	to	Elizabeth Porter	Coudon
Aug. 8 Andrew Casten	to	Jane Rowland	Coudon
" 19 John Labesvine?	to	Mary Porter	Coudon
Sept. 21 Abraham Holt	to	Jane Finley	Coudon
1790			
Jan. 1 Joseph Wagner	to	Mary Tharmegar	Coudon
1787			
Nov. 14 John Allieson	to	Elizabeth Ward	Wilmore
" 21 John Adare	to	Elizabeth Sinno	Coudon
Dec. 6 Elijah Currier	to	Margaret Brumfield	Wilmore
" 24 Reuben Harding	to	Mary Price	Coudon
" 26 John Simpers	to	Peggy Crouch	Coudon
" 29 John Galoway	to	Ann Thibetts	Coudon
1788			
Jan. 3 John Holladay	to	Rebecca Simpers	Coudon
" 7 Joseph Nevens	to	Sarah Alexander	Coudon
" 17 John Cooke	to	Sarah Parker	Coudon
" 28 William Taylor	to	Rachel Braverd	Coudon
" 29 David Hairs	to	Jamima Hughes	Wilmer
Feb. 2 Henry Spencer?	to	Ann Rutter	Coudon
" 13 Jonathan Hodgeson	to	Susannah Ford	Wilmer
Mar. 25 Lewis Miller	to	Ruth Dobson	Coudon
" 26 John Manly	to	Mary Connolly	Coudon
" 28 John Hall	to	Jean Guffy	Coudon
Apr. 4 Adam Dobson	to	Tamor Chiles	Coudon
" 11 George Ash	to	Barbary Smith	Coudon
" 23 Andrew Hughes	to	Rebecca Price	Coudon
' 24 Harman Kankey	to	Mary Hyland	Coudon
" 26 Robert Penington	to	Rebecca Price	Wilmer
" 28 Richard Miller	to	Fanny Harley	Coudon
May 7 George Werkfield	to	Rebecca Passmore	Coudon
" 20 Robert Sutton?	to	Ann Wilson	Coudon
" 26 Archibald Harvey	to	Hannah Annis	Coudon
June 3 Edward Price	to	Rebecca Beedle	Wilmer
" 13 John O'Neal	to	Rachel McLealand	Coudon
" 16 William Holmstoaff	to	Jemima Moss	G. Directions

		MAN		WOMAN	MINISTER
"	23	David Cunningham	to	Ann Ferguson	G. Directions
"	24	John Grant	to	Mary Ferguson	Coudon
July	4	Benjamin McKinsey	to	Christiana Thackery	Coudon
"	20	Tnomas Kimble Walmsley	to	Ann Mercer	Wilmer
Aug.	7	Reuben Ricketts	to	Gamore Barron	Coudon
"	27	Nathan Harris	to	Susannah Guinea	Coudon
"	30	Sidney George	to	Mary Lovittit	Wilmer
Sept.	3	Thomas Jacob	to	Mary Williams	Coudon
"	6	John Reed	to	Ann Pearce	Coudon
"	9	Robert Latham	to	Ann Dunn	Coudon
"	8	Thomas Shaw	to	Sarah Stevens	Wilmer
Oct.	9	Edmund Dougherty	to	Hannah Hines	Coudon
"	26	Joseph Wrothwell	to	Mary Biddle	Coudon
Nov.	12	John Tarnly?	to	Sina Owans	Coudon
"	13	Spencer Hottham	to	Elizabeth Morrison	Coudon
"	28	John Penington	to	Elizabeth Severson	Wilmer
Dec.	9	Richard Ford	to	Priscilla Punteley	Coudon
"	17	Samuel Montgomery	to	Susannah Furrey	Coudon
"	30	John Durgin	to	Martha Plat?	Coudon
	1789				
Jan.	20	James Grant	to	Margaret Winchester	Coudon
Feb.	7	Alexander Beard	to	Patty Sebo	Coudon
"	16	Jonathan Ballard	to	Susannah Flintham	Wilmer
"	17	Ephraim Sterling	to	Ann Carty	Coudon
"	18	John Brown	to	Rebecca Neilar	Coudon
"	25	Alexander Moody	to	Leah Moody	Coudon
"	25	David Hill	to	Rebecca Manly	Coudon
"	27	Jeremiah Cosden	to	Catherine Cosden	Coudon
Mar.	2	Peregrin Cox	to	Esther Cox	Wilmer
"	19	Joseph Adair	to	Mary Chields	Coudon
Apr.	7	Jacob Gatchell	to	Elizabeth Dunbar	Coudon
"	25	Jonathan Currier	to	Ann Craig	Coudon
May	5	George Foard, Jr.	to	Sarah Brewer	Wilmer
"	10	James Springer	to	Barbary Grey	Coudon
"	14	Hugh Montgomery	to	Mary Gibson	Coudon
"	23	George Hill	to	Elizabeth Manly	Coudon
June	2	Samuel Byard, Jr.	to	Martha Scott	G. Directions
"	15	Alexander Craig	to	Hanna Cochran	Coudon
"	17	John James	to	Rebecca Lusby	Coudor
"	17	Thomas Richardson	to	Mary Keithley	Coudon
"	18	Richard Davis	to	Elizabeth Davis	Coudon
"	18	Alexander McDonnell	to	Elizabeth Carty	Coudon
"	30	William Grace	to	Elizabeth Moore	Coudon
July	30	James Keysen	to	Elizabeth Offley	Bissitt
Aug.	6	Abraham Anderson	to	Sarah Pogue	Coudon
"	7	James Roach	to	Ann Thackery	Coudon
"	25	Samuel McElwee	to	Margaret Burke	Coudon
"	25	Richard Evans	to	Rebecca Thompson	Coudon
"	29	Robert Crouch	to	Sarah Chew	Coudon
Sept.	5	Nathaniel Crossett?	to	Zephroa Crisfield?	Coudon
"	17	Joseph Briscoe	to	Gracey Jacob	Coudon
"	23	Joseph Hemphill	to	Jane Moody	Coudon
"	29	Charles Hincky	to	Sarah Stalcup	Coudon
Oct.	28	John Hukill	to	Rebecca Thackery	Coudon
Nov.	4	Samuel Pennington	to	Sarah Etherington	Coudon
"	17	Francis Partridge	to	Hannah Gilpin	Coudon
"	21	Robert Caldwell	to	Jean Patton	Coudon
"	24	Edward Parsley	to	Priscilla Mulsey	Coudon
"	24	Morton Conner	to	Susannah Lynch	Coudon
"	24	William Couch	to	Margaret Hollingsworth	Coudon

	MAN		WOMAN	MINISTER
" 30	John Underwood	to	Jean Caste	Coudon
Dec. 2	Alexander Morrison	to	Jean Hill	Coudon
" 22	Nicholas G. Manley	to	Millisent Kankey	Coudon
" 24	Nathan Bean	to	Martha Brooks	Coudon
" 25	John Kirk	to	Sarah Roberts	Coudon
" 24	Joseph Frem	to	Mary Hunter	Coudon
" 31	John Ewing	to	Jean Mague	Coudon
1790				
Jan. 2	Jacob Groves	to	Francina Bohannan	Coudon
" 4	Nathaniel Ramsey	to	Charlotte Hall	Ireland
" 11	Justine Alexander	to	Sarah Owens	Coudon
" 22	Edward McVeigh	to	Isabel Jenny	Coudon
Feb. 2	John Moore	to	Mary Holt	Coudon
" 8	Benjamin Pearce	to	Ann Ruley	Coudon
" 8	Samuel Beedle	to	Sarah Flinter	Coudon
" 8	William Todd	to	Elizabeth Maybar	Coudon
Mar. 1	Abel Bond	to	Elizabeth Booth	Coudon
" 12	James Manley	to	Lidia Liason	Coudon
" 11	James Simms	to	Ann Gillespie	G. Directions
" 16	William Reynolds	to	Millison Wattson	Coudon
" 22	William Savin	to	Araminta Hudgson	Coudon
" 23	John Thompson	to	Hannah Evans	Coudon
" 30	Levi Willson	to	Elizabeth Eliott	Coudon
Apr. 12	Thomas Kelly	to	Mary Connally	Coudon
" 13	John Manley	to	Susannah Cox	Coudon
" 15	William Forster	to	Rachel Stalcup	Coudon
" 20	Thomas Walmsley	to	Rebecca James	Coudon
May 5	William Homes	to	Rachel Wingate	Coudon
" 6	Peregrine Chick	to	Margaret Turner	Coudon
" 3	Samuel Hood	to	Mary McGrew	Coudon
June 5	John Lashu	to	Hannah Maud Cayhan	Coudon
" 8	John Daw Crouch	to	Mary Dollison	Coudon
" 9	Lancelott Todd	to	Rachel Jewell	Coudon
" 11	James Willey	to	Jean Shaw	Coudon
" 28	William Sharp	to	Mary Smith	Coudon
July 5	David Archibald	to	Mary McMackmaster	Coudon
" 14	Edward Thomas	to	Ann Brumfield	Coudon
" 31	Nicholas Ceal	to	Catherine Nowland	Coudon
Aug. 7	Thomas Patton	to	Millecent Rice	Coudon
" 7	Joseph Springer	to	Elizabeth Donnagan	Coudon
" 12	John Duffey	to	Martha Hance	Coudon
" 20	William McDowell	to	Jean Dougherty	Coudon
Sept. 16	William Howard	to	Rebecca Rutter	Coudon
" 21	Thomas Severson	to	Sarah Mercer	Coudon
" 29	Henry Bennett	to	Hannah Johnson	Coudon
Oct. 7	George Dobson	to	Mary Anderson	Coudon
" 8	Henry McCoy	to	Dorcas Alexander	Coudon
" 6	John Carty	to	Elizabeth Nowland	Coudon
" 12	James Henry	to	Ann Ruley	Coudon
" 18	Ebenezer Kelly	to	Rachel Foster	Coudon
" 28	Jonathan White	to	Mary Slycer	Coudon
Nov. 2	James Manley?	to	Keziah Murphy	Coudon
" 15	John Rudulph	to	Elizabeth Kimble	Coudon
" 20	James Fulton	to	Margaret Savin	Coudon
Dec. 10	William Gregg	to	Elizabeth Webb	Coudon
" 23	John Burran	to	Eleanor Burran	Coudon
" 23	Robert Coudon Walmsley	to	Mary Hines	Bissett
" 27	James Thompson	to	Margaret McCreary	Coudon
" 27	John Huddabuck	to	Mary Ferguson	Coudon
" 28	Daniel Gillespie	to	Elizabeth Milligan	Coudon

	MAN		WOMAN	MINISTER
" 27	Ephraim Longe	to	Elizabeth Cusex	Coudon
" 28	Elijah Eliason	to	Tabitha Bristow	Coudon
" 30	Thomas Lacky	to	Judith Pusey	Coudon
1791				
Jan. 17	James Ford	to	Jemimah Longe	Coudon
" 17	Hugh Grant	to	Mary Marshall	G. Directions
Feb. 10	Peter Ryland	to	Hester Pearce	Coudon
" 10	Robert Parker	to	Lydia Rogers	Coudon
Mar. 1	William Willson	to	Elizabeth Cammoran	Coudon
" 1	Robert Irwin	to	Catherine Nugent	Coudon
" 3	Peter Abrahams	to	Elizabeth Cammoran	Coudon
" 8	William Smiley	to	Martha McCreary	G. Directions
" 21	David McCrea	to	Eleanor Smith	Coudon
" 23	David White	to	Rachel Kirk	Coudon
" 29	William Rowbuck	to	Sabray Bean	Coudon
" 31	John Chambers	to	Hannah Taylor	Coudon
Apr. 5	Edward Savin	to	E'izabeth Sluyter	Coudon
" 25	Frisby Lloyd	to	Maria Chew Ward	Bissett
May 19	Robert Hayward	to	Sarah Willice	Coudon
June 4	William Cather	to	Ann Sweeney	Coudon
" 7	James Griffith	to	Lina Wattson	Coudon
" 9	Levi Kirk	to	Amelia Mullin	Coudon
" 13	Moses Levey, Esq.	to	Mary Pearce	Coudon
" 13	Joseph Willson	to	Jean Willocks	Coudon
" 25	George Fowler	to	Ann McCracken	Coudon
July 5	Thomas Yeoman	to	Elizabeth Cunningham	Coudon
" 14	John Short	to	Mary Johnson	Coudon
" 22	Thomas Walmsley	to	Elizabeth Pogue	Bissett
Aug. 6	William Cord	to	Mary Masfield	Coudon
July 28	Peregrine Briscoe	to	Ann Rickett	Coudon
Aug. 24	William Huston	to	Susannah Boyd	Coudon
Sept. 2	James Robinett	to	Dolly Ann Harwood	Coudon
" 22	John Crouch	to	Cornelia Chrisfield	Coudon
" 27	James Hill	to	Ann Cavender	Coudon
Oct. 3	Isaac Thomas	to	Naomi Boggs	McCreary
Sept. 5	Robert Simms	to	Elizabeth Ewing	Coudon
Oct. 12	Joshua Reynolds	to	Rachel Brown	Coudon
" 14	James Ramsey	to	Elizabeth Haslet	Coudon
" 17	Henry Peterson	to	E'izabeth George	Bissett
Nov. 7	Charles Maffitt	to	Elizabeth Logue	Coudon
" 24	John Chandley	to	Sarah Brown	Coudon
" 30	William Ward, Sr.	to	Rachel Walmsley	Bissett
Dec. 7	William Keatley	to	Mary Beadley?	Coudon
" 13	David Henderson	to	Sarah Kimble	Coudon
" 19	Peter Mullet	to	Mary Flannggin	Coudon
" 20	Jesse Jaquet	to	Sarah Brumfield	Coudon
" 21	Nathaniel Cooper	to	Ann Crockett	Coudon
" 26	William Crouch	to	Kezia McClune	Coudon
1792				
Jan. 6	James Simm	to	Mary Gillespie	Coudon
" 9	David Swesey	to	Olive Milligan	Coudon
" 11	James McCorkal	to	Mary Jones	Coudon
" 28	Henry Hukill	to	Elizabeth Foster	Coudon
Feb. 4	William Fulton	to	Esher Alexander	Coudon
" 7	John Kidd	to	Elizabeth Williams	Coudon
" 18	James Cochran	to	Sarah Fulton	Coudon
" 21	Ferderick Ellsbury	to	Lydia Foster	Coudon
Mar. 10	James Lowry	to	Catharine Elliott	Coudon
" 14	Edward Wingate	to	Rebecca Cazier	Coudon

		MAN		WOMAN	MINISTER
"	14	Joseph Arbuckle	to	Catherine Guy	Coudon
"	24	Jacob Biddle	to	Sarah Ford	Coudon
"	28	John Brooks	to	Margaret Kirpatrick	Coudon
Apr.	9	William Whittam	to	Margaret Moore	Coudon
May	15	Charles S. Bunting	to	Fannie Price	Coudon
"	16	John Campbell	to	Polly Evans	Coudon
"	21	Joshua Rutter	to	Ann Bryson	Coudon
"	21	Allen Steel	to	Ruth Sharp	Coudon
"	26	Sampson George Hyland	to	Elizabeth Morgan	Coudon
June	12	Andrew Bryan	to	Hannah French	Coudon
"	18	Peter Springer	to	Mary Ann Penington	Bissett
"	26	Charles McDermott	to	Hannah Neuguent	Bissett
July	14	John Bristow	to	Susannah Hukell	Bissett
"	31	Francis Wilson	to	Priscilla Gray	Bissett
"	31	Joseph Philips	to	Elizabeth Scott	Bissett
Aug.	11	John Wheeler Smith	to	Rebecca Harley	Bissett
"	18	John Donal	to	Tina Beedle?	Bissett
"	30	Pearce Veal	to	Polly Knight	Bissett
Sept.	4	Joshua Wills	to	Ann Costela	Bissett
"	5	James McBride	to	Deborah Thompson	Bissett
Oct.	1	Adam Hinchman	to	Mary Passmore	Bissett
June	18	Zebulon Oldham	to	Ann Hutchinson	Ireland
Sept.	14	William Coale	to	Elizabeth Reed	G. Directions
Oct.	3	Peregrine Savin	to	Mary Jarvis	Duke
"	4	Robert Hey	to	Elizabeth Makin	Duke
"	5	James Roach	to	Elizabeth Sappington	Duke
"	8	Andrew Turner	to	Elizabeth Hollyday	Duke
"	11	Frederick Hiller	to	Hannah Trew	Duke
Nov.	1	Oliver Bing	to	Ann Logan	Duke
"	14	Solomon White	to	Priscilla Buchanan	Duke
"	30	Daniel Cuddick	to	Elizabeth O'Danly?	Duke
Dec.	21	Michael Bryant	to	Nancy Thompson	Duke
"	22	Jacob Jones	to	Isabella MeKewn	Duke
"	25	Jonathan Feddis	to	Rebecca Ryland	Duke
"	25	Thomas Ryland	to	Mary Cann	Duke
"	31	John Makin	to	Mary Savin	Duke
	1793				
Jan.	14	John Ruley	to	Elizabeth Pearce	Duke
"	19	John Matthews	to	Catharine Williams	Duke
"	21	Edward Penington	to	Henrietta James	Duke
"	23	Benjamin Benson Geers	to	Sarah Hendrickson	Duke
"	28	Joseph Parker	to	Margery Price	Duke
Feb.	5	Robert Smith	to	Polly Savin	William Duke
"	20	John Cazier	to	Martha Ford	William Duke
"	26	William Manley	to	Rachel Jackson	William Duke
Mar.	14	John Sulivan	to	Elizabeth Cornelius	William Duke
"	15	Aaron McNail	to	Mary Cashore	William Duke
"	17	Christopher Rosback	to	Mary Cashore	William Duke
"	23	Robert Ewing	to	Peggy Ewing	William Duke
"	25	Rowland Mehaffey	to	Elizabeth Colmery	William Duke
"	25	Francis Smith	to	Eleanor Hannah	William Duke
"	28	Benjamin Price	to	Sarah Matilda Coppen	William Duke
Apr.	10	Andrew Gorden	to	Margaret McCoy	William Duke
"	26	Francis Reynolds	to	Sarah Logue	William Duke
May	2	William Works	to	Rebecca Tully	William Duke
"	2	John Fitcher	to	Mary Fields	William Duke
"	16	Samuel McCullough	to	Mary Hall	William Duke
"	28	Rev. Wm. Duke	to	Hester Coudon	Coleman
June	26	Joseph Wallace	to	Margaret Whann	William Duke
"	26	Moses Nesbitt	to	Martha Bell	William Duke

		MAN		WOMAN	MINISTER
"	30	Veazey Edwards	to	Jean Richardson	William Duke
July	13	Wm. Campbell	to	Elizabeth Bing	William Duke
"	24	Jesse Foster	to	Sarah Lewis	William Duke
Aug.	3	Amos Swesey	to	Henry Cresfield	William Duke
"	5	Alphonso Cosdon	to	Alethia? Asbethere Money	William Duke
1792					
Oct.	25	George Simcoe	to	Mary Baker	William Duke
Dec.	2	John Rawlings	to	Mary Knight	William Duke
1793					
July	3	Cornelius Empson	to	Hannah Oldham	William Duke
Feb.	5	William McIntire	to	Jane Brookins	William Duke
"	14	James Farias	to	Elizabeth Moody	William Duke
"	19	John Scott	to	Jane Hull	William Duke
May	2	James Magee	to	Elizabeth Quail	William Duke
Oct.	11	John Mercer	to	Rebecca Davis	William Duke
"	29	Benjamin Hersey	to	Mary Smith	William Duke
"	30	Richard Key Heath	to	Mary Hall	Mr. Ireland
Nov.	12	Hugh Ragan	to	Elizabeth McMaster	William Duke
"	13	Edward Brumfield	to	Margaret Corbet	William Duke
"	14	George Wolsey	to	Sarah Brooks	William Duke
Dec.	10	Hance Severson	to	Rebecca Price	William Duke
"	17	John Gears	to	Sarah Heisler	William Duke
"	27	Joseph Davis	to	Susanna Hendrickson	William Duke
"	28	Joshua Ward	to	Sarah Veazey	William Duke
Jan.	1	Isaac Holden	to	Ann Cole	William Duke
"	6	William Bateman	to	Martha Brown	William Duke
"	7	Joseph Cunningham	to	Mary Templen	William Duke
"	7	Daniel Crosson	to	Catharine Brumfield	William Duke
"	9	John Ricketts	to	Mary Rutter	William Duke
"	10	Edward Henry Veazey	to	Rebecca Ward	William Duke
"	17	Peter Collins	to	Sarah Henry	William Duke
"	18	John Bennett	to	Elizabeth Mitchell	William Duke
"	27	Benjamin Hartshorn	to	Isabella McClure	William Duke
Feb.	8	Jeremiah Baker	to	Rebecca Mauldin	William Duke
"	10	Daniel Riggs	to	Sarah Davis	William Duke
"	13	Richard Clayton	to	Martha Richardson	William Duke
1794					
Feb.	10	Thomas Evans	to	Ann Broxen	William Duke
"	15	David Arnold	to	Sarah Gears	William Duke
Mar.	1	Hyland Hendrickson	to	Elizabeth Tyson	William Duke
"	6	William McCoy	to	Mary Ann Henderson	William Duke
"	11	Johnothen Glasgow	to	Elizabeth Milligan	William Duke
"	15	Titen Leads Kimball	to	Dorcas Wallace	William Duke
"	19	James McClure	to	Jane Hamilton	William Duke
"	26	John Crawford	to	Ann Boyce	William Duke
Apr.	2	Humphrey Pugh	to	Ann Chick	William Duke
"	12	Alexander Taggart	to	Martha Patrick	William Duke
"	21	Joseph Oldham	to	Mary Little	William Duke
May	9	John Wardell	to	Jane McCullough	William Duke
"	16	John Peerie	to	Sophia Fee	William Duke
"	20	David Gillmore	to	Margery Crossen	William Duke
"	21	Wm. Whann	to	Jane Maffitt	William Duke
"	27	Wm. Simpers	to	Sarah Elliott	William Duke
June	2	Samuel Counsel	to	Margaret Craddock	William Duke
"	23	Reuben H. Knight	to	Araminta Boots	William Duke
"	23	Isaac Wilcox	to	Jane Thomas	William Duke
July	19	Thomas Keatley	to	Catharine Moody	William Duke
"	23	David Fulton	to	Elizabeth Savin	William Duke

MAN		WOMAN	MINISTER
Oct. 6	John Wheeler to	Margaret Daily	William Duke
" 15	Edward McHaffey to	Margaret Hemphill	William Duke
" 18	Edward Tilden to	Mary Gooding	William Duke
" 21	John Milligan to	Catherine Williams	William Duke
" 11	James Templin to	Mary Chapple	William Duke
" 19	John Miller to	Rebecca Davis	William Duke
Nov. 19	Nathaniel Chew to	Margaret Rogers	William Duke
" 29	Daniel Norris to	Eleanor Nesbitt	William Duke
Sept. 9	Samuel Kirkpatrick to	Elizabeth Kirkpatrick	William Duke
Nev. 24	John Fisher to	Jane McMaster	William Duke
Dec. 10	Andrew Bargoe to	Susan Miles	William Duke
" 13	Ephraim Price to	Sarah Simpers	William Duke
" 22	Richard Brookings to	Margaret Matthews	William Duke
" 22	Richard Hall to	Ann Donnigan	William Duke
" 23	Wm. Thompson to	Hosannah Penington	William Duke
" 27	Wm. Logue to	Ann Smith	William Duke
1795			
Jan. 26	Peter Hossinger to	Jane McCoy	William Duke
" 27	Wm. Craig to	Elizabeth Wyatt	William Duke
" 28	James Veazey to	Polly Kerr	William Duke
Feb. 10	James Sherer to	Jane Mackey	William Duke
Mar. 7	Archibald Gordon to	Lydia McMin	Wiliam Duke
" 12	Thomas Beedle to	Araminta Alexander	William Duke
" 14	Robert Penington to	Elizabeth Moody	William Duke
" 17	Tobias Biddle to	Sarah Ford	William Duke
" 23	Edward Mercer to	Elizabeth Greenwood	William Duke
Apr. 2	Robert Swan to	Polly Ricketts	William Duke
" 3	Benjamin Ruley to	Rachel Pearce	Duke
" 14	Peter Egner to	Susannah Willson	Duke
" 14	Thomas Miller to	Elizabeth Wilson	Duke
" 14	Andrew Hall to	Fanny Stewart	Duke
" 20	John Chandlee to	Margery Kankey	Duke
" 28	John Egner to	Catherine Hukins	Duke
May 4	James Mercer to	Ann Groves	Duke
" 18	William Lasselle to	Ann Greenwood	Duke
June 12	Rev. Wm. Price to	Mary Ryland	Duke
" 17	William Smith to	Elisabeth Oldham	Duke
" 19	Stephen Kankey to	Rebecca Cox	Duke
" 18	Francis Bellow Chandler to	Ann Biddle	Duke
July 16	Isaac Hall to	Mary Bowman	Duke
Aug. 22	John Crookshanks, Jr. to	Tempy Chandley	Duke
Sept. 22	Walter Fullam to	Mary O'Donald	Duke
" 24	Isaac Bowen to	Rebecca Veazey	Duke
Oct. 1	Dennis James Nowland to	Mary M. Foard	Duke
" 7	Richard McClure to	Rebecca Woodland	Duke
" 7	Daniel Vansant to	Rebecca Hays	Duke
Nov. 5	Edward Burrows to	Leah Ryan	G. Directions
Sept. 3	James Burgoyne to	Catherine Green	Duke
" 10	Robert Creswell to	Jane Meak	G. Directions
Oct. 20	Levi Cully to	Esther Smith	Duke
" 29	William McCreary to	Margaret Glenn	Duke
Nov. 3	John Hasson to	Rachel Barrett	Duke
" 7	Lewis Hyer to	Julia Ann Whitaker	Duke
" 7	James McClure to	Eve Hyer	Duke
" 16	John Fordain to	Mary Whittam	Duke
" 17	Reuben Simpers to	Sarah Lewis	Duke
Dec. 2	David Griffith to	Ann Whann	Duke
" 10	Simon Johnson to	Sarah Short	Duke
" 10	John McCracken to	Sarah McClain	Duke
" 12	Peregrine Biddle to	Martha Bateman	Duke

MAN			WOMAN	MINISTER
1796				
Jan.	6	David Sutton to	Rachel Pearce	Duke
"	7	William C. Penington to	Catherine Ricketts	Duke
"	13	Lanty Meloney to	Mary Lewis	Duke
"	14	Edward Phillips to	Hannah Johnson	Duke
"	14	William McCollough to	Franscini Bowen	Duke
"	22	Philip Fox to	Elizabeth Brumfield	Duke
"	22	Haines Leviason to	Martha Davis	Duke
"	26	Wm. Roberson to	Ann McCracken	Duke
Feb.	6	John McNeil to	Alethea Powell	Duke
"	9	Benjamin Barnaby to	Rebecca Greenwood	Duke
"	10	Samuel Beedle to	Ann Richardson	Duke
"	16	Wm. Beeks to	Margaret Crookshanks	Duke
"	17	John Robinson to	Rachel Hukill	Duke
"	17	Hezekiah Batten to	Ann Robinson	Duke
"	24	Jacob England to	Elizabeth Short	Duke
"	29	Fredus Aldridge to	Catherine Cosden	Duke
Mar.	1	John Kirkpatrick to	Rachel Moody	Duke
"	5	Nicholas Chambers to	Rebecca Bravard	William Duke
"	10	Andrew Penington to	Sarah Ricketts	William Duke
"	15	James Stuart to	Lydia Miller	William Duke
"	16	Alexander Cay? to	Hannah McCollough	William Duke
"	21	Thomas Lackey to	Rebecca Dickinson Grant	Duke
May	2	John Davis to	Ann Lynch	William Duke
"	4	Barzzelly Boggs to	Sarah Dunbarr	William Duke
"	7	William Fergerson to	Sarah Mackey	William Duke
"	25	Charles Hinckey to	Rebecca Johnson	William Duke
"	28	Nicholas Spencer to	Margaret Currier	William Duke
June	15	Thomas Clark to	Elizabeth Wimble	William Duke
"	20	James Rawlings to	Mary Jaquette	William Duke
"	23	John Rutter to	Ann Webb	William Duke
"	28	William McGrath to	Ann Bailey	William Duke
July	20	William Hodgson to	Ann Jones	William Duke
Aug.	1	Benjamin McKenny to	Elizabeth Knight	William Duke
"	15	James Frazirr to	Sarah Barr	William Duke
"	27	John Davis to	Sarah Leak	William Duke
Sept.	12	George Knight to	Millicent Price	William Duke
Oct.	5	Robert Cameron to	Elizabeth Creswell	William Duke
"	6	William Reeley to	Mary Lum	William Duke
"	11	Samuel McCrea to	Jane Stevenson	William Duke
"	17	Hugh Steel to	Hester Boyd	William Duke
"	26	Rudolph Gonce to	Elizabeth Headner	William Duke
"	28	Henry Suppile to	Susannah Meekins	William Duke
Nov.	1	Richard Mansfield to	Ann Cosden	William Duke
"	3	John Dennis to	Ann Thomas	William Duke
"	9	Empson Gordon to	Hannah Slycer	William Cosden
"	15	Wm. Alexender, Esq. to	Margaret Partridge	William Cosden
"	15	John H. Tolan to	Margaret Loftis	William Cosden
Dec.	1	Peregrine Boyer to	Ann Bullock	William Cosden
"	10	Richard Parkerson to	Elizabeth Robert	William Cosden
"	13	Isaac Israel to	Elizabeth Robert	William Cosden
"	21	Benjamin E. Price to	Ann Morgan	William Cosden
'	22	David Higgins to	Rachel Wallace	William Cosden
"	31	Joseph Ford to	Martha Allender	William Cosden
1797				
Jan.	12	James Jackson to	Elizabeth Miller	William Cosden
"	23	Wm. Farris to	Eleanor Hukell	William Cosden
"	28	Barthollemew Lyons to	Sarah Riggs	William Cosden
Feb.	6	Peter Miles to	Rebecca Crow	William Cosden
"	13	Josiah Foard to	Hannah Lawrenson	William Cosden

		MAN		WOMAN	MINISTER
"	27	Joseph Penington	to	Ann Penington	William Cosden
Mar.	7	James Manley	to	Mary Hart	William Cosden
"	13	John Price	to	Ann Bouldin	William Cosden
"	13	John Bell	to	Ann Lashley	William Cosden
"	15	James Alexander	to	Margaret Alexander (Craig)	Cosden
"	22	John Boozer	to	Ann Alexander	William Cosden
"	27	Nicholas Wingate	to	Franscina Kankey	William Cosden
"	22	James Polke	to	Tamer Howard	William Cosden
"	23	Daniel Sherredine	to	Ann Russell	Mr. Ireland
Apr.	3	Charles Beaston	to	Mary Biddle	William Cosden
"	6	John D. Thompson	to	Sophia Baxter	William Cosden
"	8	Joseph Harlen	to	Abigail Boggs	William Cosden
"	11	Benjamin Benson	to	Mary Hendrickson	Cosden
"	19	Benjamin Riley	to	Rachel Hendrickson	Cosden
"	24	Matthew King	to	Mary Ewing	Cosden
"	27	James Porter, Jr.	to	Mary Benson	Cosden
"	27	William Moore	to	Margaret Wiley	Cosden
May	3	Chas. McDermott	to	Mary Roach	Cosden
"	6	John Robinson	to	Grace Pennington	Cosden
"	10	Joseph Joyce	to	Mary Wearum	Cosden
"	24	James Cloney	to	Bridget O'Donnally	Cosden
June	3	Thomas Crozier	to	Cornelia Ford	Cosden
"	8	Septimus Claypoole	to	Elizabeth Polk	Ireland
"	27	John Lockerman	to	Margaret Logue	Cosden
"	27	James Kidd	to	Rebecca Lyon	Cosden
"	28	John Tyson	to	Sarah Ogleviee	Cosden
July	4	Chas. Ramsey	to	Sarah Clendening	Cosden
"	22	Abraham Lucus	to	Sarah Hunter	Cosden
Aug.	5	Thomas Steele	to	Ann Simpson	Cosden
"	6	Gilbert Fox	to	Sarah Lenttel Veazey	Cosden
"	7	Benjamin Cosden	to	Janet Carter	Cosden
"	28	John Comegys	to	Ann Comegys	Cosden
"	29	Henry Sullivan	to	Mary Grace	Cosden
Sept.	2	Matthias Ruth	to	Franscina Simpson	Cosden
"	5	Robert Carson	to	Sarah Armstrong	Cosden
"	6	Jacob Oldham	to	Rachel Watkins	Cosden
"	20	John Gilpin	to	Mary Hollingsworth	Cosden
Oct.	5	James Fulton	to	Catherine Alexander	Cosden
"	28	William E. Sewell	to	Fanny Russell	Cosden
"	30	John Rock	to	Sarah Everett	Cosden
"	30	Dennis McCauley	to	Tabithia Everett	Cosden
"	30	Samuel Coale	to	Ann Gatchell	Bayten
Nov.	7	John Oglevas	to	Elizabeth Baker	Cosden
"	11	Robert Moody	to	Catherine Sadler	Cosden
"	16	William Means?	to	Rebecca Garish	Cosden
Dec.	2	Hyland Price	to	Martha Riswell	Cosden
"	7	Nathan Hanson	to	Mary Ann Watson	Cosden
"	12	Thomas Young	to	Sarah Johnson	Cosden
"	18	James Maxwell	to	Elizabeth Patten	Cosden
"	19	James Bowdoin Robins	to	Elizabeth Horsey	Cosden
"	25	Dr. William Miller	to	Sophia Cox	Cosden
"	27	James Gillespie	to	Eleanor Kilpatrick	Cosden
	1798				
Jan.	9	William Bair	to	Aramento Turner	Cosden
"	10	Jacob Freeman Abbott	to	Elizabeth Comegys	Cosden
"	18	Thomas Foster	to	Ann Harley	Cosden
"	18	John Alfond	to	Mary Davey?	Cosden
"	29	Samuel Reily	to	Sarah Pearce	Cosden
"	29	John Boulden	to	Sarah Richardson	Cosden

		MAN		WOMAN	MINISTER
"	31	Tilghman Jackson	to	Elizabeth James	Cosden
Feb.	2	James Odonald	to	Catherine Reynolds	Cosden
"	6	William Taylor	to	Margaret Waltons	Cosden
"	7	Henry Gribbon	to	Catherine Cardwell	Cosden
"	8	Philip Black	to	Margaret Redgrave	Cosden
"	10	Samuel Gay	to	Margaret Maxwell	Cosden
"	21	Joshua Meekens	to	Rose Mooney	Cosden
"	21	Joseph Maston	to	Cassey Bell	Cosden
"	22	John Hindman	to	Rachel Knight	Cosden
Mar.	3	William Reynolds	to	Jane Conway	Cosden
"	7	Samuel Harkness	to	Susannah Alexander	Cosden
"	10	Hannen Bolden	to	Margaret Stephenson	Cosden
Apr.	5	John Short	to	Elizabeth Manley	Cosden
"	12	Mark Alexander	to	Elizabeth Gilpin	Cosden
May	5	Charles William Hartley	to	Elizabeth Harrison Ward	Cosden
"	9	Isaac Allman	to	Sarah Coudon	Cosden
"	26	Richard Boulden	to	Mary Harding	Cosden
"	31	William Gaddiss	to	Sarah Crouch	Cosden
June	9	Isaac Redgrave	to	Millicent Cox	Cosden
"	12	Ebenezer Eliason	to	Rebecca Carman	Cosden
"	21	John Carpenter	to	Alithea Aldridge	Cosden
July	12	George Ash	to	Sarah Pusey	Cosden
"	17	Edward Wingate	to	Elizabeth Kankey	Cosden
"	24	Zebulon Beaston	to	Asaneth Thomas	Cosden
Aug.	4	Samuel Marrs	to	Rebecca McKinney	Cosden
"	8	William Evans	to	Rebecca Karr	Cosden
Sept.	18	John Kearn	to	Frances Ferguson	Cosden
Oct.	7	John Ferguson	to	Mary Price	Cosden
"	25	Joseph Hendrickson	to	Elizabeth Turner	Cosden
Nov.	17	James Alexander	to	Julian Hitchcock	Cosden
"	24	Abraham Williams	to	Margaret Cameron	Cosden
"	27	William Milligan	to	Sarah Milligan	Cosden
"	27	John Kile	to	Eleanor Vance	Cosden
Dec.	31	Thomas Pryor	to	Mary Willson	Cosden
"	19	David Springer	to	Mary Ann McCoy	Cosden
"	22	Robert Williams	to	Elizabeth Stephenson	Cosden
"	25	William Crow	to	Rebecca Cosden	Cosden
"	27	George Rice	to	Rachel Manley	Cosden
"	28	Benedict Pennington	to	Sarah Redgrave	Cosden
1799					
Jan.	14	Edward Cosden	to	Elizabeth Hendrickson	Cosden
"	23	Spencer Price	to	Ann Moody	Cosden
"	29	John Altzee	to	Mitcah Hart?	Cosden
Feb.	5	Nathan Pearson	to	Ann Bolton	Cosden
"	8	Richard Hukill	to	Mary Jackson	Cosden
"	21	Thomas Quigley	to	Mary Ann Hall	Cosden
"	28	John Hyland Price	to	Amelia Montgomery	Cosden
Mar.	12	Zebulon Kankey	to	Aramenta Montgomery	Cosden
"	26	Joseph Williams	to	Mary Scott	Cosden
Apr.	1	Hyland Biddle Pennington	to	Edith Hendrickson	Cosden
"	8	Samuel Wallace	to	Frances McCoy	Cosden
May	20	Dr. John King	to	Jane Irwin	Cosden
"	8	John Culbertson	to	Sarah Foster	Cosden
"	14	William Davis	to	Rebecca Ward	Cosden

License granted by Joseph Baxter since May 1, 1798

1798					
May	24	John McCoy	to	Agnes Brown	General D.
Dec.	6	John Bryson	to	Elizabeth Keir	General D.
"	12	Jeremiah Larkin Leslie	to	Sarah Hill	General D.

Date	MAN		WOMAN	MINISTER
1799				
Feb. 13	Joseph Cunningham	to	Elizabeth Watson	Geeneral D.
May 27	Benjamin K. McKinsey	to	Susanna Barr	Cosden
" 28	Thomas Wingate	to	Mary Wingate	Cosden
June 10	Nicholas Hyland	to	Ann Hyland	Cosden
" 10	Philipp Fox	to	Alice Shepard	Cosden
" 13	Andrew Anderson	to	Margaret Pennington	Cosden
July 2	Thomas Orr	to	Mary Gatchell	General D.
" 7	Daniel Richardson	to	Elizabeth Hart	Cosden
" 23	William Money	to	Arimenta Morgan	Cosden
" 31	Alexander Williams	to	Deborah Roach	Cosden
Aug. 15	George Rea	to	Catherine Logan	Cosden
" 19	Robert Standley	to	Ann Hall	Cosden
" 27	Levi Biddle	to	Sarah Boultin	Cosden
" 27	David Short	to	Sarah Lorch	Cosden
" 31	Dr. John Groome	to	Elizabeth Wallace	Cosden
Sept. 5	John McCullough	to	Margaret Martin	Cosden
" 24	Henry Marshall	to	Elizabeth Newgent	Cosden
" 25	Charles Veitch?	to	Mary Blackburn	Cosden
Oct. 9	Charles J. Bunting	to	Ann Grant	Cosden
" 15	Thomas Crouch	to	Rebecca Patten	Cosden
" 18	John Gray	to	Mary Pouge	Cosden
" 24	Philip Roach	to	Elizabeth Manley	Cosden
Nov. 3	William Barker	to	Elizabeth McGairly	Cosden
" 6	Charles Foard	to	Mary Mauldin	Cosden
" 6	Charles Beaston	to	Rachel Thackery	Cosden
Dec. 4	Stephen Owens	to	Charlott Edenor	Cosden
" 11	Thomas Howard	to	Mary Casho	Cosden
" 19	James Wallace	to	Lency Bouldin?	Cosden
" 25	William Cantley	to	Rebecca Burns	Cosden
" 26	Robert Hindman	to	Mary Mann	Cosden
" 28	Dr. William C. Ellis	to	Rebecca Spraat	Cosden
1800				
Jan. 2	Thomas Price	to	Millicent Price	Cosden
" 2	Joseph Stall	to	Elizabeth Alexander	Cosden
" 7	Aguillo Richard	to	Margaret Cox	Cosden
" 18	Thomas Janes	to	Mary Whittam	Cosden
" 25	John Hicks	to	Ann Brister	Cosden
" 31	Samuel Boree?	to	Catherine McCoy	Cosden
Feb. 5	James Rigan	to	Hannah White	Cosden
" 25	Jacob Wilcox	to	Mary Morgan	Cosden
" 27	John Kirk	to	Elizabeth Underwood	Cosden
Mar. 1	William Garrett	to	Mary Williams	Cosden
" 8	Samuel Johnson	to	Millescent Crisfield	Cosden
" 15	Elisha Kirk	to	Hannah Mullin	Cosden
" 28	Thomas McMullan	to	Sarah Little	Cosden
" 29	Edward Pennington	to	Rebecca Beaston	Cosden
" 29	John George	to	Margaret Hart	Cosden
" 31	Robert Hildwal	to	Martha McCullough	Cosden
" 31	William Buchanan	to	Mary Dever	Cosden
Apr. 9	Robert Wilkison	to	Margaret McCullough	Cosden
Nov. 25	Barney Bartley	to	Ann Bell	Cosden
Dec. 10	John Gillespie	to	Margaret Brown?	Cosden
Jan. 18	Thomas Burns	to	Ann Patterson	G. Directions
Feb. 17	John Tomlinson	to	Ann Cox	G. Directions
Mar. 27	Peter Harding	to	Eleanor Williams	G. Directions
Apr. 10	John Gottier	to	Elizabeth Booth	Cosden
" 21	Robert Kirkpatrick	to	Barbara Rodenhein	G. Directions
" 24	Daniel Lobes?	to	Ann Scott	Cosden
" 26	George Hedency	to	Ann Price	Cosden

		MAN		WOMAN	MINISTER
May	1	James Partridge	to	Mary Gilpin	G. Directions
"	13	William Ewing	to	Nancy Turner	G. Directions
"	27	Thomas Ford	to	Elizabeth McColley	Cosden
"	29	Peter Israels	to	Margaret Wilcox	Cosden
"	31	William Guy	to	Rebecca Maxwell	Cosden
June	4	John Bowlay	to	Sarah Creswell	Cosden
"	5	Samuel Anderson	to	Amelia Hemphill	Cosden
"	9	Edward Lewis	to	Margaret Crow	Cosden
"	18	Spencer Beedle	to	Elizabeth Richardson	Cosden
"	24	Alexander Scott	to	Hannah Howard	Cosden
"	30	James Smith	to	Ann Buckwith	Cosden
"	30	Samuel Harkness	to	Elizabeth Simmons	Cosden
July	23	George Banan	to	Mary Anderson	Cosden
June	23	David Boyd	to	Patty Boyer	Cosden
Aug.	16	David Tull	to	Anne Addams	Cosden
"	16	Joseph Mills	to	Letia Childs	Cosden
"	11	William Potts	to	Elizabeth Israels	Cosden
"	21	Thomas Williams	to	Agnes Hartshorn	Cosden
"	21	John McCracken	to	Elizabeth Hukill	Cosden
"	26	John Cannon?	to	Hannah Williams	Cosden
"	28	Edward Gracie	to	Ann Anderson	Cosden
"	28	James Benson	to	Mary Penis	Cosden
Sept.	6	Thomas Roberts	to	Sarah Price	Cosden
"	11	Nathaniel Tipton	to	Mary Gibson	Cosden
"	10	Evan Morgan	to	Margaret McDonald	Cosden
Oct.	10	William Groves	to	Rebecca Logan?	Cosden
Nov.	4	David Gatchell	to	Sally Stokeley	Cosden
"	6	Isaac Jones	to	Elizabeth Conoley	Cosden
"	18	Dennis Vanhorn	to	Tempy Pennington	Cosden
"	24	Noleto Jones	to	Mary Boyer	Cosden
"	25	Robert Crouch	to	Hannah Creawes	Cosden
Dec.	1	John Thompson	to	Elizabeth Bird	Cosden
"	3	John Hollen	to	Sarah Laird	Cosden
"	9	Benjamin Wilson	to	Elizabeth Chick	Cosden
"	10	Thomas Miller, Sr.	to	Eleanor Wollex	Cosden
"	20	David Culbertson	to	Clarissa Brevard	Cosden
"	22	Peter Tigard	to	Mary Ereand	Cosden
"	25	John Wright	to	Ann Mayhught	Cosden
"	29	Charles Ford	to	Sarah Montgomery	Cosden
	1801				
Jan.	1	John Prower	to	Jane Prower	Cosden
"	13	James Manly	to	Ann Ford	Cosden
"	20	Thomas Slagle	to	Jane Black	Cosden
"	21	Frederick White	to	Ann Simpers	Cosden
"	24	Rudolph Gonce	to	Ann Cox	Cosden
"	24	Ingry Thompson	to	Mary Holton	Cosden
"	28	John S. Moffitt	to	Mary Moffitt	Cosden
"	28	William Patterson	to	Elizabeth Money	Cosden
"	30	Sylvester Nowland	to	Elizabeth Hawkins	Cosden
"	31	Richard Whartz	to	Margaret Justice	Cosden
Feb.	4	James Miller?	to	Eleanor Hall	Cosden
"	16	William Commegeys	to	Eliza Ward	Cosden
"	17	Philip A. Barton	to	Eliza Jay	Cosden
"	20	Putman Ewing	to	Jane McCleland	Cosden
"	23	Henry Pearce	to	Elizabeth H. Ward	Cosden
Mar.	5	William Richardson	to	Sarah Hughes	Cosden
"	7	Levi Johnston	to	Mary Boucher	Cosden
"	10	William Hays	to	Mary McMannis	Cosden
"	18	Thomas Bell	to	Anna Hamelton	Cosden
"	18	Richard Bratcher	to	Ann Maria Short	Cosden

		MAN		WOMAN	MINISTER
"	21	Thomas Yeamans	to	Margaret Grace McGaw	Cosden
"	26	Jonas McCluser	to	Maria McC.ain	Cosden
Apr.	8	Elijah Eliason	to	Mary Savin	Cosden
"	14	George Walmsley	to	Sarah Everson	Cosden
"	14	Andrew Gordon	to	Elizabeth Ogle	Cosden
"	14	William Whan	to	Elizabeth Gillespie	Cosden
"	29	John Crouch	to	Jane McClure	Cosden
May	12	George Turner	to	Eliza Hattea?	Cosden
"	13	Vatchel Terry Price	to	Araminta Ann Hendrickson	Cosden
"	22	Gassaway Watkins	to	Milcha Allfree	Cosden
"	29	Adam Wilkinson	to	Eliza Donell	Cosden
"	30	Benjamin Tyson	to	Rosanna Simpers	Cosden
June	3	Levi Shattuck	to	Cassandra Graham	Cosden
"	20	Jacob Price	to	Millicent Hendrickson	Cosden
"	26	David Cummings	to	Elizabeth Catherg	
July	1	Charles T. Bivens	to	Martha Pennington	
"	8	James Sloan	to	Elizabeth Collins	
"	18	Robt. Johnson	to	Deborah Boucher	
"	27	Samuel Aikin	to	Rachel Corby	
"	30	Alexander Alexander	to	Ann Barr	
Aug.	8	Wm. Helmstarff	to	Hester Allen	
"	13	Geo. Cully	to	Ann Barr	
"	19	Joseph Ho t	to	Rachel Tyson	
"	19	Joseph Brown	to	Priscilla Thomas	
"	24	Edward Porter	to	Mary Patterson	
Sept.	4	James Lake	to	Ann Segars	
"	11	Johnson Porter	to	Elizabeth Pearce	
"	12	Robert Cook	to	Catherine Kilpatrick	
"	17	Thomas Bricison	to	Susannah Sterling	
Oct.	10	Joseph Bolton	to	Althea Roberts	
"	14	Joseph Walker	to	Mary Thomas	
"	24	Peter Graham	to	Margaret Stalkup	
"	29	Francis Harvey	to	Rachel Scott	
"	31	Jos. McCreary	to	Eleanor McCreary	
"	31	William Rich	to	Mary Wilson	
"	31	Reuben Boulden	to	Sarah Beaston	
Nov.	18	Abner? Scoll (Scott)	to	E'izabeth Montgomery	
"	18	Richard Keatley	to	Elizabeth Barnett	
"	23	James Steel	to	Ann Evans	
"	26	Edward Jackson	to	Mary Fox	
"	29	John Evans, Jr.	to	Eliza Marshall	
Dec.	5	Emery Cox	to	Mary Clark	
1802					
Jan.	5	John Thompson	to	Hannah Follers	
"	19	James Aikens	to	Margaret Matthews	
"	25	John Faytor?	to	Mary McDowell	
"	25	Nathan Ireland	to	Rachel Bristow	
Feb.	3	Thomas Roach	to	Margaret Pugh	
"	13	William Wilcox	to	Mary Sherer	
"	16	Elisha Gatchell	to	Susannah Ewing	
"	17	William Foard	to	Elizabeth Beaston	
Mar.	1	Thomas Patten	to	Martha Meeke	
		Thomas Sprorten	to	Catherine Abrahams	
"	5	Benj. Sluyter	to	Ann Wirt	
"	7	Nathan Tyson	to	Mary Thompson	
"	12	Samuel McKay	to	Susan Etherington	
"	12	Harman Husband	to	Mary Wingate	
"	30	Jesse Haltham	to	Rachel Pennington	

MAN				WOMAN	MINISTER
Apr.	5	John Coppin	to	Anna Craig	
"	19	Benjamin Craige	to	Eliza Redgrave	
May	8	John Beeks	to	Rachel Crissfield	
"	15	James Wilcox	to	Mary Conwell	
"	20	Francis Segars	to	Mary Grimes	
"	21	Richard Beaston	to	Ann Beaston	
"	25	James Allen	to	Sarah Stephens	
"	29	John Howard	to	Martha McCracken	
"	29	Cornelius Vansant	to	Jane Price	
		John Young	to	Rachel Ashbaugh	
June	8	Nathan Bouldin	to	Mary Foard	
"	17	Richard Savin, Sr.	to	Mary B. Pennington	
"	21	Thomas Smith	to	Jane Kidd	
July	3	Thomas Miller	to	Abby George	
"	6	Edward Stokes	to	Margaret Conway	
"	19	Nathan Prockton	to	Millicent Ganish	
"	28	Patrick Collins	to	Margaret Donaldson	
"	28	John Little	to	Ann Crookshank	
"	29	Peregrine Severson	to	Ann Stephens	
Aug.	7	Michael Hague	to	Elizabeth Lusby	
"	12	William Sheppard	to	Eliza Bittle	
"	21	John Kirk	to	Mary Thompson	
Sept.	3	John Wallace	to	Ann McFarley	
"	23	Thomas Price	to	Sarah Gears	
"	27	Robert Smiley	to	Nancy Johnson	
Oct.	4	Israel Evans	to	Abbe Alexander	
"	4	Robert John	to	Catherine Pennington	
"	21	James Evans	to	Martha Gillespie	
Nov.	6	Benjamin Thomas	to	Margaret Rylett	
"	12	Richard Hall	to	Hannah Logan	
"	24	Henry Keathly	to	Ann Hitchcock	
"	25	Edward Hanna	to	Rebecca Proctor	
"	26	William Pearce	to	Sarah Arratt	
Dec.	1	Joseph Bowen	to	Sylvia Evans	
"	5	John Hasson	to	Agnes Meek	
"	5	John Sappington	to	Sophia Severson	
Dec.	8	Jacob Hyland	to	Elizabeth Thackery	
"	30	William Winstandley	to	Ann Lusby	
"	30	Nathaniel Cleaver	to	Margaret Page	
	1803				
Jan.	5	Thomas Woppleton	to	Betsy Tyson	
"	11	Raymond Beetle	to	Polly Morton	
"	4	Joseph Bayard	to	Rachel Myers	
Feb.	5	Robert Black	to	Sarah Parsley	
"	22	Caron Burgoin	to	Rebecca Cantley	
"	23	George Willson	to	Sarah Thompson	
"	25	Henry Hayes	to	Elizabeth Pogue	
Mar.	17	Benjamin Alexander	to	Rebecca McLure	
"	21	John George	to	Mary Tyson	
"	22	James Berry	to	Ann E. Severson	
"	23	John Bryan	to	Mary Foster	
"	24	William Rice	to	Milcabe Owens	
"	29	David Dickey	to	Ann Moffett	
"	31	Thomas Pennington	to	Batris- R. Brewer	
Apr.	4	James Lowry	to	Ann Belfour	
"	11	James Pennington	to	Rebecca Welsh	
"	23	David Cunningham	to	Katie Tomlinson	
"	26	David Fulton	to	Martha Alexander	
"	27	Samuel Morford	to	Polly Bailey	

MAN			WOMAN	MINISTER
" 30	John Williams	to	Mary Bennett	
May 11	Roger Hammill	to	Hannah Stewart	
" 13	Moses Ross	to	Jenny Biggs	
" 19	John Cashner	to	Rebecca Davis	
" 21	Thomas Logan	to	Jenny Medoll	
Jan. 20	William Pearce	to	Sarah Baxter	Rev. Mr. Reese
May 27	William McCracken	to	Ruthy Richardson	
" 30	John Mitchell	to	Elizabeth Williams	
" 31	William Winchester	to	Betsy Crawson	
June 2	Richard Mahan	to	Mary Short	
" 7	William Boulden	to	Margaret Taylor	
" 18	William Deween	to	Elizabeth Dickson	
" 23	John Coale	to	Jane Beaston	
" 28	Benjamin Owens	to	Elizabeth Currier	
" 29	James McCracken	to	Ann Armstrong	
July 20	Jacob Latman?	to	Amelia Millbourne	
" 27	James Camron	to	Letitia Smith	
Aug. 6	George Niblick	to	Sarah Webb	
" 15	John Mullen	to	Margaret McMaster	
" 22	Thomas Mahan	to	Jean Rock	
" 29	James Janney	to	Margaret Gillespie	
" 30	Isaac Lancaster	to	Rebecca Pennington	
Sept. 1	Arnold Hodgson	to	Patty Bevins	
" 10	Samuel Hill	to	Nancy Phillips	
" 23	Benjamin Pearce	to	Nancy Houston	
" 23	Jesse Holt	to	Margaret Hemphill	
" 24	Sampson G. Hyland	to	Elizabeth Bristow	
Oct. 10	Thomas Boyer	to	Hetty Wallace	
" 25	Joseph Harlan	to	Amelia Abrams	
" 26	Spencer Etherington	to	Eleanor Beck	
Nov. 9	Peter Goodwin	to	Eleanor Scott	
" 13	Isaac Taylor	to	Sarah Manley	
" 16	Harry Sluyter	to	Siney Wirt	
" 23	Thomas Ferguson	to	Catherine Montgomery	
Dec. 2	George Morrison	to	Rebecca Maguire	
" 6	Isaac Sterling	to	Mary Crow	
" 14	Moses Cannon	to	Sarah Massett	
" 14	Thomas Rutter	to	Ann Willis	
" 22	James Nixon	to	Catherine Moody	
" 31	Jacob Bateman	to	Mary Adair	
1804				
Jan. 2	John Allman	to	Martha Jewell	
" 2	John Wood	to	Patty Everett	
" 9	Enos Howell		Ann Beaston	
" 16	John Richardson	to	Ann Lum	
" 18	Fredus Robinson	to	Sarah Gears	
" 18	Thomas Robinson	to	Rebecca Moss	
" 21	Aldridge Robinson	to	Tabitha Page	
Feb. 11	Caleb Read	to	Polly Greenwell	
" 14	William Low	to	Isabella Nash	
" 23	Robert Wright	to	Margaret Cantwell	
" 25	Robert Walsh	to	Margaret Cather	
Mar. 8	Michael Ruley	to	Henny Crossley	
" 14	James Willson	to	Rebecca Cromwell	
" 17	Isaac Biddle	to	Elizabeth Aldridge	
" 23	Alexander Wilson	to	Mary Hyland	
" 23	Wm. MacKelney	to	Margaret Moore	
" 23	John Clark	to	Elizabeth V. Miller	
" 27	Henry Fowler	to	Susan Pearce	

MAN			WOMAN	MINISTER
Apr.	2	Samuel Burlin to	Jane Sterrett	
"	7	Levi G. Foard to	Ann Bayard	
"	11	Isaac Lum to	Amelia Crow	
May	1	George Davidson to	Catherine Thomas	
"	9	Jesse Holt to	Anne Tyson	
"	9	John Pearce to	Rebecca Sappington	Davis
"	14	Christopher Little to	Mary Simcoe	Davis
"	17	Andrew Egan to	Ruth Conway	Davis
"	17	William Waggener to	Sarah Jackson	Davis
"	26	Macey Francis to	Anne Thomas	Davis
June	4	Lambert Veasey to	Araminta Money	Davis
"	6	Joseph Richardson to	Sophia Harkin	Davis
"	12	Joseph Boulton to	Rebecca Batemon	Davis
"	14	Peregrine Greenwood to	Martha Welsh	Davis
"	22	Joseph Bouldin to	Ann Simpers	Davis
Aug.	9	Jacob Wilson to	Rachel McClary	Davis
"	21	William Brumfield to	Elizabeth Owens	Davis
Oct.	31	Stephen Owens to	Mary Ann Gaunce	
"	31	Joseph Polloch to	Ann Mathews	
Nov.	6	Charles Beaston to	Sara Crow	
June	28	Benjamin Pennington to	Sara Roberts	Davis
July	15	William Ford to	Mary Robnet	Davis
"	19	Nathan Foster to	Susan Bryson	Davis
"	21	Thomas Melvolin? to	Elizabeth S. Chambers	Davis
"	31	John McCullough to	Ester Williams	Davis
Aug.	30	Peregrine Severson to	Elizabeth Stephens	
"	30	Richard Hukill to	Edder Wingate	
"	30	George D. Handy to	Mary Alden	
Sept.	1	Daniel Brumfield to	Lydia Watson	
"	21	William Freeman Abbott to	Elizabeth Williamson	
"	28	William Milburn to	Rebecca Lowe	
"	28	Thomas H. White to	Mary Key Heath	
Oct.	11	James McIntosh to	Ann Pearse	
"	18	John Scott to	Isabella Rammage	
Dec.	14	William Smith to	Margaret Brooks	
Nov.	6	Nathan Blake to	Polly Abrams	
"	15	Charles Buckwith to	Sarah? Goldsborrough	
"	24	Zachery Gray to	Sarah Callender	
"	28	Samuel Owens to	Mary Lassell	
Dec.	13	Thomas McLaughlin to	Jane Barr	
"	18	Samuel McDowell to	Rebecca Matthew	
"	18	Samuel Price to	Hannah Greenwood	
"	19	Simon Dennison to	Christiana Hitchcock	
"	23	Lewis Thomas to	Margaret Campbell	
1805				
Jan.	3	David Alexander to	Charlotte Rogers	
"	5	Lambert Foard to	Ann Hamm	
"	7	Hyland Price to	Rebecca Wingate	
"	8	Peter McKenney to	Blanch Owens	
"	10	Henry Stedham to	Elizabeth Rutter	Handy
"	7	John Evans to	Susannah Buckworth	
"	19	Charles Clark to	Jane Wollocks	Handy
"	19	Enoch Cloud to	Margaret Hamphile	Handy
"	28	Isaac Foster to	Martha Cazier	Davis
Feb.	5	Joseph Sorret to	Arminta Manly	Handy
"	7	Richard Pennington to	Hukell	Davis
"	16	Andrew Bryan to	Elizabeth Parkinson	Davis
"	18	Daniel O'Donnel to	Jane Dunker	Davis
"	27	Thomas Russell to	Esther Russell	

	MAN		WOMAN	MINISTER
Mar. 6	George Gillespie	to	Mary McClelland	McGraw
" 6	John Piper	to	Eliza Bowman	McGraw
" 8	Joseph Smith	to	Elizabeth Pennington	McGraw
" 9	William Smith	to	Elizabeth Grace	
" 12	George Benjamin	to	Sara Taylor	
" 13	James Wilson	to	Jane Cunningham	
" 20	George Simpson	to	Polly Taylor	
" 21	John Hitchcock	to	Jane Short	
" 25	Thomas Clark	to	Priscilla Parsley	Hindman
Apr. 1	Robert H. Archer	to	Mary Stump	Hindman
" 3	Robert Ratcliff	to	Susannah Carpenter	Hindman
June 29	John Cresewell	to	Agnes Hood	Hindman
May 6	Brinton Johns	to	Elizabeth Mitchell	Hindman
" 20	Harthsel Hessey	to	Elizabeth Brady	Davis
" 22	Robert Donaldson	to	Orpah Logan?	Davis
" 27	Joseph Hendrickson	to	Ann Guffey	McGraw
June 6	Thomas Culbertson	to	Elizabeth Ashbaw	Hindman
" 11	Owen Murphy	to	Ann Philips	Hindman
" 22	John Etherington	to	Rebecca Price	Davis
July 1	Clement Guytor	to	Mary Bateman	Hindman
" 2	Thomas Leech	to	Ruth Thomas	Hindman
" 2	Michael Nuomee	to	Mary Couden	Hindman
" 10	Thomas Watson	to	Hester Beck	Handy
" 17	John Foard	to	Rebecca Kankey	Handy
Aug. 6	Peregrine L. Lynch	to	Catherine Reese	Davis
" 6	William Comby	to	Sarah Stedham	Davis
Sept. 8	Joseph Harris?	to	Mary Walmsley	Davis
" 13	John Thackery	to	Eliza Roach	Hindman
" 26	John Lusby	to	Ann Walmsley	Davis
Nov. 4	James Scott	to	Elizabeth B. Casho	Davis
Sept. 26	John Newton	to	Elizabeth Carpenter	Davis
Nov. 18	Jesse Money	to	Ann Jones	Davis
" 14	Richard Bryson	to	Catherine Hindman	Robinson
" 19	Dr. Richard L. Davis	to	Julian N. Veasey	Davis
" 19	Nicholas Vandagrift	to	Mary Biddle	Handy
" 28	Jonathan Short	to	Rebecca Shields	Handy
Dec. 7	Adam Wilkinson	to	Elizabeth Hussleton	Handy
" 11	John Donathy	to	Mary Dodds	Handy
" 12	Peregrine Briscoe	to	Elizabeth Rollison	Davis
1806				
Jan. 4	Joseph Biggs	to	Oma Hayes	Handy
" 9	Patrick Foy	to	Jane Smith	Handy
" 15	Isaac D. Watson	to	Sarah Baker	Handy
" 16	Augustine Sc—y	to	Sarah Othosot or n	Davis
Feb. 8	John Cochran	to	Amelia Lum	Davis
" 11	James Couson	to	Jamimah Hughes	Handy
" 12	Stephen Veazey	to	Amelia Dawson	Handy
" 13	William Ricketts	to	Mary Whann	Hindman
" 17	Andrew Willox	to	Letitia Willson	Hindman
" 19	James W. Munigan	to	Racheal Armstrong	Handy
" 26	John W. Klinton	to	Elizabeth Fulton	Handy
" 27	William Hollingsworth	to	Ann Black	Reed
Mar. 17	Thomas Matthews	to	Margaret Cosgrove	Hindman
" 20	Andrew Stalkeep or kup	to	Rachel Hitchcock	Handy
" 22	Ramond Biddle	to	Fanny Miller	Handy
" 10	Levi Oldham	to	Milcha Rowley	Handy
Sept. 5	James Lomax	to	Sarah Ewing	McGraw

	MAN		WOMAN	MINISTER
1805				
Dec. 5	James Christie	to	Mary Stende	McGraw
" 26	Geo. Gillespie	to	Sarah Hall	McGraw
" 26	Thomas Kelly	to	Celia Egan	McGraw
1806				
Jan. 16	Wm. Cameron	to	Deborah Williams	McGraw
Mar. 6	Matthew Cameron	to	Mary Russell	McGraw
" 15	James B. Porter	to	Martha M. Culley	McGraw
" 6	Walter Songwell	to	Nelly Scott	Hindman
Apr. 23	William Walmsley	to	Rebecca James	Davis
" 29	John Carruthers	to	Ann Everitt	Handy
" 29	Zachariah B. Graham	to	Rebecca Lewis	Handy
" 29	Robert Lochard	to	Ebby Brown	Handy
May 1	John Porter	to	Eliza Comegys	Davis
" 1	James Patridge	to	Hannah Hollingsworth	Hindman
" 22	Andrew Boyce	to	Mary Bristow	Hindman
" 27	John Griffith	to	Alathea Cosden	Handy
June 5	John M. Shields	to	Jane McCreery	Handy
July 16	John Linton	to	Martha Rawlings	Handy
" 25	John Davis	to	Ann Thompson	Handy
Aug. 6	Henry McCauley	to	Ann McCauley	McGraw
" 6	James Morgan	to	Henrietta Maria Ward	Davis
" 20	John Barnes	to	Ann Warren	Davis
" 25	Benjamin Smith	to	Marian Chick	Davis
" 27	Lambert Sewell	to	Amelia Aldridge	Handy
Sept. 2	Samuel Aldridge	to	Margery George	Handy
" 10	John Hyland	to	Margery Mauldin	Handy
" 10	Joshua Bennett	to	Allibena Bennett	Handy
" 11	William Hamitlon	to	Margaret Culbertson	Handy
" 22	Thomas Scott	to	Rosanna Tyson	Handy
" 24	Elijah McCray	to	Jane Bath	Handy
" 25	John Stephenson	to	Mary Long Porter	McGraw
" 25	James Cummings	to	Mary Reynolds	McGraw
Oct. 4	George Price	to	Terry Owens	Davis
" 6	Hugh T. Ferguson	to	Martha Corbett	Davis
" 22	Fisher Smith	to	Ann Manley	Handy
Nov. 15	John Johnson	to	Margaret Alexander	Handy
" 25	John Boyd	to	Mary Currey	Handy
Dec. 1	Robert Wilson	to	Ann Jamison	Handy
" 9	John Tomlinson	to	Isabella McKeowen	Handy
" 24	Jacob Lum	to	Rebecca Alexander	Davis
" 27	Alexander Patterson	to	Priscilla Stephens	Hindman
" 29	Israel Alexander	to	Rebecca Culley	Hindman
" 30	Zacharias Derickson	to	Margaret McGuire	Hindman
" 30	George Ricketts	to	Rachel Hewitt	McFerrell
1807				
Jan. 3	John Wimble	to	Rachel Thompson	Handy
" 6	John Ward Junior	to	Margaret Worthington	Handy
" 8	Benjamin McVey	to	Rebecca Baker	Handy
" 12	Elihu Roach	to	Emily Crouch	Handy
" 13	John W. Etherington	to	Sarah Wingate	Handy
" 13	Nathan Boulden	to	Frances H. Wallace	Davis
" 15	John Sparrowgrove	to	Isabella Anges	McGraw
" 17	Ebenezer Watts	to	Henrietta Hukill	Davis
" 20	John Rawlings	to	Elizabeth McCleland	Handy
" 21	William Logan	to	Margaret Corbay	Handy
" 22	John Thomas Slicer	to	Deborah Kirk	McGraw
" 24	Moses Cannon	to	Ann Hendrickson	Handy

		MAN		WOMAN	MINISTER
Feb.	4	Matthew Alexander	to	Ann Tyson	Hindman
"	4	William Reynolds	to	Francina Bravard	Hindman
"	11	Isaac Phillips	to	Priscilla Hill	Handy
"	18	Stephen Bayard	to	Ann Wirt	Handy
"	25	Levi Quinsley	to	Margaret Beaks	Handy
"	25	Charles G. Black	to	Sarah Baily	Handy
"	25	Emmor Knight	to	Hester Haines	Handy
Mar.	3	Nathan Tyson	to	Catharine Crouch	Handy
"	6	Samuel Buckwith	to	Mary Eppell?	Handy
"	11	Jonathan Johnson	to	Elizabeth Boyd	Handy
"	6	Samuel Ramsay	to	Margaret Stephenson	McGraw
Apr.	6	Joseph White	to	Ruth Henderson	McGraw
Mar.	17	Thomas Simpers	to	Jane Burke	Handy
"	25	Josiah Johnson	to	Ann Baxter	Handy
"	28	John McCoy	to	Eleanor Lockman	Handy
"	30	James H. Colmary	to	Sarah Bennett	Handy
"	17	John McClenahan	to	Sarah Morrison	Handy
Apr.	2	Edward O'Harrow	to	Mary Hill	Handy
"	10	William Welsh	to	Ann Lemmon	W. Davis
"	11	John Maslen	to	Ann Hendrickson	W. Davis
"	15	John Oldham	to	Elizabeth Mahan	W. Handy
Jan.	12	Sampson George	to	Eliza Campbell	W. Hindman
"	12	Alexander Morrison	to	Mary Biddle	W. Hindman
May	7	Samuel Coudon	to	Jean Kerr	W. Hindman
"	12	John Postle	to	Rachel Vandyke	W. Davis
"	22	George Turner	to	Sarah Hynson	W. Davis
"	27	Thomas Cox	to	Mary Redgrove	W. Davis
"	30	John Smith	to	Francina W. Lary	W. Handy
"	30	Andrew Smith	to	Ann Hodgson	W. Davis
June	3	Jacob Roach	to	Betsy Pugh	W. Handy
"	3	John Spence	to	Jane Morrisson	W. Handy
"	16	Henry Miller	to	Sarah Taylor	
"	19	Nathan Lochtin	to	Ann Gorrill	W. Handy
"	23	John Armstrong	to	Sarah Dun	W. Handy
"	25	James Stevenson	to	Mary Black	M. Davy
"	29	Jamy? McVey	to	Martha Kidd	McGraw
"	30	John Bouldin	to	Ann Farij?	M. Davy
July	1	Edmund Burke	to	Mary Johnson	W. Handy
"	11	Alexander Sturgeon	to	Charlott Ferguson	W. Handy
"	15	David Pearson	to	Margaret Huey	W. Handy
"	18	William Slaughter	to	Amelia Bateman	W. Handy
"	21	Thos. P. Sappington	to	Elizabeth Evern	M. Davy
Sept.	5	John Kearns	to	Jane Adder	W. Davis
"	18	Reubin Reynolds	to	Henrietta Cromwell	W. McGraw
"	21	George Mather	to	Eleanor Barrington	W. Handy
"	29	John Gonell	to	Eleanor Willox	W. Hindman
Oct.	1	Barney Gainor	to	Sarah Ashbaugh	W. Handy
"	14	Robert Lusby	to	Anna M. Money	W. Davis
"	28	Henry Lowe	to	Mary Moore	W. Handy
Nov.	5	James Phillips	to	Ann McCauley	W. Handy
"	5	John Brown	to	Margaret Leech	W. Handy
"	10	Sinclair Lancaster	to	Mary Hukin	W .Davis
"	16	David Whann	to	Margaret Maffitt	W. Duhi
"	18	Joseph Chalk	to	Isabella Hewey	W. Handy
"	26	Edward I. Jones	to	Ann Jones	W. Handy

	MAN		WOMAN	MINISTER
Dec. 2	James M. Young	to	Sarah Waram	W. Handy
" 3	John Roberts	to	Sarah Wiley	W. Dvisa
" 5	Jacob Black	to	Margaret Mahan	W. Handy
" 5	James Blackistone	to	Jemima Foard	W. Davis
" 7	Henry Spence	to	Esther Davidson	W. Handy
" 15	George Young	to	Rachel Hendrickson	W. Davy
" 17	Joseph Crofford	to	Lydia Harvey	W. Davy
" 17	Charles McCray	to	Sarah Taylor	W. Handy
" 21	Jesse Irvine	to	Nancy Garrish	W. Handy
" 21	John Smith	to	Mary Taylor	W. Handy
" 22	Samuel Philips	to	Rachel Lowe	W. Handy
" 23	Henry Simpers	to	Jemima Kilgore	W. Handy
" 31	Joseph Etherington	to	Sarah Lusby	W. Davy
1808				
Jan. 1	John Burd	to	Mary Dickson	W. Davis
" 2	William Woodall	to	Rebecca Bristoe	W. Handy
" 2	Robert Carson	to	Margaret Blakey	W. Handy
" 5	Hugh Fulton	to	Ann Rammage	W. Hindman
" 9	John McCauley	to	Elizabeth McCauley	W. McGraw
" 13	Stephen George	to	Mary Simpers	W. Handy
" 18	Ira Roach	to	Margaret Crouch	W. Handy
" 21	Thomas Moody	to	Margaret Stokes	W. Davis
" 26	Charles Carey	to	Beulah Tyson	W. Handy
" 28	Hugh Brown	to	Catherine Greaves	W. Handy
" 30	William Moore	to	Mary Morgan	W. Handy
Feb. 3	Azra Churchman	to	Eliz. W. Clenachan	W. Handy
" 9	Abraham Bowland	to	Mary W. Clenichan	W. Handy
" 10	William Lusby	to	Eleanor Etherington	W. Davis
" 11	George Everon	to	Rebecca Dixon	W. Davis
" 19	George Smith	to	Milcah Watkins	W. Davis
" 24	Benjamin Craig	to	Rebecca Robertson	W. Davis
Mar. 2	Michael Lunn	to	Martha Manley	W. Handy
" 3	Jacob Egner	to	Elizabeth Kinkead	W. Farrett
Apr.	John Johnson	to	Lydia Stokes	W. Handy
Feb. 25	James Fulton	to	Hannah Simpers	W. Handy
" 25	Hugh Jackson	to	Elizabeth Whitelock	W. Handy
Mar. 14	Thomas Scott	to	Nancy Ewing	W. Handy
" 19	Benjamin Pennington	to	Mary Pugh	W. Davy
" 23	John Etherington	to	Eleanor Gillespie	W. Davis
" 29	John Devenport	to	Martha Coulson	W. Davis
" 31	Joseph Veazey	to	Ann Worth	W. Davis
Apr. 2	William Young	to	Margaret Davidson	W. Handy
" 2	Adam Short	to	Alathea Carpenter	W. Handy
" 2	Thomas Mackey	to	Catherine Evans	W. Davis
Mar. 10	Robert Leech	to	Elizabeth Johnston	W. Hindman
" 10	James McCormeck	to	Ann Orr	W. McGraw
" 10	Joshua Harlan	to	Deborah Cather	W. McGraw
" 10	Joseph Brown	to	Rachel Brown	W. McGraw
" 10	Thomas Williams	to	Jane Cameron	W. McGraw
" 10	Abner Kirk	to	Sarah Stephenson	W. McGraw
May 4	William Clark	to	Julia Ann Mercer	W. Davis
" 5	John Booth	to	Isabella Longwin?	W. Davis
" 17	Fredus Aldridge	to	Rebecca Hyland	McGraw
" 19	Nicholas Price	to	Mary Evans	Davis
" 28	Isaac Lorte	to	Millescent McLlure	Davis
June 8	Abraham Biddle	to	Mary Lowry	Davis
" 10	Phillip Plummar	to	Edy May	Davis

MAN				WOMAN	MINISTER
July	5	William Damsell	to	Elizabeth Harvey	Hindman
"	8	McKinney	to	Elizabeth Riggs	Davis
"	12	Nathan McVey	to	Elizabeth Matthews	Paid
"	14	Moses Scott	to	Mary Kinkaid	Duke
"	19	Lewis Harlan	to	Louisa Ann Cromwell	McGraw
Aug.	5	Samuel Hemptton	to	Delilah Steel	McGraw
"	10	John Devlin	to	Margaret Murphy	Duke
Sept.	21	Charles Pearson	to	Mary Kelly	Duke
"	21	James Mercer	to	Elizabeth Money	Davis
"	22	James Cook	to	Rebecca Chambers	Duke
"	24	Moses Cannady	to	Sarah Biggs	Duke
"	27	John Calloway	to	Elizabeth Connoly	McGraw
Oct.	30	William Reeves	to	Jane Taylor	McGraw
"	14	John Runk	to	Jeminah Ross	Davis
"	19	William Hukill	to	Elizabeth Roach	Duke
Nov.	10	John Burke	to	Elizabeth Johnston	Duke
"	22	Peregrine Ward	to	Mary Ruley	Davis
Dec.	6	John Foard	to	Catherine Hedrick	McGraw
"	14	Samuel Rutter	to	Rebecca Rogers	McGraw
"	21	William Redmond	to	Lucretia Dunlap	McGraw
"	24	Edward Crouch	to	Elizabeth Hogen	Duke
"	27	Robert Hayes	to	Betsy Bristoe	Davis
"	27	Samuel Wirt	to	Francena Byard	Davis
1809					
Jan.	3	William Price	to	May Howell	Duke
"	10	Isaac Moore	to	Sarah Veach	Duke
"	21	John Thompson	to	Ally Nelson	Duke
"	23	Jonas Dixon	to	Sarah Etherington	Davis
"	23	Richard Simpson	to	Mary Nowland	McGraw
"	31	Samuel Willson	to	Rebecca Young	Duke
"	31	Elias Cox	to	Mary Loftus	Davis
Feb.	1	James Dysart	to	Sarah Updegrove	Davis
"	7	Jacob Stephens	to	Sarah Sappington	Davis
"	8	Charles Rolliston	to	Sarah Cox	Davis
"	10	Benedict Craddoche	to	Margaret Thomas	Davis
"	14	John Jennings	to	Sarah Benjamin	McGraw
"	14	James Sewall	to	Ann Maria Rudolph	Handy
"	15	Joseph T. Grimes	to	Nancy Fowler	Duke
"	23	James Anderson	to	Netty Carpenter	McGraw
"	27	Thomas Stephens	to	May Henderson	Davis
"	27	John Henderson	to	Nina Henderson	McGraw
Mar.	1	Benjamin Dennis	to	Sarah Grahman	Davis
"	2	John Barnett	to	Sarah Keithley	McGraw
"	6	William Davis	to	Elizabeth Ford	Davis
"	8	Thomas Ryland	to	Rebecca Snow	Davis
"	9	George Remington	to	Margaret Sherman?	Duke
"	19	Sampson G. Hyland	to	Mary Williamson	McGraw
"	28	Christopher Bricks?	to	Mary W. Coudon	Davis
"	29	Joshua Pearce	to	Julia Sappington	Davis
"	30	David Wall	to	Sarah Derrickson	McGraw
Apr.	1	John Rob	to	Sarah McCummings	Davis
"	11	William Davidson	to	Lehtia Jackson	McGraw
"	11	John Vallindan	to	Elizabeth Wood	Duke
"	7	Hugh Patterson	to	Ann Etherington	Davis
"	15	Joshua Ryland	to	Rachel Brooks	Davis
"	18	Thomas Owens	to	Rebecca Simpers	McGraw
"	24	James A. Nowland	to	Sarah Morgan	Davis

MAN				WOMAN	MINISTER
1808					
Aug.	2	William Tosh	to	Eleanor Nesbit	McGraw
"	18	Henry McCollough	to	Agnes Dixon	McGraw
"	15	David Brown	to	Rebecca Kelly	McGraw
Nov.	10	John Hellough	to	Margaret Porter	McGraw
"	17	James Gillespie	to	Lawrainer Rawlings	McGraw
1809					
Jan.	12	David Gilmore	to	Elizabeth Kerr	McGraw
"	29	William Leech	to	Elizabeth McKeag	McGraw
Mar.	2	Randal Death	to	Martha McLarry	McGraw
"	25	William Radley	to	Jane Campbell	McGraw
May	10	Thomas Lewis	to	Ann Mitchell	Duke
"	11	John Puntney	to	Ann Veasey	Davis
"	22	Bernan O'Neal	to	Jane McClelland	Davis
"	23	William Smith	to	Mary Relah?	McGraw
"	30	William Ward	to	Ann Sproat	Davis
June	1	William G. Richardson	to	Julia Lum	Davis
"	12	John H. Ford	to	Sophia Cosden	Duke
"	15	Thomas Miller	to	Elizabeth Simpson	McGraw
"	28	John Scott	to	Ann Crouch	McGraw
July	5	Robert A. Sewart	to	Priscilla E. Manly?	McGraw
"	10	John Johnston	to	Agnes Gallagher	McGraw
"	18	William Curl	to	Martha McGee	Duke
"	24	Isaac Beetle	to	Mary Hughs	Davis
Aug.	31	Joel Hayes	to	Rachel Bristow	Davis
1808					
Aug.	18	John Creswell	to	Tabitha Gitchel	McGraw
1809					
Sept.	7	Robert Watson	to	Jane Orr	Rev. Mr. Duke
"	21	James Wingate	to	Mary Ward	Rev. Mr. Davis
"	28	John Anderson	to	Elizabeth Roberts	Rev. Mr. Davis
Oct.	2	John Harry	to	Mary Short	Rev. Mr. Duke
"	3	George Dixon	to	Mary Houck	Rev. Mr. Duke
"	24	William Stewart	to	Hetty Alexander	Rev. Mr. McGraw
Nov.	23	Thomas Simpers	to	Hannah Camblin	Rev. Mr. McGraw
"	15	Manley Keene	to	Sarah Hodgson	Rev. Mr. Davis
"	27	John Ireland	to	Ann Penix	Rev. Mr. Davis
Dec.	2	Charles Buckwith	to	Hannah Carpender	Rev. Mrfl Davis
"	12	John N. Black	to	Nancy Hasson	Rev. Mr. McGraw
"	14	John Stalcup	to	Lydia Crookshanks	Rev. Mr. McGraw
"	14	Alexander Hasson	to	Martha Crawford	Rev. Mr. Duke
"	14	Joseph Ash	to	Ann Wingate	Rev. Mr. Duke
"	24	Matthias Allen	to	Charity Caulk	Rev. Mr. Duke
"	30	Nathan Farrow	to	Elizabeth Holton	Rev. Mr. Davis
1810					
Jan.	1	Joseph Phillips	to	Rachel Biddle	Rev. Mr. McGraw
"	1	Thomas Cork?	to	Betsey Yeamans	Rev. Mr. McGraw
"	8	Fredy Ryland	to	Elizabeth Ewing	Rev. Mr. Duke
"	8	James Hayes	to	Elizabeth Bowen	Rev. Mr. Duke
"	16	Thomas Whiteside	to	Rebecca Morgan	Rev. Mr. Farrell
"	20	David Robinson	to	Maria Hollis	Rev. Mr. Davis
"	23	Joshua Joyce	to	Ann Hyland	Rev. Mr. McGraw
"	23	Samuel Burnite	to	Rachel Kilgore	Rev. Mr. Duke
"	26	Samuel McCoy	to	Elizabeth Murphy	Rev. Mr. Duke
"	30	William Bayham	to	Ann Pearce	Rev. Mr. Duke
Feb.	7	Harmon Phillips	to	Mary Reed	Rev. Mr. Davis
"	10	Peregrine Cox	to	Sarah Davis	Rev. Mr. Davis

MAN		WOMAN	MINISTER
Mar. 10	Thomas Shaw	to Ann Vail	Rev. Mr. Davis
" 22	John Vandegrift	to Elizabeth Sterling	Rev. Mr. Davis
" 29	Noble Biddle	to Rachel Veazey	Rev. Mr. Davis
" 31	Benjamin Price	to Ann Maria Price	Rev. Mr. Davis
" 31	Jonah Tyson	to Larrey? Tyson	Rev. Mr. Davis
Apr. 18	Nathan Vansant	to Catherine Dodson	Rev. Mr. Davis
" 23	Joseph Cummings	to Ann Hill	Rev. Mr. Davis
" 25	Mathias Egnor	to Jane Davidson	Rev. Mr. McGraw
1809			
Apr. 20	Robert Cather	to Hannah McCullough	Rev. Mr. McGraw
May 28	John McGowan	to Rebecca Thompson	Rev. Mr. McGraw
Sept. 28	Hugh McCoy	to Elizabeth Fulton	Rev. Mr. McGraw
Nov. 1	David Cunningham	to Elizabeth Gillespie	Rev. Mr. McGraw
" 2	John Conrad	to Jane Rodney	Rev. Mr. McGraw
Dec. 8	John Dixon	to Mary Homer	Rev. Mr. McGraw
" 17	John Fox	to Mary Owens	Rev. Mr. McGraw
1810			
Jan. 18	Robert Kerr	to Mary Healy	Rev. Mr. McGraw
Mar. 8	Peter Langdon	to Agnes Kerr	Rev. Mr. McGraw
Apr. 5	William Mackey	to Hannah McCullough	Rev. Mr. McGraw
" 12	Levi Childs	to Amelia Coulson	Rev. Mr. McGraw
May 3	James Boulden?	to Eva Short	Rev. Mr. Duke
June 13	Thomas McCall	to Sarah Brown	Rev. Mr. McGraw
" 26	George Beaston	to Abigail Morgan	Rev. Mr. Davis
July 14	Thomas Pennington	to Sarah Ward	Rev. Mr. Davis
" 17	Daniel McLaughlin	to Elizabeth Lynch	Rev. Mr. McGraw
Jan. 17	John Shaw	to Sarah Richardson	Rev. Mr. McGraw
Aug. 10	Daniel Booth	to Hannah Bowan	Rev. Mr. McGraw
Sept. 5	William Winchester	to Ann Oldham	Rev. Mr. McGraw
" 11	Henry Alexander	to Esther Johnson	Duke
" 19	Robert Hitchcock	to Ebby Clark	Davis
Oct. 4	Joseph Marshall	to Sarah Broom	Duke
" 9	Thomas Roach	to Alice Lynch	Duke
" 20	John Sappington	to Catherine Everson	Davis
Dec. 5	Stephen Mahan	to Elizabeth McCauley	McGraw
" 13	William Penington	to Amelia Hyland	Duke
" 21	William Craig, Jr.	to Mary Hyland	Davis
" 31	Richard H. Kepling	to Charlotte Hall	Davis
1811			
Jan. 2	John Palmer	to Jane Carruthers	Duke
" 7	Hugh Brown	to Ariminta Foard	Duke
" 21	Edward Todd	to Mary McCartney	Duke
" 23	Johnson Hyland	to Margaret Loran	Duke
Feb. 11	Charles Kelly	to Deborah Lesslie	McGraw
" 5	William Walker	to Elizabeth Whitaker	McGraw
" 11	Hezekiah Bostic	to Elizabeth Webb	McGraw
" 19	Samuel Gatts	to Mary Moore	McGraw
Mar. 6	John Baker	to Mary Edmondson	McGraw
" 20	Edward Grievy	to May Warner	Davis
" 23	James Shirkey	to Mary Bell	Davis
" 27	Samuel Anguish	to Mary Leason	McGraw
" 30	Nathaniel Burke	to Elizabeth Roddey	McGraw
Apr. 16	Henry Penington	to Rebecca Beetle	Duke
" 1	John Louhan	to Elizabeth Boyd	McGraw
" 2	Jacob Ash	to Sarah Casho	Duke
" 6	Joshua Smith	to Jane Watson	McGraw
" 15	Jonathan Greenwood	to Rebecca Benson	Davis
" 20	Thomas Dixon	to Elizabeth Murphy	Davis

		MAN		WOMAN	MINISTER
"	25	Thomas Tyson	to	Catharine Walraven	Duke
"	26	Isaac Parker	to	Maria Veazey	Davis
May	15	Mark Arthur	to	Ann Hart	Duke
"	18	Richard Robnat	to	Mary Bryton	Duke
"	21	George Wilson	to	Milliscent Proctor	Duke
"	23	Laurence Simmons	to	Elizabeth Foard	Davis
June	1	Henry Patterson	to	Elizabeth Penington	Davis
"	5	Elihu Ewing	to	Ann Smith	McGraw
"	5	Moses Rutter	to	Ebby Keithley	Duke
"	13	Jonathan Keithley	to	Catharine Crooks	Duke
"	13	George Seo?	to	Sarah Alcock	Duke
"	15	William Milligan	to	Susannah Nevin	Duke
"	17	Noble Veazey	to	Mary Ford	Davis
"	20	Joseph Couden	to	Margaret S. Biddle	Duke
"	22	Hezekiah Dowland	to	Mary Bigs	Duke
"	22	James O'Donald	to	Elizabeth Sappington	Duke
"	25	Benjamin Price	to	Elizabeth Hartley	Davis
"	28	Augustine Beedle	to	Rachel Ruley	Davis
July	1	Thomas McIntire	to	Maggy Philips	Duke
Aug.	3	Henry Elliott	to	Nancy Conway	MaGraw
"	11	John Clark	to	Rebecca Richardson	Duke
"	22	John Henderson	to	Ann Benson	Davis
"	24	Joseph Richardson	to	Mary Culverson	Duke
"	27	Henry Clark	to	Elizabeth Grant	Duke
Sept.	12	Thomas W. Coudon	to	Elizabeth Buchanan	Duke
Oct.	2	Joseph Davis	to	Amelia Sappington	Davis
"	20	William Foard	to	Sarah Cox	Davis
"	29	George W. Lightner, Esq.	to	Eliza A. Springer	Davis
"	31	John Israel	to	Margaret Simpson	Davis
Nov.	4	James Jester	to	Mary Updegrave	Davis
"	5	Richard Hill	to	Margaret Browne	Davis
"	9	Christopher McClure	to	Catharine Moore	Davis
"	18	James McGregor	to	Jane French	Davis
"	21	James Nowland, Jr.	to	Rebecca Morgan	Davis
Dec.	6	Edward Luster	to	Julia Pearce	Davis
"	11	James Ramsey	to	Sarah Wilson	Duke
"	17	Francis Gillespie	to	Rebecca Nowland	McGraw
"	17	John Biddle	to	Elizabeth Vance	Duke
"	19	Doct. David Davis	to	Ann Mercer	Davis
"	19	William Wilson	to	Rebecca Bettle	Duke
"	23	Andrew Rigs	to	Margaret Alexander	Magraw
"	28	Peregrine Hendrickson	to	Rebecca Pearce	Davis
"	30	William Morgan	to	Mary Walmsley	Davis
"	30	Thomas Jackson	to	Elizabeth Manley	Duke
	1812				
Jan.	2	Nicholas C. Hyland of Edward	to	Jane Hart	Duke
"	14	Joseph Davis	to	Catharine Pennington	Davis
"	29	James Vaunce	to	Sarah McClary	Davis
Feb.	3	Jacob Wilson	to	Grace York	Magraw
"	5	James M. Craig	to	Agnes Killmerry	Magraw
"	5	Frisby P. Lloyd	to	Sarah Ann Robinson	Davis
"	5	John Anderson, Jr.	to	Elsey Jamison	Magraw
"	17	Jonathan Pacher	to	Mary Hynes	Magraw
"	19	David Haveris	to	Jane Gribbon	Magraw
"	22	John Killiman	to	Hannah Keys	Magraw
"	21	Howard Roach	to	Jane Moody	Magraw
Mar.	3	David Short	to	Mary Segars	Magraw
"	4	Jacob Stephens	to	Sarah Sappington	Magraw
"	5	James Matthews	to	Grace Broom	Magraw
"	9	James Chesney	to	Ann McCauley	Magraw

MAN			WOMAN	MINISTER
" 9	Stephan Hyland	to	Maria Kinkey	Magraw
" 10	William Gallaher	to	Sarah Vance	Magraw
" 20	Samuel Roth	to	Rebecca Pennington	Magraw
" 31	William Roberson	to	Rebecca Webb	Magraw
Apr. 1	Thomas Taylor	to	Priscilla Baddor	Magraw
" 7	Henry James Smith	to	Rebecca McCauley	Magraw
" 11	Benjamin McKenney	to	Sarah Letty?	Magraw
" 17	Nicholas Frank	to	Eliza Ruley	Magraw
" 21	John Price	to	Emeline Ward	Magraw
" 24	George Davis	to	Deborah Price	Magraw
1810				
July 31	John Arnerica	to	Kaziah Mackey	
Sept. 13	James P. Weight	to	Mary Kerr	
Oct. 24	John Whitelock	to	Agnes Gore	
Nov. 15	Richard Griffee	to	Mary Barrett	
1811				
Jan. 4	John Death	to	Mary Ann McClary	
Mar. 14	John Abrams	to	Eleanor Rawlings	
June 17	Reuben Hawkins	to	Mary Harvey	
July 4	David Edmonson	to	Mary Stevenson	
	John Whitelock	to	Agnes Girl	
Sept. 19	Robert Evans	to	Rebecca Patterson	
" 19	William Grist	to	Lydia Brown	
Nov. 26	Jesse Williams	to	Sarah Green	
Dec. 5	Cyrus Oldham	to	Eleanor Evans	
Feb. 6	Jonathan Ray	to	Deborah Williams	
" 13	Thomas Knight	to	Nancy Kirk	
1812				
Mar. 17	William McCann	to	Mary Smith	
Apr. 9	Joshua Gibson	to	Catherine Cunning	
" 14	John Harris	to	Martha Hindman	
June 17	Thomas Watson	to	Elizabeth Leich	Magraw
" 18	Samuel Hewitt	to	Jane Willson	Magraw
July 7	William Roliston	to	Martha Miller	Magraw
" 15	Cornelius McDonald	to	Sarah Kyle	Magraw
" 28	John Buchanan	to	Mary Allcorn	Magraw
Aug. 18	Thomas Jones	to	Ann Vandegrift	Magraw
" 22	Samuel Genness	to	Sarah Alexander	Magraw
Sept. 2	Richard Robinson	to	Lucy Moore	Magraw
" 23	John Johnson	to	Margaret Foster	Magraw
Oct. 15	John Jones	to	Rebecca Foard	Magraw
Sept. 24	Thomas Veazy	to	Mary Wallace	Magraw
Oct. 15	Edmund Brown	to	Rebecca Beetle	Magraw
" 20	Thomas Calhoun	to	Jane McKinney	Magraw
" 29	John Jarekind	to	Esther Jones	Magraw
" 31	John McCoy	to	Elizabeth Williams	Magraw
Nov. 4	Able Marple	to	Harriet McVey	Magraw
" 10	Jeremiah Currin?	to	Hannah Hall	Megraw
Dec. 1	Thomas Lewis	to	Catherine McCannan	
" 5	Dan Hendrick	to	Mary Hinson	Megraw
" 12	John Sutton	to	Hannah McCauley	Megraw
" 14	Hugh Cosgrove	to	Priscilla Jones	Megraw
" 31	Tobias Rudolph	to	Maria Hayes	Megraw
" 31	Solomon Barroll?	to	Henrietta Cox	Megraw
1813				
Jan. 8	John Arrants	to	Sarah Young	Megraw
1812				
Dec. 24	Andrew Cross	to	Rachel Wallace	
" 31	Eli Coulson	to	Jane Egan	

MAN			WOMAN	MINISTER
1813				
Jan. 6	John Cooper	to	Ann Cammell	
" 21	Allen Kirk	to	Mary McCullough	
" 28	Thomas Burnsides	to	Catherine Moore	
Mar. 11	Samuel McCullough	to	Rachel McGallaty	
" 18	Levi Kirk	to	Rachel Kirk	
Apr. 8	James Horner	to	Agnes McGaraty	
June 8	Thomas H. Morgan	to	Julia L. Hall	
Aug. 1	James Orr	to	Sally Ramsey	
" 19	David M. Farr	to	Mary Lyon	
Sept. 23	Henry Booth	to	Ann Wade	
1814				
Jan. 18	William Richardson	to	Catherine Hall	
Feb. 14	James Evans	to	Mary Patterson	
" 24	Andrew McCullough	to	Jane Williams	
Mar. 24	James Magaraty	to	Aisler Shields	
Apr. 19	Samuel Hogg	to	Rebecca Baker	
Oct. 20	James McDowell	to	Elizabeth Cummings	
Nov. 1	Levi Williams	to	Agnes Carr	
Dec. 29	Jacob Shank	to	Harriett Garrett	
" 29	George Kidd	to	Mary Hogg	
1815				
Jan. 5	George Clark	to	Eleanor Smith	
Mar. 23	John Carter	to	Jane Fulton	
Apr. 11	John Marshell	to	Sarah Calwell	
May 4	Jacob Conrad	to	Margaret Rodney	
" 11	James Jones	to	Mary Boyd	
1816				
Jan. 22	John T. Wirt	to	Sarah A. Bayard	
" 22	Charles Badger, Jr.	to	Ann Morgan	
May 2	John Taylor	to	Rebecca McArrough	
" 4	John Huttan	to	Lydia Keitley	
" 7	Edward Lester	to	Elizabeth Beetle	
1813				
Nov. 24	Thomas Beetle	to	Mary Vandigrift	McGraw
" 27	William Conway	to	Isabella Armour	McGraw
	Stephen Heveim	to	Mary Ann Fulum	
Dec. 8	William Cosgrove	to	Ann Harlan	McGraw
	Elisha Simmons	to	Sarah Veazey	
" 22	John Lynch	to	Julia Clark	McGraw
" 23	Benjamin Mauldin	to	Sarah Thomas	McGraw
" 24	William Meyers	to	Mary B. Crookshank	McGraw
" 25	John Meyers	to	Sarah Thompson	Davis
" 29	Andrew Holt	to	Mary Crouch	McGraw
	Ephraim Alexander	to	Catherine Johnson	McGraw
1814				
Jan. 11	William Marshall	to	Mary Gibson	McGraw
" 14	Alexander Grace	to	Ann Blackstone	McGraw
" 17	Noble Davis	to	Rachel Ruley	McGraw
" 18	Philip Harding	to	Aurelia Giles	McGraw
" 18	Jacob Varriluden	to	Ann Gwinn	McGraw
" 27	James Morgan	to	Elizabeth Porter	McGraw
Feb. 3	James Fatman	to	Elizabeth Ginn	McGraw
" 23	Robert Logan	to	Jane McCullough	McGraw
" 23	William Pattison	to	Sarah Morston	Magraw
" 26	Thomas Wallace	to	Mary Jackson	McGraw

	MAN		WOMAN	MINISTER
Apr. 5	Richard Miller	to	Mary Poltson	McGraw
" 10	James Redgrave	to	Harriet Welch	McGraw
" 11	James Willerston	to	Mary Steel	McGraw
" 12	Joseph Thomas	to	Elizabeth Sergant	McGraw
Mar. 10	Charles Rutter	to	Mary Gillespie	McCauley
Apr. 27	Samuel Wood	to	Rachel Thomas	McGraw
May 6	Andrew Boulden	to	Frances Foard	McGraw
" 11	Robert Hart	to	Ann Joice	McGraw
" 17	Owen Devlin	to	Jane Morgan	McGraw
" 23	Thomas Brison	to	Rebecca Short	McGraw
" 25	Jesse Holliday	to	Milly Crouch	McGraw
" 28	Philip Jenkins	to	Casander Shatterick	McGraw
June 2	Levi Craig	to	Elizabeth Hevering	McGraw
" 15	George Bennett	to	Darcas Lum	McGraw
" 20	Enoch Bennett	to	Ann Welch	McGraw
July 7	Henry Bennett	to	Margaret Roach	McGraw
" 7	Thomas Deer	to	Margaret Ba:d	McGraw
" 26	William Short	to	Rebecca McDonald	McGraw
Aug. 11	John Taylor	to	Mary Wilson	McGraw
" 15	Joseph Brian	to	Susan Louisa Mason	McGraw
" 15	Robert Cameron	to	Mary Marns	McGraw
" 18	Philip Brady	to	Elizabeth Butler	McGraw
" 24	Thomas Garrett	to	Hannah P. Scott	McGraw
Sept. 20	William Robinson	to	Araminta Bristoe	McGraw
" 26	Thomas Taylor	to	Elizabeth Wiley	McGraw
Oct. 25	John Scott	to	Lucinda Ames	McGraw
Nov. 1	John Winchester	to	Mary Severson	McGraw
" 19	Benjamin Abbott	to	Sarah McCoy	
" 22	Jason Cook	to	Elizabeth Hiller	McGraw
" 22	John Lum	to	Sophia Boulden	McGraw
" 26	William Morgan	to	Jane Jones	McGraw
Dec. 5	John Fisher	to	Sarah Black	McGraw
" 6	Alexander Alexander	to	Ann Mahaffay	McGraw
" 13	Frisby L. Biddle	to	Maria Ford	McGraw
" 14	Robert Galloway	to	Mary McCleary	McGraw
" 15	Thomas Biddle	to	Anne McKinsey	Duke
" 17	Joseph Arrants	to	Ann Pearce	McGraw
" 20	Nicholas Lusby	to	Rebecca Etherington	McGraw
" 25	Benjamin McCay	to	Mary Blackston	McGraw
" 29	James Johnson	to	Mary Armstrong	McGraw
1815				
Jan. 4	Thomas McIntire	to	Mary Thomas	McGraw
" 18	Joshua Hyland	to	Margaret Crouch	McGraw
" 25	Doct. John Veazey	to	Sarah Ward	McGraw
Feb. 1	James Hudson	to	Maria Ward	McGraw
" 14	John Kirk	to	Elizabeth Meakings	McGraw
" 28	Nicholas Hyland	to	Ruth McCracken	McGraw
Mar. 8	William Miller	to	Lydia B. Eliason	McGraw
" 24	Andrew Alexander	to	Jane Stalhap	Duke
Apr. 5	James Gorrell	to	Mary Ryan	Duke
" 13	Tobias Beetle	to	Tamar Boulden	Duke
" 13	John M. Johnson	to	Susan Ricketts	McGraw
" 27	Thomas Stradley	to	Mary Scanlan	McGraw
" 30	John Davis	to	Mary Owens	Duke
Mar. 10	Charles Rutter	to	Mary Gillespie	
May 5	Floyd Bailey	to	Amelia Holliday	
" 26	John Jackson	to	Rachel Campbell	
Sept. 15	Jacob Berkins	to	Mary Johnson	

MAN				WOMAN	MINISTER
1815					
Feb.	23	George Hinds	to	Millicent Lowrey	
May	2	Benjamin Thomas	to	Mary Short	Duke
"	16	Nicholas Price	to	Sarah Vansant	McGraw
"	14	John Todd	to	Margaret McCartney	McGraw
"	16	James Arrants	to	Martha Bristoe	McGraw
"	22	Daniel Vansant	to	Catharine Hays	McGraw
"	23	George Roch	to	Jane Wilson	McGraw
"	30	Archibald M'Corkle	to	Elizabeth Moore	McGraw
"	31	Charley Maxwell	to	Sarah McCoy	McGraw
June	17	John S. Merritt	to	Mary Cliffen	Davis
"	20	Tobias Biddle	to	Elizabeth Boulden	Duke
"	22	Henry Chamberlaine	to	Henrietta E. Gale	Davis
July	23	Richard Swift	to	Sarah Foard	McGraw
"	28	James Chambey?	to	Elizabeth Johnson	McGraw
"	29	Richard Swift	to	Salicia Welsh	Duke
Aug.	4	Levy Palmer	to	Nancy Lynch	Duke
"	7	Robert Lowery	to	?Elydia Grahame	Davis
"	8	Alphonse Cilloney	to	Margaret Crookshanks	Davis
"	9	Thomas Rowe	to	Abigail Davidson	Davis
"	10	Charles Murray	to	Mary Hemphill	Duke
"	22	Richard Jones	to	Ann Jackson	McGraw
"	21	William Clawson	to	Eliza Tyson	Farrell
"	31	John Davidson	to	Elizabeth Ricketts	Duke
Sept.	25	John Joennans?	to	Mary Grant	McGraw
Oct.	3	John Lusby of Thos.	to	Emeline Neal	Davis
1816					
Oct.	7	John Connely	to	Ann Freame	Davis
1815					
Oct.	17	James Carrol	to	Elizabeth Lee	Davis
"	18	Jethro Johnson	to	Ann Winchester	McGraw
"	27	Joshua Greenwald?	to	Mary Bird	Duke
Nov.	23	Andrew McIntire	to	Mary Simpers	Chambey
Dec.	5	Samuel Anderson	to	Margaret Scarborough	Duke
"	6	William Grace	to	Eliza Price	Duke
"	12	Robert Jones	to	Amelia Milburn	Duke
"	13	Jacob Tyson	to	Rebecca Simpson	Duke
"	25	John Garrett	to	Ann Hill	McGraw
1816					
Jan.	6	Benjamin Knock	to	Ann Martin?	Davis
"	9	John Barnet	to	Amelia Chilson	McGraw
"	21	Fredus Owens	to	Araminta Price	Davis
"	24	John Jones	to	Elizabeth Harrend	Duke
"	24	Henry Pennington	to	Araminta Biggs	McGraw
Feb.	2	Nickolas Plummer	to	Sarah Boswell	Duke
"	3	William Patterson	to	Eliza Benson	
"	5	John O. Iler	to	Sarah Pennington	McGraw
"	5	Samuel Johnston	to	Elizabeth Sutton	McGraw
"	7	Samuel McKenney	to	Catharine Burk	Duke
"	9	Robert F. Smith	to	Susannah Cousden	Bell
"	9	Benjamin Meekings	to	Elizabeth Lucus	Duke
"	14	James McCullough	to	Delia Pennington	Duke
"	19	Fredus Price	to	Ann Benson	Davis
Mar.	7	Ebenezer Simpson	to	Sophia Ash	Farrell
"	9	Thomas Ricketts	to	Jane Egnor	Duke
"	12	Edward Wilson	to	Francis Bennett	Farrell
"	20	Allen Brown	to	Rachel Wilson	Davis
"	30	James Matthews	to	Margaret Martin	McGraw

MAN		WOMAN	MINISTER
Apr. 3	Isaac Mingling to	Elizabeth Wilcox	Duke
" 4	Henry Baker to	Eliza Jane Adair	Davis
" 9	Andrew Crow? to	Ann Ford	Duke
" 16	Samuel Wright to	Elizabeth Williams	Duke
" 20	Levin Ehillipy (Phillips)? to	Eliza Griffith	Duke
" 25	Robert McLaughlin to	Jane Mahan	Duke
July 9	Edward Hughes to	Phebe Harris	
Sept. 17	John J. Porter to	Mary Ann Toy?	
Nov. 5	Jacob Eainter to	Mary Reves	
" 5	George Bohemer? to	Eliza Painter	
May 28	Andrew Lynch to	Margaret Taylor	Duke
" 17	William Mackey to	Jane Mackey	Graham
June 6	Daniel McKenny to	Ellenor Derumple	Duke
July 4	William Mahan to	Elida Farley	Duke
" 22	Jonathan Simpers to	Amelia Ford	McGraw
" 29	John Goforth to	Ann Brookings	Duke
" 29	James McCauley to	Margaret S. Alexander	Duke
Aug. 1	George Foster to	Maria Stoops	Duke
" 9	William Hackett to	Sarah Foard	Sewell
" 10	John Denny to	Sarah Severson	McGraw
" 17	Enoch McGreedy to	Mary Jones	McGraw
" 31	William Biggs to	Margaret Matson	McGraw
Sept. 3	Joseph Hudson to	Mary Ann McIntire	Tenel
" 10	Charles Badger to	Ann Morgan	Coombs
" 21	William McClung to	Sarah Wilson	Duke
Oct. 1	Joseph Ryland to	Margaret McMullen	Duke
" 2	Robert Young to	Elizabeth Steel	Duke
" 17	John Wiley to	Ann Harvey	Duke
Nov. 9	Charles Rutter to	Sarah Campbell	Duke
" 11	Joseph Davis to	Mary Ann Biddle	Duke
" 11	Samuel Little to	Mary Pitnin	Duke
" 20	William Brumfield to	Amilea Owens	Duke
" 30	Nathan Lackland to	Mary Ann Harlan	McGraw
Dec. 19	Lewis Harlan to	Esther Boyd	Lane
	Alexander McCullough to	Mary Dickson	Lane
" 31	Elisha Reynolds to	Sarah Taylor	Lane
1817			
Mar. 20	Benjamin M. Davis to	Jane Kidd	Magraw
Apr. 17	Abraham Hard to	Margaret Thompson	Lane
May 13	John Y. Walmsley to	Harriet Simcoe	Lane
June 5	Elijah Reynolds to	Eliza Ednector	Lane
July 20	William H. Pierce to	Ann Fleming	Duke
" 28	John Willis to	Rebecca Kilgars	Duke
Aug. 4	James Scott to	Margaret Hutton	Duke
" 7	Thomas Wingate to	Frances Lum	Duke
" 12	John Lusby to	Sarah Maraland	Duke
" 20	Robert Davidson to	Elizabeth Fleming	Duke
" 27	William Carretson to	Mary Marnes	Duke
Sept. 1	John Grant to	Jane Miller	Duke
1	James Currier to	Mary Ann Holmes	Lane
" 2	John Penington to	Amelia Snow	Duke
" 2	John McCaig to	Ann Holt	Duke
" 13	Sam. H. Freeman to	Harriet Foard	Duke
Oct. 6	Daniel Megredy to	Mary Reynolds	Goforth
" 16	Richard Boyd to	Elizabeth Alexander	Duke
" 22	James Gillespie to	Susan Breakley	Duke
" 30	Greenbury Purrnell to	Ann Hinman	Sharpley
Dec. 1	William Simco to	Rebecca Cazier	Sharpley
" 3	John H. Penington to	Mary Ann Carty	Duke
" 6	Levi Craig to	Rebecca Roley	Duke

		MAN		WOMAN	MINISTER
"	9	Benjamin Atwell	to	Rebecca Moore	Duke
"	30	David Fulton	to	Ann C. Hull	Dicky
"	31	Richard Bristow	to	Ann Robinson	Duke
1818					
Jan.	8	William Alexander	to	Rebecca McKenny	Serby
"	8	Thomas Jones	to	Maria Kilpatrick	Duke
"	19	Isaac Tyson	to	Emily Janney	Duke
"	19	Hyland J. Penington	to	Rebecca Wroth	Duke
"	21	Christopher Vandergrift	to	Ann Limman	Duke
"	31	George Standley	to	Elizabeth O'Dondley	Duke
Feb.	4	Lamuse Beetle	to	Rebecca Hackett	Duke
Mar.	12	Daniel Riggs	to	Catherine Ringler	Duke
"	13	Samuel Marns	to	Sarah McCreary	Duke
"	19	Matthias Tyson	to	Ann Mingling	Duke
"	25	Richard Simpers	to	Eliza Short	Duke
"	25	John Turner	to	Sarah Young	Duke
Apr.	3	William Matthews	to	Francina Bouchell	Duke
"	8	Robert W. Fee	to	Ann Moore	Duke
"	16	Cornelius Smith	to	Hannah Reynolds	Duke
"	25	William James	to	Emiline Price	Duke
"	25	Joshua Hudson	to	Sina Bayard	Chambers
"	27	John George, Jr.	to	Rosanna Crouch	Duke
May	7	Richard Simpers	to	Eliza Beard	Duke
"	27	Richard Flintham	to	Jemima Bryan	Duke
1819					
Jan.	1	Samuel Rutter	to	Agnes Banetey	Magraw
"	22	Wm. E. Dorsey	to	Catherine Lightner	Magraw
Feb.	12	Francis A. Warner	to	Ann J. Herron?	Magraw
Mar.	3	Samuel Kerr	to	Rebecca Rawlings	Magraw
"	19	James Hamilton	to	Catherine Graham	Magraw
1816					
Dec.	10	Stephen Clark	to	Elizabeth Cooling	Duke
"	11	Levi Tyson	to	Catherine Wilson	Magraw
"	11	William Curry	to	Elizabeth Crawford	Magraw
"	24	Hazea Terry	to	Aramenta Creswell	Magraw
"	30	George Fulton	to	Rebecca Carathey	Magraw
1817					
Jan.	2	George Kenbead	to	Catherine Johnson	Duke
"	8	William Etherington	to	Millison Redgrave	Duke
"	15	John Ward Jones	to	Ann Neal	Duke
"	17	Robert Jackson	to	Sarah Williams	Duke
"	17	James Hemhill	to	E'ydia Moody	Duke
"	20	James I. Carratt	to	Catherine Lee	Duke
"	29	Elicy Lee	to	Ann Hackett	Duke
Feb.	3	Andrew Harvey	to	Elydia McCauley	Duke
"	4	Thomas Cully	to	Amelia Griffin	Duke
"	7	John Holliday	to	Aasina Brown	Duke
"	8	Robert Penington	to	Frances Roberts	
"	19	Thomas Britanham	to	Ann Griffith	Duke
"	22	Stephen Bayard	to	Letitia Armstrong	Duke
Mar.	17	John Scarborough	to	Rachel Harvey	Duke
"	17	John Manley	to	Naomi Sineperd	Duke
May	10	Wm. Ruple	to	Ann Clark	Duke
"	1	Benjamin McKinzie	to	Elizabeth Purnell	Duke
"	3	John Gamble	to	Elidia Johnson	Duke
"	14	John Jones	to	Mary Ford	Duke

	MAN		WOMAN	MINISTER
June 2	Thomas Foster	to	Margaret McLelland	Sharplay
" 3	Parker Barnard	to	Ann Freeman	Duke
" 9	Thomas B. Veazey	to	Ann Ward	Duke
" 9	Moses Whitelock	to	Rebecca Brickley	Magraw
" 1	John Maxwell	to	Sarah Ann Hutton	Duke
" 13	Lawerence Collins	to	Margaret Greenwood	Duke
" 16	James Crawford	to	Rebecca Cathers	Duke
" 24	James McMullen	to	Sarah Whitelock	Duke
" 24	George Wilson	to	Eliza Wilson	Duke
July 2	John Hannon	to	Hannah Rooch	Duke
" 27	James McDowell	to	Sarah Can (Carr)?	Magraw
1815				
Aug. 3	Alexander Boyd	to	Mary Gibson	Lane
1817				
Aug. 10	Robert Kerr	to	Mary Rawlings	Lane
1815				
Oct. 12	Isaih Brown	to	Sarah Morris	Lane
Dec. 21	John Burris	to	Elizabeth Whitelock	Lane
" 25	Charles Wallace	to	Sarah Stenete (Sterett)?	Lane
1816				
Feb. 15	William Gifford	to	Mary Barnett	Lane
Mar. 7	James Thompson	to	Ann McCullough	Lane
" 14	John Brickley	to	Sarah Barrett	Lane
" 19	John McKinney	to	Elizabeth M. Nesbitt	Lane
" 24	John St—.	to	May Williams	Lane
Apr. 25	George Leslie	to	Jane Balchford	Magraw
June 6	Abie Whitaker	to	Sarah Orr	Lane
" 6	Edward Whitelock	to	Mary Cross	Lane
	William Gorrell	to	Elizabeth Reyon	Lane
" 13	Samuel Ewing	to	Rebecca McDowell	Lane
July 4	John Adams	to	Mary Reed	Lane
Aug. 14	Samuel Clendenin	to	Mary Alexander	Lane
Oct. 1	James Galbraith	to	Rebecca Wilson	Lane
1817				
Dec. 1	William Simco	to	Rebecca Cazier	Sharpley
" 3	John A. Pennington	to	Mary Ann Carty	Duke
1818				
Jan. 9	John Veach	to	Rachel Mariott	Magraw
" 12	George Price	to	Ann Conley	Magraw
" 19	Nicholas Hart	to	Milcah Crouch	Magraw
" 25	William Thomas	to	Margaret Hyland	Magraw
" 28	Samuel Roberts	to	Elizabeth Price	Magraw
" 30	Henry Ball	to	Eliza Maffitt	Magraw
Feb. 3	William Dacey	to	Rebecca Dacey	Magraw
" 3	Lewis Thomas	to	Ann Pennington	Magraw
" 15	William Ramsey	to	Martha McVey	Magraw
" 27	John McIntire	to	Elizabeth Philips	Magraw
Mar. 3	John Simpers	to	Mary Simpers	Magraw
" 3	John Wilson	to	Elizabeth Wyeth	Magraw
" 6	Lewis Hall	to	Eliza Lamet	Magraw
" 11	William Hays	to	Hannah Thomas	Magraw
" 13	Zebulon Mauldin	to	Rebecca Arrants	Magraw
" 16	Jesse Updegrove	to	Margaret Tyson	Magraw
" 17	Augustus Stoops	to	Sarah Foster	Magraw
" 18	Dan Rayhnor	to	Eleanor Willock	Magraw
" 20	Philip Luning	to	Hannah Tolson	Magraw
" 27	Elijah Hill	to	Rachel Crothers	Magraw

	MAN		WOMAN	MINISTER
Apr. 28	Samuel M. Cullough	to	Mary McVey	Magraw
May 12	William Perry	to	Ann Carr	Magraw
" 19	James Riddle	to	Jane McCartney	Magraw
June 1	Robert McCray	to	Elizabeth Roberts	Magraw
" 8	Edward Alexander	to	Hannah Hitchcock	Thomas
" 9	Joseph Grant	to	Susan Crouch	Magraw
" 23	Levi Milburn	to	Sarah Sewall	
July 1	John Hueston	to	Susannah Cummings	Magraw
" 3	Henry E. Coleman	to	Henrietta M. Loyd	Magraw
" 16	Thomas Dixon	to	Rachel Crouch	Magraw
Aug. 3	Benjamin Milburn	to	Catharine Boyes	Magraw
" 12	Waters Chilson	to	Emily Roach	Magraw
" 17	Sam Badders	to	Catharine Kerr	Magraw
" 26	John Wills	to	Mary Mahon	Magraw
" 26	Benjamin Veazy	to	Rebecca Ginny	Magraw
Sept. 6	Jesse Janney	to	Maria Taylor	Magraw
" 13	Nathan Owens	to	Julia Simpers	Magraw
Oct. 6	Hector MacKennan	to	Ann Vance	Magraw
" 6	John Cray	to	Elizabeth Hukill	Magraw
" 11	Charley Humphreys	to	Jane Crawford	Magraw
" 13	James Jackson	to	Ava? Hodge	Magraw
" 21	John Vint	to	Mary Ramsey	Magraw
Nov. 17	Samuel Smith	to	Margaret MaClenethen	Magraw
Mar. 25	Richard Simpers	to	Eliza Short	Rev. Mr. Duke
" 19	Mathias Tyson	to	Ann Mingling	Rev. Mr. Duke
" 25	John Turner	to	Sarah Young	
Apr. 3	William Mathews	to	Francina Bouchelle	Rev. Mr. Duke
" 8	Robert W. Fee	to	Ann Moore	Rev. Mr. Duke
" 16	Cornelius Smith	to	Hannah Reynolds	Rev. Mr. Duke
" 25	William James	to	Emeline Price	Rev. Mr. Duke
" 25	Joshua Hudson	to	Sina Bayard	Rev. Mr. Chambers
" 27	John George, Jr.	to	Rosanna Crouch	Rev. Mr. Duke
May 7	Richard Simpers	to	Eliza Beard	Rev. Mr. Duke
" 27	Richard Flintham	to	Jemima Bryan	Rev. Mr. Duke
Jan. 1	Samuel Rutter	to	Agnes Barrett	
" 22	William E. Dorsey	to	Catherine M. Lightner	Rev. Mr. Duke
Feb. 12	Francis A. Warner	to	Ann Jefferson	Rev. Mr. Duke
Mar. 3	Samuel Kerr	to	Rebecca Rawlings	Rev. Mr. Duke
" 19	James Hamilton	to	Catherine Graham	Rev. Mr. Duke
" 19	Jehoachim Brickley	to	Agnes R. Moore	Rev. Mr. Duke
" 31	William Smith	to	Sarah Lyle	Rev. Mr. Duke
" 31	Warren? Reynolds	to	Jane Bulin	Rev. Mr. Duke
June 11	Stephen Crouch	to	Jane Pennington	Rev. Mr. Duke
" 16	Abraham D. Mitchell	to	Jane T. Evans	Rev. Mr. Duke
" 26	John L. Ewing	to	Elizabeth Cook	Rev. Mr. Shockley
July 3	Joseph Grubb	to	Ann Murphy	Rev. Mr. Duke
" 18	Moses N. Cannon	to	Mary Biddle	Rev. Mr. Duke
" 21	William Alexander	to	Ann Richardson	Rev. Mr. Duke
Aug. 18	John Bates	to	Mary Martin	Rev. Mr. Duke
May 20	Benjamin Woodrow	to	Maria Currier	Rev. Mr. Duke
Sept. 8	Isaac Benjamin	to	Rebecca Alexander	Rev. Mr. Duke
" 9	William Davis	to	Mary McDonald	Rev. Mr. Duke
" 16	Andrew Quinley	to	Mary Multel	Rev. Mr. Ferrell
" 17	William Thompson	to	Rebecca Gillespie	Rev .Mr. Duke
Oct. 2	Richard Wingate	to	Elizabeth Smith	Rev. Mr. Chambers
Nov. 9	Edward Wright	to	Ann Tilletson	Rev. Mr. Duke
Nov. 11	Thomas Carroll	to	Saharh Graham	Rev. Mr. Duke
" 12	William Ward	to	Sarah Parkinson	Rev. Mr. Duke
" 17	Benjamin Bowers	to	Ann Thomas	Rev. Mr. Duke
" 18	John McKinney	to	Eliza Wood	Rev. Mr. Duke

	MAN		WOMAN	MINISTER
Dec. 1	Adam Anderson	to	Elizabeth White	Rev. Mr. Duke
" 2	William Nickle	to	Betsey Harris	Rev. Mr. Duke
" 9	Alphonso Money	to	Mary Ruley	
" 9	William Manly	to	Ann Rutter	Rev. Mr. Duke
" 10	William Hewitt	to	Ann Purnell	Rev. Mr. Duke
" 17	Jacob R. Hewitt	to	Mary E. Lowry	Rev. Mr. Duke
" 29	John Collis	to	Rebecca Severson	Rev. Mr. Magraw
" 2	Wm. Nickle	to	Betsy Harris	Mr. Duke
" 9	Alphonso Money	to	Mary Ruleys	Mr. Nire
" 9	Wm. Manley	to	Ann Rutter	Mr. Duke
" 10	William Hewite	to	Ann Currica	Mr. Duke
" 18	Jacob R. Hewite	to	Mary E. Lowry	Mr. Duke
" 29	John Coolie	to	Rebecca	Mr. Nepan
1819				
Jan. 13	John Richards	to	Ann Guy	Mr. McGraw
" 18	John Rarrick	to	Fanney Penington	Mr. Duke
" 27	Hugh Boyd	to	Margaret Keitley	Mr. Early
" 28	John Marcus	to	Sarah Reed	Mr. Duke
Feb. 11	John George Sen.	to	Elizabeth Johnson	Mr. Duke
" 16	David Steel	to	Mary Hall	Mr. Graham
" 24	Alexander Boyd	to	Sarah Leslie	Mr. Duke
" 25	Andrew Riggs	to	Martha Morgan	Mr. Duke
Mar. 9	Nathaniel Wiley	to	Margaret Kidd	Mr. Woolson
" 13	Andrew Alexander	to	Margaret Crouthers	Mr. Terrell
" 16	Elias Pennington	to	Elizabeth Shields	Mr. Duke
" 18	William Johnson	to	Jane Hitchcock	Mr. Duke
" 18	Eli White	to	Ann Brickley	Mr. Duke
" 23	John Wingate	to	Sarah Austin	Mr. Sharpley
	Reece Crookihanky	to	Margaret Cameron	
" 29	John Lightmer	to	Rebecca Frey	Mr. Magraw
" 29	Henry Brisban	to	Julia Ann Lightner	Mr. MaGraw
" 31	Frisby Henderson	to	Mary H. Gilpin	Mr. Bele
Apr. 13	John Briscoe	to	Henrietta Reynolds	Mr. MaGraw
" 14	Benjamine Atwell	to	Deborah Hayse	Mr. Duke
" 26	David Austin	to	Lipborah Heath	Mr. Sharpley
" 26	John Cooper	to	Hannah Watson	Mr. MaGraw
" 27	Eli Janney	to	Esther Lackland	Mr. Duke
" 29	James Lynch	to	Mary Conley	Mr. Duke
May 4	Joseph Pugh	to	Rebecca Price	Mr. Sharpley
" 5	John Russell	to	Margaret Coney	Mr. MaGraw
June 3	William Simpers	to	Mary Ann Dunn	Mr. Duke
" 7	Ebanizer Welch	to	Rebecca Money	Mr. Sewell
" 8	Victor Currier	to	Mary Burrows	Mr. MaGraw
" 23	Daniel Wright	to	Sarah Smith	Mr. Duke
Aug. 10	Abraham Watson	to	Hannah Owens	Mr. MaGraw
" 14	George W. Cochran	to	Rebecca Crouch	Mr. MaGraw
Sept. 5	William Knight	to	Marie Jones	Mr. Duke
Oct. 27	Henry D. Miller	to	Ann Dowerty	Mr. Duke
" 28	John McClary	to	Ann Gallaway	Mr. Chambers
Nov. 3	George Ford	to	Ann Savin	Mr. Ninde
" 3	Elisha J. Hitchcock	to	Ann Roach	Mr. Duke
" 8	William Lansborough	to	Elizabeth Crossn	Mr. MaGraw
" 10	Robert Williams	to	Mary Barrett	Mr. Duke
" 16	Amas Miles	to	Ann Lowery	Mr. MaGraw
" 18	John L. Taylor	to	Ann Beaston	Mr. Terrell
" 24	William Jamison	to	Hannah Menghing	Mr. Sharpley
Dec. 1	John Lourey	to	Mary Ann Clark	Mr. Sharpley
" 14	Andrew Biddle	to	Louise McGregor	Mr. Chambers
" 14	John Mercer	to	Nancy Bennett	Mr. Williams
" 15	Andrew Egan	to	Hester Corbett	Mr. Goforth

	MAN		WOMAN	MINISTER
" 21	Thomas Thomas	to	Ann Sewall	Mr. Duke
" 21	Robert A. C. Lusby	to	Elizabeth Price	Mr. Duke
Jan. 13	John Richard	to	Ann Guy	Rev. Mr. Magraw
" 18	John Ranick	to	Tammy Pennington	Rev. Mr. Duke
" 27	Hugh Boyd	to	Margaret Kealty	
" 28	John Marcus	to	Sarah Reed	Rev. Mr. Duke
Feb. 11	John George, Sr.	to	Elizabeth Johnson	Rev. Mr. Duke
" 16	David Steele	to	Mary Hall	Rev. Mr. Graham
" 24	Alexander Boyd	to	Sarah Leslie	Rev. Mr. Duke
" 25	Andrew Riggs	to	Martha Morgan	Rev. Mr. Duke
Mar. 9	Nathaniel Willy	to	Margaret Kidd	Rev. Mr. Woolston
" 13	Andrew Alexander	to	Margaret Crouthers	Rev. Forrell
" 16	Elias Pennington	to	Elizabeth Shields	Rev. Mr. Duke
" 18	William Johnson	to	Jane Hitchcock	Rev. Mr. Duke
" 18	Eli White	to	Ann Brickley	Rev. Mr. Duke
" 23	John Wingate	to	Sarah Austen	Rev. Mr. Sharpley
	Reece Crookihanky	to	Margaret Cameron	
" 29	John Lightner	to	Rebecca Frey	Rev. Mr. Magraw
" 29	Henry Brisban	to	Julia Ann Ligtner	Rev. Mr. Magraw
" 31	Frisby Henderson	to	Mary H. Gilpin	Rev. Mr. Bele
Apr. 13	John Briscoe	to	Henrietta M. Reynolds	Magraw
" 14	Benjamin Atwell	to	Dehorah Hayes	Rev. Mr. Duke
" 26	John Cooper	to	Hannah Watson	Rev. Mr. Magraw
" 26	David Austin	to	Lipborah? Heath	Sharpley
" 27	Eli Janney	to	Esther Lackland	Rev. Mr. Duke
" 29	James Lynch	to	Mary Conley	Rev. Mr. Duke
May 11	Joseph Pugh	to	Rebecca Price	Rev. Mr. Sharpley
" 5	John Russell	to	Margaret Coney	Rev. Mr. Magraw
June 3	Wm. Simpers	to	Mary Ann Dunn	Rev. Mr. Duke
" 7	Ebenezer Wells	to	Rebecca Money	Rev. Mr. Sewall
" 8	Victor Currier	to	Mary Burrows	Rev. Mr. Magraw
" 23	Daniel Wright	to	Sarah Smith	Rev. Mr. Duke
Aug. 10	Abraham Watson	to	Hannah Owens	Rev. Mr. Magraw
" 14	George W. Cochran	to	Rebecca Crouch	Rev. Mr. Duke
Sept. 3	William Knight	to	Maria Jones	Rev. Mr. Duke
Oct. 27	Henry D. Miller	to	Ann Dowerty	Rev. Mr. Duke
" 28	John McClary	to	Ann Galloway	Rev. Mr. Chambers
Nov. 3	George Ford	to	Ann Savin	
" 3	Elisha J. Hitchcock	to	Ann Roach	Rev. Mr. Duke
" 8	Wm. Landsborough	to	Elizabeth Crossan	Rev. Mr. Magraw
" 10	Robert Williams	to	Mary Barratt	Rev. Mr. Duke
" 16	Amos Miles	to	Ann Lowrey	Rev. Mr. Magraw
" 18	John S. Taylor	to	Ann Beaston	Rev. Mr. Forrell
" 24	Wm. Jamison	to	Hannah Meughing?	Rev. Mr. Sharpley
Dec. 1	John Lowrey	to	Mary Ann Clark	Rev. Mr. Sharpley
" 14	Andrew Biddle	to	Louise McGregor	Rev. Mr. Chambers
" 14	John Mercer	to	Nancy Bennett	Rev. Mr. Williams
" 15	Andrew Egan	to	Hester Corbitt	Rev. Mr. Goforth
" 21	Thomas S. Thomas	to	Ann Sewall	Rev. Mr. Duke
" 21	Robert C. Lusby	to	Elizabeth Price	Rev. Mr. Duke
" 27	Isaac Nowland	to	Rachel White	Rev. Mr. Magraw
" 28	Stephen McKinney	to	Ann Letby	Rev. Mr. Duke
" 27	Isaac Nowland	to	Ann Letty	Duke
" 20	Stephen McKinney	to	Rachel White	MaGraw
1820				
Jan. 1	Samuel Otterson	to	Alice Ruby	Nyne
" 3	Edward Iler	to	Elizabeth Jackson	
" 5	Andrew Gibson	to	Mary Ann Howard	Ferrell
" 10	Robert Maklum	to	Barbara Muflete	Sharpley
" 10	James McCay	to	Mary Broughton	MaGraw

		MAN		WOMAN	MINISTER
"	10	Andrew Henderson	to	Susan Ward	Ninde
"	11	Benjamin Price	to	Elizabeth Conway	Ninde
"	17	David H. Price	to	Mary Ann Chandler	Ninde
"	17	Joseph Blunkshall?	to	Patty Willcocks	Duke
"	20	Joshua Vansant	to	Mary Benson	Nyne
"	26	Benjamine Bowen	to	Mary Garrett	Duke
		Joseph P. Ryan	to	Rosana Burris	Magraw
Feb.	2	Joseph Wimble	to	Ann Keatly	Duke
"	3	Patrick Dougherty	to	Mary Ann McCleary	Chambers
"	8	George Alcorne	to	Ann Casho	Chambers
"	14	Thomas Aldridge	to	Eliza Cazier	Sharpley
"	24	Thomas Lowe	to	Ann Simpers	Sharpley
"	23	Daniel McCauley	to	Elizabeth Harvey	Neilson
"	25	Thomas Miller	to	Anne Simpers	Torbat
"	28	John Johnson	to	Sarah Taylor	Neilson
Mar.	1	William Bristow	to	Charlotte Armstrong	Chambers
"	2	Ferdinand Taylor	to	Elizabeth Stoops	Sharpley
"	7	Eli Stubbs	to	Mary Webb	Chambers
"	9	Manlove Hayes	to	Ann Tatman	Duke
"	13	Richard Bateman	to	Mary Hand	Nine
"	16	Joseph Dennison	to	Ann Read	Duke
"	22	John C. Cameron	to	Nancy Mearns	Duke
"	22	John Tatman	to	Mary Fenelin	Duke
"	23	Davidson D. Pearce	to	Rebecca Brevard	Chambers
"	28	John Mahan	to	Abigail Nowland	Duke
"	29	William Reed	to	Amy McVey	Duke
Apr.	5	Richard Carpenter	to	Harriet Biddle	Duke
"	14	William F. Abbott	to	Millicent Williamson	Ninde
May	1	George Hayes	to	Elizabeth James	Ninde
"	8	Giles T. Langdon	to	Eliza McCutcheon	MaGraw
"	9	Samuel Sevenson	to	Sina Baker	Sharpley
"	22	Harvery Moore	to	Sarah Dougherty	Sharpley
"	24	Harman Foster	to	Ann Stagle	Sharpley
"	25	Samuel Garrett	to	Mary Ann Guiberson	Duke
"	25	Joseph Coudon	to	Ann Stump	Duke
"	30	Amos Slack	to	Maria Price	Sharpley
July	11	James Butler	to	Mary Northerman	Ninde
"	25	Daniel Ashton	to	Olevia Ferrell	Griffith
Aug.	8	Charles Jones	to	Mary Ann Hyland	Ninde
"	8	Isaac Taylor	to	Jane Hewett	Sharpley
"	14	William McBride	to	Ann Fleming	Sharpley
"	23	Peter Wingate	to	Elisa Ward	Duke
"	28	Adam Stevens	to	Elizabeth Steel	Magraw
"	28	Henry Richardson	to	Elizabeth Yeamans	Sharpley
Sept.	5	Eliha Brown	to	Ann Guy	MaGraw
"	11	John Polk	to	Elizabeth Cliff	Sharpley
"	19	Asbury Sappington	to	Anna Hevering	Nine
Jan.	1	Samuel Otterson	to	Alice Ruley	
"	3	Edward Iler	to	Elizabeth Jackson	Rev. Mr. Chambers
"	5	Andrew Gibson	to	Mary Ann Howard	Rev. Ferrell
"	10	Robert Macklum	to	Barbara Mullett?	Rev. Sharpley
"	10	James McCay	to	Mary Broughten	Rev. Mr. Magraw
"	10	Andrew F. Henderson	to	Susan Ward	
"	11	Benjamin Price	to	Elizabeth Conway	
"	17	David H. Price	to	Mary Ann Chandle	
"	17	Joseph Blunkshall?	to	Patty Wilcocks	Rev. Mr. Duke
"	20	Joshua Vansant	to	Mary Benson	
"	26	Benjamin Bowen	to	Mary Garrett	Rev. Mr. Duke
"	26	Joseph P. Ryan	to	Rosanna Burris	Rev. Mr. Magraw

Date	MAN		WOMAN	MINISTER
Feb. 2	Joseph Wimble	to	Ann Keatley	Rev. Mr. Duke
" 3	Patrick Dougherty	to	Mary Ann McClary	Rev. Mr. Chambers
" 8	George Alcorne	to	Ann Casho	Rev. Mr. Chambers
" 14	Thomas Aldridge	to	Eliza Cazier	Rev. Mr. Sharpley
" 29	Thomas Lowe	to	Ann Simpers	Rev. Mr. Sharpley
" 23	Daniel McCauley	to	Elizabeth Harvey	Rev. Mr. Wilson
" 25	Thomas Miller	to	Ann Simpers	Rev. Mr. Torbert
" 28	John Johnson	to	Sarah Taylor	Rev. Mr. Wilson
Mar. 1	Wm. Bristow	to	Charlotte Armstrong	Rev. Mr. Chambers
" 2	Ferdinand Taylor	to	Elizabeth Stoops	Rev. Mr. Sharpley
" 7	Eli Stubbs	to	Mary Webb	Rev. Mr. Chambers
" 9	Manlove Hayes	to	Ann Tatman	Rev. Mr. Duke
" 13	Richard Bateman	to	Mary Hand	
" 16	Joseph Dennison	to	Ann Reed	Rev. Mr. Duke
" 22	John C. Cameron	to	Nancy Mearns	Rev. Mr. Duke
" 22	John Tatman	to	Mary Fonelin?	Rev. Mr. Duke
" 23	Davidson C. Pearce	to	Rebecca Brevard	Chambers
" 28	John Mahan	to	Abigail Nowalnd	Rev. Mr. Duke
" 29	Richard Carpenter	to	Harriet Biddle	Rev. Mr. Chambers
Apr. 14	Wm. F. Abbot	to	Millicent Williamson	Rev. Mr. Duke
May 1	George Hayes	to	Elizabeth James	
" 8	Giles S. Langdon	to	Eliza McCutcheon	Rev. Mr. Magraw
" 9	Samuel Severson	to	Sina Baker	Rev. Mr. Sharpley
" 22	Harvey Moore	to	Sarah Dougherty	Rev. Mr. Sharpley
" 24	Harmon Foster	to	Ann Slagle	Rev. Mr. Sharpley
" 24	Samuel Garret	to	Mary Ann Guiberson	Rev. Mr. Duke
" 25	Joseph Coudon	to	Ann Stump	Rev. Mr. Duke
" 30	Amos Slack	to	Maria Price	Rev. Mr. Sharpley
July 11	James Butler	to	Mary Northerman?	
" 25	Daniel Ashton	to	Olevia Ferrell	Rev. Mr. Griffith
Aug. 18	Charles Jones	to	Mary Ann Hyland	
" 8	Isaac Taylor	to	Jane Hewitt	Rev. Mr. Sharpley
" 14	William McBride	to	Ann Flemming	Rev. Mr. Sharpley
" 23	Peter Wingate	to	Eliza Ward	Rev. Mr. Duke
" 28	Adam Stevens	to	Elizabeth Steel	Rev. Mr. Magraw
" 28	Henry Richardson	to	Elizabeth Yeamens	Rev. Mr. Sharpley
Sept. 5	Elisha Brown	to	Ann Guy	Rev. Mr. Magraw
" 11	John Pope	to	Elizabeth Cliff	Rev. Mr. Sharpley
" 19	Asbury Sappington	to	Anna Hevering	
" 25	George Stebbings	to	Elizabeth Grant	Rev. Mr. Sharpley
" 27	Samuel A. Miller	to	Lavey Tyson	Rev. Mr. Griffith
" 27	Elisha Oldham	to	Elizabeth Lilly	Rev. Mr. Griffith
Oct. 4	Henry Akison?	to	Mary Abrahams	Rev. Mr. Magraw
" 10	George Wilson	to	Elizabeth Crouch	Rev. Sharpley
" 12	Franklin Betts	to	Ann Davis	Rev. Mr. Duke
Nov. 27	Andrew Barrett	to	Jane Smith	Rev. Mr. Goforth
Dec. 8	William Torbert	to	Martha Rudulph	Rev. Mr. Sharpley
" 19	Stephen Donohoe	to	Sarah Wilcox	Rev. Mr. Sharpley
" 22	John Gamble	to	Elizabeth Reed	Rev. Mr. Sharpley
" 28	Jesse Foster	to	Elizabeth Rutter	Rev. Mr. Griffith
" 28	James Foster	to	Margery Rutter	Rev. Mr. Griffith
1821				
Jan. 4	Andrew Wilson	to	Rachel Simpers	Rev. Mr. Griffith
" 3	James Linden	to	Rebecca Groves	Rev. Mr. Griffith
" 8	Joseph Grant	to	Elizabeth McKeowan	Rev. Mr. Miller
" 15	Joshua Alden	to	Margaret Dysart	Rev. Mr. Sharpley
Dec. 24	Elias Pennington	to	Jane Grubb	Rev. Mr. Magraw
" 25	John Girvin	to	Elizabeth Jones	Rev. Mr. Sharpley
" 27	Ebenezer Hurlock	to	Sarah C. Reed	Rev. Mr. Sharpley
" 31	James Barker	to	Mary Bryson	Rev. Mr. Chambers

MAN			WOMAN	MINISTER
1822				
Jan. 3	Joseph Mathias	to	Mary Shaeffer	Rev. Mr. Sharpley
" 8	George W. Kirk	to	Maria Thompson	Rev. Mr. Magraw
" 12	William Donaldson	to	Rebecca Savin	Rev. Mr. Chambers
" 14	Baker Fritt?	to	Mary Ann Staples	
" 14	Thomas W. Smith	to	Mary Ford	Rev. Mr. Griffith
1820				
Sept. 25	George Stebbing	to	Elizabeth Grant	Griffith
" 27	Samuel R. Miller	to	Lansy Tyson	Griffith
" 27	Elisha Oldham	to	Elizabeth Lilly	Duke
Oct. 4	Henry Akison	to	Mary Abrams	MaGraw
" 10	George Wilson	to	Elizabeth Crouch	Sharpley
" 12	Franklin Betts	to	Ann Davis	Mr. Duke
Nov. 27	Andrew Barrett	to	Jane Smith	Goforth
Dec. 8	William Torbert	to	Martha Rudolph	Sharpley
" 19	Stephen Donoho	to	Sarah Wilcox	Sharpley
" 22	John Gamble	to	Elizabeth Reed	Sharpley
" 28	Jesse Foster	to	Elizabeth Rutter	Griffith
" 28	James Foster	to	Margery Rutter	Griffith
1821				
Dec. 3	John James	to	Emeline James	Ninde
" 5	Leonard Dorr	to	Mary Ginnes	Griffith
" 12	Joseph Phillips	to	Rebecca Kilgor	Duke
" 12	Samuel Jackson	to	Mary Baker	Duke
" 19	John Fisher	to	Ann Simmons	Magraw
" 20	Hugh Jones	to	Ann Kidd	Griffith
" 20	William Hukill	to	Jane Crouch	Sharpley
" 24	Elizas Penington	to	Jane Grubb	Magraw
" 25	John Garvin	to	Elizabeth Jones	Sharpley
" 27	Ebenezer Hurlock	to	Sarah Reed	Sharpley
" 31	James Barker	to	Mary Bryson	Chambers
1822				
Jan. 3	Joseph Mathias	to	Mary Shaeffer	Sharpley
" 8	George W. Kirk	to	Marie Thompson	McGraw
" 12	William Donaldson	to	Rebecca Savin	Chambers
" 14	Baker Frist	to	Mary Ann Staples	Chambers
" 14	Thomas W. Smith	to	Mary Ford	Griffith
" 16	Ephraim Sterling	to	Jamima A. Mansfield	Chambers
" 19	William Price	to	Sarah Robinson	Chambers
" 31	Joel Chamberlaine	to	Eleanor Kerr	Magraw
Feb. 6	James Faris	to	Martha Ann Boyd	Chambers
" 12	James G. Moore	to	Catherine Robinson	Sharpley
" 12	William C. Penington	to	Eliza Ann Coale	Sharpley
" 12	Patrick Ewing	to	Isabella P. Evans	McGraw
" 14	James Fairbank	to	Rebecca Osburn	Sharpley
" 20	John Manlove	to	Rebecca Hukill	Ninde
" 25	James Hart	to	Rebecca Walmsley	Griffith
" 28	Able Marnes	to	Mary Cameron	Magraw
Mar. 9	Joseph McClary	to	Jane Moore	Goforth
" 11	James Irvin	to	Susanna M. Cummings	Sharpley
" 18	John Thompson	to	Letitia Heath	Goforth
" 20	James McCracken	to	Mary Ann Garey	Russell
" 21	Robert Davidson	to	Jane McBride	Griffith
1821				
Jan. 4	Andrew Wilson	to	Rachel Simpers	Griffith
" 5	James Linden	to	Rebecca Groves	Griffith
" 8	Joseph Grant	to	Elizabeth McKeon	Miller
" 15	Joshua Alden	to	Margaret Dysart	Sharpley

		MAN		WOMAN	MINISTER
"	18	James E. Mahan	to	Margaret Whann	Magraw
"	30	Samuel C. Atkinson	to	Charlotte L. Coffield	Duke
"	30	Robert Carter	to	Mary Reynolds	Griffith
Feb.	1	David Alexander	to	Lidia Wood	Chambers
"	6	John Evans	to	Sarah Patton	McGraw
"	6	David Moore	to	Hester Russell	Duke
"	6	John Evans	to	Isabella Work	Sharpley
"	13	John L. Caruthers	to	Isabella Cord	McGraw
"	13	Philip Coale	to	Eliza Ann Walmsley	Sharpley
"	22	Jeremiah Short	to	Martha Aldridge	Griffith
Mar.	5	David Churchman	to	Rebecca Newcomer	Goforth
"	8	Robert Sutton	to	Hannah Ferguson	Sharpley
"	26	Jesse Simpers	to	Jane Miller	Griffith
"	30	James Cummings	to	Rachel Hall	Duke
Apr.	5	Noble Cox	to	Maria Tyson	Griffith
"	23	Joseph Alexander	to	Eliza Morris	Griffith
"	24	Peter Hall	to	Elizabeth Blunkhall	Sharpley
"	26	Isaac Holt	to	Mary Campbell	Wilton

Record of Marriage Licenses rendered treasurer to here amount

May	4	Michael Millegan	to	Sarah Grant	Sharpley
"	4	William Garrett	to	Ann Gregg	Sharpley
"	17	Samuel Nesbit, Jr.	to	Harriet Lyons	McGraw
"	19	James W. McCelland	to	Hester Cox	Nyne
"	28	Frances Owens	to	Charity Bryan	Sharpley
June	2	Cloud Carter	to	Rachel Miller	Griffith
"	4	William Kilgor	to	Ann Humphreys	Griffith
"	9	Edward Lister	to	Mary Dowling	Ninde
"	9	Cogle Holden	to	Sarah Bouchelle	Chambers
"	18	James Todd	to	Aramenta McCartney	Goforth
"	18	James Miller	to	Sarah Archibald	Magraw
"	21	Alexander Crowle?	to	Elizabeth Hall	Duke
"	27	William Montgomery	to	Ann Hall	Duke
"	30	Thomas Barclay	to	Sarah Campbell	Sharpley
July	2	Henry Keatley	to	Julian Lynch	Griffith
"	5	George Mahan	to	Lydia Wells	Sharpley
"	10	John Janney	to	Caroline Newland	Sharpley
"	13	James Logue	to	Sarah Copes	Osbourn
"	31	Joseph Peters	to	Hannah Shearer	Sharpley
Aug.	17	Jonathan Beans	to	Mary Morrison	Sharpley
"	27	Samuel Beattie, Jr.	to	Deborah Kelley	Goforth
Sept.	7	Charles C. Vinhekle	to	Margaret F. Williams	Duke
"	11	Jacob Egner	to	Margaret Williams	Sharpley
"	25	Samuel Crouch	to	Mary Lowe	Sharpley
"	26	Henry Work	to	Jane McDonall	Sharpley
Oct.	2	James Brown	to	Elizabeth McCarlin	Sharpley
"	25	John Adams	to	Margaret Martin	Griffith
"	30	Phineas Jones	to	Virginia Thomas	Griffith
"	30	Sidney Chandlee	to	Tobetio Price	Sharpley
"	30	Thomas Bouldin	to	Priscilla Foard	Sharpley
Nov.	14	Hezekiah Masten	to	Alethe Griffith	Sharpley
"	20	Thomas Fisher	to	Kaziah McMaster	Magraw
"	30	William Patten	to	Sarah Evans	Magraw
1822					
Mar.	21	James Sumplin	to	Mary Latman	Chambers
"	28	John Simpers	to	Frances Price	Sharpley
Apr.	14	William Jackson	to	Sarah Wilson	Woolferd
"	14	Enoch Latham	to	Ann Jester	Chambers
"	10	Andrew Price	to	Martha Ford	Chambers
"	23	John Burrows	to	Martha Whitelock	Goforth
"	30	James Roach	to	Elizabeth Farley	Sharpley

		MAN		WOMAN	MINISTER
May	1	Samuel Johnson	to	Mary Ann Savage	Duke
"	11	Richard Craig	to	Rebecca Hall	Wait
"	23	Samuel Davis	to	Cornelia Pennington	Sewall
"	24	John Ford	to	Mary Cillon	Griffith
"	28	William Purdy	to	Rebecca Simpson	Chambers
June	1	Rowille Kirk	to	Lydia Harris	Magraw
"	3	John Grace	to	Rebecca Alexander	Smith
"	5	George W. Price	to	Ann Price	Chambers
"	6	Henry B. Simpson	to	Martha Ann Walker	Chambers
"	10	James Martin	to	Sarah Spence	Sharpley
"	10	John Calvert	to	Mary Ann Rutter	Goforth
"	11	Richard Ford	to	Sarah Craig	Duke
"	22	Hanse Serverson	to	Sarah Pennington	Myne
"	29	John Sneakenburgh	to	Rachel Shroff	Magraw
July	1	William Hutton	to	Rachel Kirk	Magraw
"	2	Solomon Blake	to	Martha Collins	Ninde
"	18	Edward Veazey	to	Eliza Flake	Ninde
"	27	John Hornes	to	Annie Eliza Crow	Duke
Aug.	1	John Ryland	to	Maud Kimble	Sharpley
"	8	Joseph Richardson	to	Elizabeth Bryan	Chambers
"	12	William Graham	to	Charlotte Dixon	Duke
Sept.	2	James Wells	to	Margaret Cameron	Goforth
"	11	Samuel McMullin	to	Eliza Taylor	Magraw
"	23	John Sampson	to	Sarah Humes	Magraw
Oct.	7	William Edwards	to	Mary Gilmore	Magraw
"	17	Robert McWearles?	to	Martha Taggart	Magraw
"	18	Isaac Roddis	to	Elizabeth Cantwell	Chambers
"	21	Edward Davidson	to	Hannah Scarborough	Sharpley
Nov.	6	Thomas Calvert	to	Mary Richardson	Goforth
"	14	John Moore	to	Jane Barnes	Magraw
"	28	John Raughley	to	Mary Conlyn	Sharpley
"	29	Samuel McCrery	to	Jane Alexander	Duke
"	29	Samuel Williams	to	Jane Rutherford	Sharpley
"	29	Samuel McIntire	to	Rachel Caurthers	Duke
Dec.	2	Nathan Tyson	to	Margaret Mackey	Duke
"	6	Henry S. Stites	to	Ann McGready	Finney
"	11	Joseph Phillips	to	Elizabeth Mingling	Duke
"	18	Andrew Price	to	Jane Conlyn	Weller
"	19	William Spence	to	Martha Cloud	Sharpley
"	21	Robert Hall	to	Elizabeth Hague	Weller
"	20	Edward Pennington	to	Catharine Lusby	Weller
"	27	John McCulser	to	Rosanna Gilmore	Jackson
"	30	John Copes	to	Juliann Copes	Weller
	1823				
Jan.	8	William Cameron	to	Margaret Patten	Magraw
"	11	George Walmsley	to	Sarah Hall	Weller
"	13	James Craig	to	Eliza Manley	Chambers
"	16	William Patterson	to	Ruth Lumblin	Duke
"	28	John Perry	to	Jane Guy	Magraw
Feb.	5	Morris Davis	to	Saba Snow	Sewall
"	19	John Barclay	to	Margaret Dean	Sharpley
"	26	Robert McNitt	to	Sarah Tumlin	Chambers
Mar.	12	Thomas W. Cameron	to	Jane Alexander	Goforth
"	12	John Nesbitt	to	Jane Nesbitt	Magraw
"	17	William Carpenter	to	Nicey Tumlin	Chambers
"	18	Francis Segars	to	Elizabeth Kerr	Goforth
"	19	William G. Richardson	to	Mary Barrington	Chambers
"	25	James Hill	to	Mary Wollaston	Duke
Apr.	2	George Gonce	to	Catherine Comegys	Wilton
"	17	Thomas Holton	to	Mary Alexander	Duke

MAN			WOMAN	MINISTER
May 3	James Bowdon	to	Anna Sullivan	Duke
" 12	William Coolin	to	Sarah Calvert	Griffith
" 20	Owin Siles	to	Rebecca Johnson	Duke
" 21	Joseph Alexander	to	Mary Alden	Duke
" 21	George Foard	to	Sarah Davis	Duke
" 27	George Daily	to	Jane Hardy	Sharpley
June 7	Benjamin Biggs	to	Anne Sparks	Duke
" 12	William Jack	to	Hannah Griffee	Magraw
" 18	John Cruikshanks	to	Mary Ellis	Wilson
" 26	Samuel Hannah	to	Mary Ann Spencer	Sharpley
" 26	David Burnite	to	Sarah Moore	Rider
Aug. 11	John P. Ryan	to	Elizabeth Armstrong	Goforth
" 25	Tylus Roberson	to	Eliza McKenney	Wyat
" 26	Roderick Hevelow	to	Ann S. Price	Sharpley
Sept. 2	Samuel Gillespie	to	Hester McClellan?	Magraw
" 3	Hammond Allen	to	Rebecca Ruly	Waller
Oct. 1	James Bacum	to	Jane Bates	Chambers
" 13	Edward Whitelock	to	Catherine Hoddz	Goforth
" 27	Samuel Williamson	to	Margaret Milburn	Goforth
" 27	John Peters	to	Rebecca Grant	Griffith
Nov. 17	John Gothris?	to	Rebecca Harper	Sharpley
Dec. 3	William C. Price	to	Jane Miller	Griffith
" 9	Samuel Thomas	to	Mary Ann Cosden	Griffith
" 9	William Peters	to	Angeline Woods	Duke
" 13	George Hayes	to	Hannah Biddle	Duke
" 18	James Pugh	to	Eliza Wilson	Sharpley
" 20	Joseph Scarborough	to	Rebecca Boyd	Magraw
" 30	Levi H. Evans	to	Rachel Stump	Duke
" 30	Francis Jarvis	to	Marie Beard	Griffith
1824				
Jan. 5	William Price	to	Ann Tobitha Pugh	Sharpley
" 12	John Cameron	to	Amelia Bennett	
" 9	Spencer Biddle	to	Susan Pagh	Chambers
" 20	Alexander Maller	to	Amelia Jane Coale	Magraw
" 20	Benjamin Sergeant	to	Clarisa Bravard	Duke
Feb. 3	Jesse Hall	to	Mary Alexander	Duke
" 5	James McGee	to	Ann E. Rodney	Duke
" 9	John Ruby	to	Julian Ruby	Miller
" 9	William Pearce	to	Margaret Handy	Miller
" 11	James A. Price	to	Ocy Scarborough	Wilson
" 29	Washington Edward Moore	to	Rachel Smith	Duke
Mar. 1	Nicholas White	to	Ann M. Springer	Goforth
" 3	Outoix Jester	to	Sarah Hudson	Chambers
" 4	Samuel Boulden	to	Ruth Roberts	Chambers
" 17	Thomas E. Clayton	to	Sarah R. Laurenson	Duke
" 23	Daniel Mullen	to	Eleanor Cloward	Sharpley
" 23	William Brown	to	Eliza. Manly	Griffith
" 23	Enoch Cloud	to	Mary Ann Callahan	Chambers
" 25	Samuel C. Sample	to	Ann B. Howard	Duke
" 31	John Vandegrifth	to	Mary Fillingame	Chambers
" 31	Benjamin M. Asleip	to	Ann Moffett	Duke
" 31	James Brumfield	to	Elizabeth Hudson	Chambers
Apr. 6	James H. Boggs	to	Aseneath Beaston	Chambers
" 21	John Clark	to	Elizabeth Merritt	Chambers
" 29	William Briston	to	Ann Groves	Griffith
" 29	George Howard	to	Eliza. Jane Jones	Sharpley
May 1	John Crokshank	to	Mary Ann Pennington	Grace
" 1	John C. Murphy	to	Ann R. Price	Grace
" 6	Jesse McCrea	to	Elizabeth Fletcher	Sharpley
" 12	Robert Nes-Bitt (junior)	to	Eleanor Nes-Bitt	Magraw

		MAN		WOMAN	MINISTER
"	20	William Jones	to	Susan McKenzie	Sharpley
"	24	James Russell	to	Clarabelle McVey	Griffith
June	7	James Alexander	to	Francis Clark	Griffith
"	15	Samuel Thompson	to	Evaline Brown	Goforth
"	16	Samuel Freeman	to	Rebecca Ellsbury	Sharpley
"	17	Moses Scott	to	Elizabeth Moore	Rufell
"	23	Edward T. Bailey	to	Mary E. Woodland	Sharpley
"	26	John Filligame	to	Mary Orr	Chambers
July	1	John Watson	to	Elizabeth Sharp	Sharpley
"	2	Jesse Evans	to	Deborah Johnson	Goforth
Aug.	4	Benjamin Mauldin	to	Araminta Hyland	Griffith
"	11	George Wilson	to	Scintha Davis	Sharpley
"	11	William Little	to	Mary Holt	Sharpley
"	21	John M. Satterfield	to	Eliza Sappington	Smith
Sept.	13	William King	to	Rachel Moffett	Duke
"	13	James Marnes	to	Lavenia Oldham	Duke
"	15	Asariah Pennington	to	Rebecca Crouch	Sharpley
"	15	John White	to	Jane Hall	Rider
"	18	Hugh King	to	Elizabeth Pennington	Sharpley
"	25	James Hayes	to	Sarah Dickson	Chambers
"	28	Andrew Thompson	to	Abigail S. Johnson	Grace
"	13	Alphonso Comegys	to	Sarah E. M. Morgan	Miller
Oct.	2	Andrew Garrison	to	Mary R. Nowland	Duke
"	11	James Barnes	to	Rhoda Beaty	Magraw
"	23	Jehorchim Brickly	to	Elizabeth Thompson	Griffith
Nov.	2	Issace Reynolds	to	Mary Alexander	Griffith
"	15	James Carll	to	Rebecca Jackson	Barton
"	20	Benjamin McKinney	to	Kesiah Jones	Duke
"	22	Ambrose Price	to	Ann E. W. Porter	Waller
"	25	Thomas McCreary	to	Isabella Kilgore	Duke
"	27	Hugh Patterson	to	Elizabeth Patterson	Waller
"	29	Stephen Hamab?	to	Elizabeth Megredy	
Dec.	7	Levin Shockley	to	Sarah Johnson	Chambers
"	8	Edward Jackson	to	Ann Berry	Grace
"	10	John Ford	to	Mary Bond	Bell
"	13	James Lunney	to	Susan Keitly	Sharpley
"	15	John Sumption	to	Jane McCall	Griffith
"	20	John H. Biddle	to	Mary Bowen	Chambers
"	30	Joseph Roswell	to	Mary Sailsbury	Duke
"	30	Tobias McKensie	to	Maria Tyson	Sharpley
	1825				
Jan.	1	Uphres Biddle	to	Mary Thompson	Griffith
"	4	John Virtue	to	Maria R. Coale	Grace
"	5	William Stanton	to	Mary Evans	Russell
"	5	John D. Carter	to	Mary Ann Lowe	Sharpley
"	10	David Gilmore	to	Sarah Irvin	MaGraw
"	13	James Crothers	to	Rachel Cameron	MaGraw
"	13	Levi Hill	to	Mary Crothers	Griffith
"	25	Joseph Henry Stewart	to	Arrietta Craddock	Stephen
Feb.	5	Andrew Barrett	to	Eliza Burris?	Griffith
"	14	Thomas Bryan	to	Leah Wallace	Chambers
"	14	John V. Price	to	Ann Nowland	Miller
"	16	John B. Campbell	to	Sarah McMullen	Griffith
"	16	Thomas Rutter	to	Mary Fisher	Duke
"	21	Absolom McVey	to	Mary Edmonson	Griffith
"	24	John Gallaway	to	Margaret A. Gashore	Sharpley
Mar.	1	William Norris	to	Louisa Whitlock	Smith
"	3	Benjamin Mercer	to	Casandra White	Stephenson
"	9	William H. Davis	to	Margaret Worthington	Waller
"	9	Jeremiah Eliason	to	Ann Killen	Chambers

		MAN		WOMAN	MINISTER
"	14	William Little	to	Hannah Simcoe	MaGraw
"	15	Stephen Davis	to	Caroline Smith	Sharpley
"	16	William Boulton	to	Mary Buckhanan	Chambers
"	17	Joseph W. Miller	to	Martha Whann	Sharpley
"	17	John C. Williams	to	Susanna Biddle	Magraw
"	2	Edward T. Bailey	to	Mary E. Woodland	Duke
"	22	John Jordon	to	Elizabeth Farran	Sharpley
"	22	John McCrea	to	Margaret Kinkead	Duke
"	29	David Jennis	to	Rebecca Davidson	Sharpley
Apr.	5	Iasiah H. Gilpin	to	Martha T. Moffet	Duke
"	13	Samuel Whitlock	to	Elizabeth Loftis	Duke
May	3	James McNit	to	Martha Tumblin	Chambers
"	6	Eber Smith	to	Nancy Gilmore	MaGraw
"	16	Seborn Grant	to	Sarah Worth	Rider
"	22	Morris Flinn	to	Elizabeth Farral	Duke
"	24	Joseph George	to	Sarah Clark	Wilson
"	27	Abraham F. Pennington	to	Elizabeth Reed	
June	1	George Davidson	to	Ann E. Haines	MaGraw
"	13	James A. Williamson	to	Sarah W. Williamson	Miller
"	14	Samuel R. Hogg	to	Rachel Boulden	Gilbert
"	20	Robert Nesbitt Jr.	to	Elinor Hindman	MaGraw
July	5	James B. Herbert	to	Mary Ann Baker	Duke
"	12	Samuel Logan	to	Margaret McCall	McGraw
"	18	Isaac McClay	to	Margaret Burnite	Sharpley
"	18	Richard Boulden	to	Mary Ann Herrington	Chambers
"	20	Patrick Murphey	to	Catherine Cavender	Duke
"	27	Samuel Briley	to	Mary May	Chambers
Aug.	22	Nathaniel Simpers	to	Hannah Crouch	Miller
Sept.	5	Edward B. Gibbs	to	Margaret Bowen	Smith
"	13	Samuel Buenes	to	Susan Taylor	Sharpley
"	23	Joseph Sumption	to	Mary Kilpatrick	Sharpley
"	24	William Grant	to	Ann Alexander	Duke
"	27	John Ash	to	Ruth Ann Smythers	Sharpley
"	28	Samuel Taylor	to	Janetta Cunnay	MaGraw
Oct.	3	James Forman?	to	Eleanor Slaven	Duke
"	4	William H. Maffitt	to	Elizabeth Daugherty	Duke
"	11	Joseph Strawbridge	to	Eliza Oldham	Graham
"	15	Jefferson W. White	to	Grissell Currier	MaGraw
"	25	Lewis Bristow	to	Elizabeth Bostick	Sharpley
"	27	Moses Rumsey	to	Rebecca Brown	Goforth
Nov.	26	Noah Frieze	to	Rebecca Thompson	Talley
Dec.	3	Elias B. Glenn	to	Rachael Ann Taylor	Sharpley
"	5	John McGee	to	Mary Stewart	Duke
"	19	Henry B. Broughton	to	Isabella S. Evans	Magraw
"	19	John Glenn	to	Pheby Knight	Sharpley
"	20	Daniel M. McCauley, Jr.	to	Rachael Beard	Wilson
"	21	Joseph Hall	to	Charity Scarborough	Sharpley
"	29	Andrew Ramsey	to	Mary Thompson	Magraw
"	31	William Ferguson	to	Henrietta Mary Porter	Davis
1826					
Jan.	2	John Heath	to	Susanne Moore	Goforth
"	5	Andrew Were	to	Mary Murphey	Goforth
"	5	Robert Robertson	to	Ann Eliza Williams	Davis
"	10	George Lewis	to	Mary Laurenson	Sharpley
"	11	John Cameron	to	Margaret Lynch	Talley
"	11	Samuel Cummings	to	Mary Perre	Graham
"	11	Isaac Johnson	to	Susan Curry	Barratt
"	16	Thomas Holland	to	Margaret Egner	Woolford
"	25	Jeremiah Baker	to	Mary Campbell	Magraw

		MAN		WOMAN	MINISTER
Feb.	4	Alfred C. Nowland	to	Phebe Pennington	Duke
"	8	Benjamin Reynolds	to	Alsey Johnson	Sharpley
"	8	John Cooper	to	Jane Little	Magraw
"	9	John Short	to	Sarah Grant	Sharpley
"	14	James Proctor	to	Rebecca Hadney	Duke
"	18	Myron Terry	to	Margaret Gamble	Sharpley
"	18	Thomas Evans	to	Mary Hall	Sharpley
"	26	James Pennington	to	Caroline Davis	Smith
"	28	John O. Ferry	to	Susan Alexander	Duke
Mar.	6	William Campbell	to	Nancy Weir	Goforth
"	8	John Caldwell	to	Rebecca Price	Smith
"	8	Ruben Lake	to	Deborah Cameron	Tally
"	16	Hugh Boyd	to	Margaret Fox	Magraw
"	17	Samuel Harris	to	Maria Hudson	
"	25	Samuel Clark	to	Catherine Hitselberger	Magraw
"	25	Hugh Marnes	to	Nancy Cochran	Graham
"	27	Samuel Hayes	to	Edith Emeline Biddle	Smith
"	28	Francis B. Gottier	to	Rebecca Wingate	Duke
Apr.	3	William J. Brown	to	Ann M. Evans	Russell
"	12	Isaac Robinson	to	Mary Iler	Wyat
"	20	Nicholas Smith	to	Ann Dougherty	Phinfatra
"	26	John McNeal	to	Sarah Craig	Woolford
		Copy made and sent to treasurer the 1st May			
May	8	Corbon Cooley	to	Jane Johnson	Griffith
"	13	Philip Craig	to	Ann A. Lee	Duke
"	20	John Venort	to	Elizabeth Thompson	Goforth
"	23	William Hogg	to	Jane Moffitt	Graham
"	25	Thomas Wingate	to	Millicent Hyland	Barrett
"	27	William Lowey	to	Rachel Richardson	Duke
June	1	Amos Slack	to	Mary Boyce	Barrett
"	3	Francis Owens	to	Sophia O'Brien	Reyngedd
"	6	Robert McMillin	to	Deborah Williams	Magraw
"	6	John F. Crouch	to	Merrey Strong	Barrett
"	8	William Brumfield	to	Amelia Owens	Magraw
"	10	James Mulholland	to	Margaret Veasey	Page
"	22	Samuel Williams	to	Rebecca McVey	Barrett
"	27	Francis Atkinson	to	Hettie Logan	Barrett
July	6	John Thomas Cameron	to	Sarah Ballan	Magraw
"	11	William Hutson	to	Mariah Robinson	Duke
"	26	James Lowery	to	Mary Simpers	Page
Aug.	1	Barney Mullen	to	Elizabeth Barnes	Goforth
"	10	Joseph Whitelock	to	Mary Hodge	Barrett
"	29	George W. Oldham	to	Susan A. Biddle	Duke
"	29	John McCord	to	Susan Kean	Woolford
"	30	Samuel Maxwell	to	Eliza Russell	Duke
Sept.	13	Edward B. Foard	to	Sarah Severson	Smith
"	19	Thomas Moffitt	to	Araminta Cozier	Wallace
"	19	William Dennison	to	Sarah Logan	Barrett
"	27	William Steigal	to	Rebecca Ann Smith?	Barrett
Oct.	25	Francis Goleober	to	Agnes McCullough	Goforth
"	30	William Bennett	to	Elizabeth McCall	Barrett
Nov.	9	John B. Pitt	to	Eliza Mackey	Graham
"	14	Edward Webb	to	Martha Alexander	Magraw
"	20	William Colmery	to	Rachel Oliver	Goforth
Dec.	5	Andrew McCue	to	Mary Kiney	Magraw
"	12	Samuel Crouch	to	Mary McKenney	Barrett
"	19	Robert Gillespie	to	Margaret Nesbitt	Magraw
"	20	John C. Anderson	to	Sarah Watson	Duke
"	20	William Gibson	to	Catherine Hughs	Graham

	MAN		WOMAN	MINISTER
" 20	William Edmondson	to	Maria White	Beem
" 27	John Rutter	to	Sarah B. Lorritt	Barrett
1827				
Feb. 1	Joseph Keetley	to	Catherine White	Barrett
" 6	William Lusby	to	Francis A. Cochran	Wilson
" 10	Francis Boyd	to	Sarah Patterson	Barrett
" 12	Robert M. Walmsley	to	Margaret Beard	Wilson
" 11	John Noland	to	Mary Warbutton	Beem
" 16	Gideon Lusby	to	Rosetta H. Benson	Higgins
" 22	Christopher Little	to	Ann Moffitt	Magraw
" 27	Allen Maxwell	to	Hannah Hutton	
Mar. 3	Arthur Clendenin	to	Susan Ricketts	
" 8	John Yeamans	to	Mary Grant	
" 13	Francis Roch	to	Ann Smith	
" 13	Benj. B. Chambers	to	Caroline J. Pearce	
" 19	Richard Abrams	to	Letitha Alexander	
" 29	Umphrey Riddle	to	Rachel Crouch	
" 31	John Jackson	to	Ann Craig	
" 31	William Brown	to	Mary Robinson	
Apr. 19	Robert Virtue	to	Rebecca Roach	
" 26	Jacob C. Howard	to	Araminta Hyland	
May 12	James Smith	to	Mary Griffee	
" 21	John Cantwell	to	Mary Clark	
" 24	John Anderson	to	Eliza Jane Megee	
" 27	John Niblock	to	Mary Jane Blakeley	
" 30	John Conegan	to	Mary Ashen	
" 31	Michale Rieley	to	Amelia Haway	
June 5	Andrew Marnes	to	Margaret Cameron	
" 11	Henry Templeman	to	Sarah Smithers	
" 11	James Walton	to	Mary Wallace	
July 5	Henry Jamar	to	Caroline Shiplie	
" 26	James Morrow	to	Sophia Thompson	
Aug. 4	Samuel Bostic	to	Sarah Garrettson	
" 8	John Gamble	to	Ann Barnes	
" 13	Robert Armstrong	to	Catharine Marshall	
" 14	William Keetley	to	Mary Penington	
" 15	William Conlin	to	Lueina Barwick	
" 20	Samuel Severson	to	Henrietta Price	
" 23	Samuel Burden	to	Lydia Myrphey	
" 24	Charles Newland	to	Sarah Martin	
Sept. 11	Andrew Barrett	to	Rosanna Laritt	
" 11	Antoire Dupellee	to	Ester Gibson	
" 17	George Landces	to	Margaret Price	
Oct. 6	James Anderson	to	Maria Simpson	
" 10	John Aldridge	to	Eliza Gottier	
" 8	William Hollingsworth	to	Mary Eliza Evans	
" 11	William Grace	to	Jane Roach	
" 16	Robert Archibald	to	Levina Trump	
" 20	George H. Moore	to	Julia Ann Wilson	
" 23	Jos. Marrcee	to	Anna M. Brown	
" 26	Patrick Onley	to	Maria Milligan	
Nov. 6	John Cazier	to	Ann Haines	
" 12	James Alexander	to	Isabella Gay	
" 14	Nicholas Lotman	to	Ann Rutter	
" 12	Robert Alerton	to	Mary Pogue	
" 14	John Campbell	to	Temperance Pearson	
" 26	Richard Moore	to	Ann Phillips	
" 29	William Pannell	to	Mary Ann Oldham	
Dec. 4	James Pritchard	to	Mary Johnston	
" 4	Andrew Kidd	to	Sarah Ring	
" 4	John Marshall	to	Margaret McKinley	

MAN			WOMAN	MINISTER
" 10	John Brickley	to	Mary Thompson	
" 17	John Kinkead	to	Louisa Ash	
" 19	John Foard	to	Elizabeth Simpers	
" 20	Daniel Gillespie	to	Mary Currier	
" 26	Samuel Hall	to	Ella Tyson	
1828				
Jan. 3	Henry Martin	to	Ann Brown	
" 9	John Lockard	to	Dollie Ann Tyson	
" 15	John McIntire	to	Hanna Murrey	
" 19	George Grady	to	Judy Precall (Pascall)?	
" 22	Thomas A. Roberts	to	Augusta Veazey	
" 23	Aaron Keeck	to	Mary E. Thompson	
" 30	Hazlet Logan	to	Ann Murphey	
" 30	Joshua Ward	to	Rebecca Veazey	
Feb. 13	William Thompson	to	Catharine Blake	
" 18	Charles Willey	to	Elizabeth Bond	
" 19	Henry Wallen	to	Julia McDaniel	
" 28	William Green	to	Eliza Taylor	
" 28	David Gilmore	to	Elizabeth White	
Mar. 1	Benj. Elliott	to	Mary Rock	
" 8	Thomas Taylor	to	Margaret Saw	
" 10	William Moore	to	Margaret Steele	
" 17	Joseph Harlan	to	Margaret Scott	
" 19	Isaac Trimble	to	Rebecca Moore	
" 25	George Shannon	to	Ellen Rutter	
" 26	Sylvester McGee	to	Catharine Welch	
" 31	John H. Price	to	Deborah Canlyn	
Apr. 2	Samuel Nickle	to	Catharine M. Porter	
" 3	John W. McCall	to	Eliza Hawkins	
" 4	Thomas Garrett	to	Elizabeth Aulden	
" 10	Henry G. Simpers	to	Ann Simpers	
" 21	Arthur Clark	to	Rachel Thackery	
" 22	William Jones	to	Lydia M. McKinsey	
May 1	John Ravick	to	Magery Wilson	
" 3	Henry E. Gatchell	to	Elizabeth Simpson	
" 5	John Gallaher	to	Susan Logan	
" 6	Arthur Alexander	to	Catherine Abrahams	
" 19	Richard Dean	to	Sarah Morrow	
" 19	Morgan Price	to	Harriet Veazey	
" 22	John Keath	to	Mary Bergoin	
" 22	Robert Hayes	to	Nelly Etherington	
	Omitted			
1828				
Mar. 26	Peregrine F. Lloyd	to	Letitia Smith	Goforth
May 26	Samuel Smith	to	Amelia Barratt	Barratt
" 26	George Grant	to	Hannah Ann Whann	Hodskie
June 3	Hugh Kelly	to	Sarah White	Graham
" 4	George Evans	to	Deborah Drennon	Sharps
" 5	Samuel Howard	to	Esther Ann Webb	Barratt
" 12	William Robinson	to	Ann Maria Aldridge	Barratt
" 16	Jeremiah Steel	to	Eliza Wright	Barratt
" 18	Charles Parker	to	Harriet Carter	Barratt
" 18	Levi Todd	to	Mary Ann Reynolds	Barratt
" 23	Hasson Lynch	to	Hannah McElwee	Barratt
" 28	James T. Kidd	to	Frances Christie	Goforth
July 8	Joseph Gibson	to	Jane E. Knight	Goforth
" 16	John F. McGilton	to	Phebe Bayless	Magraw
" 16	Benjamin Vandever	to	Margaret S. Lyon	Goforth
" 17	Samuel Cray	to	Ann Price	Barratt

	MAN		WOMAN	MINISTER
Aug. 2	Jacob Woollehan	to	Margaret Veach	Cooper
" 13	Andrew Huggins	to	Elizabeth Egnor	Woolford
" 16	Andrew Brickley	to	Mary Campbell	Magraw
" 16	John Burk	to	Mary Grace	Barratt
" 18	Lewis McKey	to	Rachel Woosten	Smith
" 20	Thomas Reece	to	Ann Price	Duke
" 27	Thomas J. Foster	to	Rebecca Slagle	Barratt
Sept. 26	Samuel Gillespie	to	Susan Shroff	Goforth
" 26	Nicholas Murphey	to	Mary McCall	Barratt
Oct. 7	Watson Scarborough	to	Jane Wright	Barratt
" 13	William Rider	to	Rachel Davis	Goforth
" 20	Charles Brookings	to	Eliza Johnson	Goforth
Nov. 5	Hezekiah Foard, Jr.	to	Mary Ann Hyland	Barratt
" 10	John McCullough	to	Elizabeth McVey	Graham
" 11	John R. Price	to	Rachel R. Walmsley	Duke
" 11	Harrison T. Bullen	to	Mary Price	Duke
" 27	George Biddle	to	Rebecca Johnson	Barratt
Dec. 2	George Reed	to	Ann Biddle	Hodskie
" 17	Joseph Greer	to	Rachel Bowen	Barratt
" 30	William Dennison	to	Mary Ann Burrows	Goforth
1829				
Jan. 5	Harman Foster	to	Frances Jan?	Barratt
" 6	Thomas Wilson	to	Susan Mingline	Duke
" 6	Henry Whitlock	to	Grace? Jackson (Grissell)	Magraw
" 7	William Cameron	to	Ann Maria Oldham	Duke
" 13	Levi Kirk	to	Elizabeth Gray	Barratt
" 13	Thomas Boulden	to	Ann Thomas	Woolford
" 13	Thomas W. Skirven	to	Margaret B. Greenwood	Smith
" 26	Richard Keeler	to	Sarah Maxwell	Magraw
Feb. 3	William Robinson	to	Julia Ann Aldridge	Barratt
" 10	Benoni Nowland	to	Margaret Miller	Barratt
" 16	John McCracken	to	Martha Jane Cazier	Sharpe
" 17	Joseph T. Stoops	to	Ann Maria Law	Woolford
Mar. 2	Thomas Bouchelle	to	Mary M. Bayard	Duke
" 10	George Deal	to	Mary Ann Tibbitt	Duke
" 18	Jonathan Gillespie	to	Mary Ann Sturgeon	Goforth
" 18	Alexander Kirk	to	Christia Ann Bristow	Barratt
Apr. 2	Caleb Steel	to	Jane Smith	Barratt
" 9	Robert E. Hogg	to	Caroline Purnell	Duke
" 28	Rudulph Bennett	to	Sarah Jane Roach	Russell
May 13	Alexander Curry	to	Martha Cunningham	Russell
" 21	Edmund Brown	to	Martha Simpson	Barratt
June 15	Alfred B. Thomas	to	Alice O. Donald	Effenie
July 11	Robert Gerry	to	Hannah E. Reynolds	Ayres
Sept. 1	George Grant	to	Sophia Lowery	Barratt
" 22	Lewis Price	to	Salina Carman	King
" 29	Adam Little	to	Elizabeth Campbell	Magraw
Oct. 8	James N. Mercer	to	Millicent Ann Lum	Barratt
" 8	David Simpers	to	Mary Armstrong	Barratt
" 8	Samuel R. Clayland (Kent)	to	Mary Eliza (McDonough Kent	Duke
" 17	George R. Pearce	to	Julia Ann Ward	Sitgrieves
" 24	William Simmons Wood	to	Amelia Pennington	Duke
" 24	John Lancaster	to	Mary Lum	Rider
" 26	George W. Black	to	Mary Price	King
" 7	John Denney	to	Mary Ann Pearce	Rider
Dec. 16	Reuben Segers	to	Margaret A. Alden	Duke
" 19	John W. Morgan	to	Mary Gale	King
" 19	Benjamin Cox	to	Elizabeth Ethrington	King
" 21	Edward Pearce	to	Rachel Burke	Barratt
" 23	John Baldwin	to	Mary Ann Orr	Ayres
" 28	William R. Moore	to	Martha Linton	Ayres
" 28	William Simpers	to	Elizabeth Pryor	Barratt

		MAN		WOMAN	MINISTER
1830					
Jan.	2	Nicholas George	to	Milliscent Wingate	Barratt
"	6	Samuel Hasson	to	Elizabeth Allexander	Magraw
"	13	William Henry Pryor	to	Ann Gray	Barratt
"	13	Joseph Worth	to	Margaret Grant	Barratt
"	30	John Pantry	to	Mary Jane Patterson	King
Feb.	2	John Keatly	to	Margaret Culberson	Barratt
"	8	James W. Rutter	to	Margery Wilson	Barratt
"	9	John H. Graham	to	Rachel Alexander	Miller
"	10	Richard Griffee	to	Mary Smith	Magraw
"	11	William Logan	to	Harriett Rutter	Goforth
"	18	Benjamin Walmsley	to	Cornelia Ford	Griffith
"	22	Alfred Nowland	to	Mary A. Biddle	Duke
Mar.	1	James Ford	to	Margaret Davis	Duke
"	1	John Henderson	to	Rebecca Groves	Duke
"	1	Benjamin F. Johnson	to	Mary McCullough	Magraw
"	12	Andrew Nickle	to	Mary C. Harlan	Magraw
"	15	John E. Simpers	to	Ann McCauley	Griffith
"	19	John E. Powley	to	Esther Haines	Ayres
"	29	James Brown	to	Margaret Williams	Magraw
"	30	William Gillespie	to	Emeline Lomans	Griffith
"	30	John Slack, Balto., Md.	to	Eliza Evans, New Castle, Del.	Duke
Apr.	6	Reuben Lake	to	Rachel Boice	Barratt
"	9	John Cleaver	to	Philena Baker	Griffith
"	9	John Harvey	to	Abigail Janney	Smith
"	12	Nicholas Vandegrift	to	Elizabeth Fillingame	Duke
"	13	Charley Bruce	to	Mary Eliza Death	Magraw
"	20	Stephen Hyland of W.	to	Elizabeth Jane Hyland	Duke
May	5	Evan Morgan	to	Martha Gibson	Goforth
"	15	William Johnson	to	Millicent Watson	Griffith
"	17	John R. Barwick	to	Emily Ann Hudson	Duke
June	8	Thomas Hayes	to	Rebecca Smith	Mahan
"	10	Samuel Decham, N. Cas., Del.	to	Mahala Crouch, N. Cas., Del.	Duke
Aug.	14	John Brown	to	Edith Foster	Duke
"	26	Caleb W. Cloud	to	Eliza Kean	Duke
Sept.	21	Patricious Finnegan	to	Jane Gallaher	Reece
"	22	Lavi Lottman	to	Mary Rutter	Goforth
"	30	William Leavis?	to	Ann Maria Lovitt	Goforth
"	30	Francis Gordon	to	Hetty Reynolds	Griffith
"	29	John T. Knight	to	Margaret Ann Denison	Goforth
Oct.	5	Jacob Holden	to	Margaret Boulding	Hodson
"	20	Samuel Fisher	to	Jane Scott	Griffith
"	21	Richard Thomas	to	Sarah Johnson	Hodson
"	26	Samuel Severson	to	Sarah Denny	Barratt
Nov.	2	Samuel Perry	to	Susan Giberson	Hodson
"	8	William Grant	to	Araminta M. Denny	Barratt
"	8	William H. Wilson	to	Catharine Foster	Rider
"	9	Ranselen Biddle	to	Mary Egnor	Hodson
"	10	Lloyd Bailey	to	Jeusha Harvey	Hodson
"	13	Joseph Miller	to	Margaret Warburton	Mahan
"	23	John McCreary	to	Sophia Perry	Graham
"	26	William Reed	to	Mary White	Duke
Dec.	4	Isaac N. Sidwell	to	Jane Keatley	Griffith
"	15	Elijah Moore	to	Mercie Davis	Griffith
"	16	Lambert D. Nowland	to	Ann Maria Ford	Duke
"	16	John Roberts	to	Harriet Bowen	Duke
"	16	James Ruley	to	Alice Alterson	Duke
1831					
Jan.	6	David Taylor	to	Elizabeth Gorrell	Goforth
"	6	John A. Johnson	to	Sarah Wallace	Barratt
"	8	George D. Hollace	to	Lydia Ann Hackett	Duke

		MAN		WOMAN	MINISTER
"	12	John W. Holt	to	Elizabeth Gallaher	Duke
"	11	Noble Pennington	to	Henrietta E. Morgan	Duke
"	18	Joseph Carter	to	Sarah A. Reynolds	Duke
"	19	John Thompson	to	Jane Lum	Barratt
"	24	Samuel Jackson	to	Ann Cunningham	Goforth
"	24	Robert Price	to	Araminta Coffin	Duke
"	31	Richard Fillingame	to	Mary Biddle	Smith
May	9	William Bristow	to	Martha Arrants	Barratt
"	19	William Lewis	to	Sarah Aldridge	Barratt
"	23	Nicholas Clark	to	Margaret Ann Little	Barratt
"	28	Reuben Taylor	to	Rachel Ward	Barnes
"	31	Joseph Ricketts	to	Rebecca Murphy	Smith
June	1	William Ferguson	to	Maria Grant	Barratt
"	6	Richard Hudson	to	Letitia Mills	Barnes
"	9	James Davis	to	Rachel Davis	Barratt
"	15	Jacob Price	to	Martha Wilson	Duke
July	13	Ambrose Knapp	to	Rachel Touchstone	Duke
"	13	John Little	to	Eliza Clark	Barratt
"	16	Hugh McConkey, Jr., Lan., Pa.	to	Mary Henry Cecil Co., Md.	Duke
"	19	James Simmons	to	Elizabeth Clark	Barnes
"	19	Enoch Boyd	to	Catharine Ann Mahan	Warburton
"	20	Richard Currier	to	Rebecca Benjamin	Goforth
Aug.	16	Joel Evans	to	Margaret Scott	Rees
"	17	James McVey	to	Elizabeth Shockley	Barnes
Sept.	5	William E. G. Graham	to	Mary Ann Lewis	Barratt
"	8	Samuel Davis	to	Eliza Vansant	Duke
"	20	James Crouch	to	Mary Crouch	Barratt
Oct.	10	Levi Boulden	to	Margaret S. Boulden	Smith
"	18	John Tigna	to	Deborah Ann Jones	McCarroll
"	22	John D. Turner, N. Cas., Del.	to	Amelia Margaret Pearce	Duke
"	25	Allen Anderson	to	Esther McCullough	Magraw
Nov.	7	Jones Matthias	to	Hetty Ann Alexander	Duke
"	14	Rowland Ellis	to	Elizabeth Hyland	Rees
"	16	John Steel	to	Sarah Patten	Magraw
"	16	John Hayes	to	Sarah Ann Money	Duke
"	16	Joseph Hacket	to	Henrietta Pennington	Duke
"	26	Isaac M. Chesbrough, Bal.,C.	to	Mary Jones, Elkton, Md.	Rees
"	26	Samuel W. Staples	to	Louisa H. Nowland	Rees
"	29	Robert Richie, N. Y. Sta.	to	Annet Owens	Magraw
Dec.	9	William Tamnay	to	Rachel Griffie	McCarroll
"	12	Matthew C. Pearce	to	Eliza Jane Groome	Rees
"	21	William Pannel?	to	Sarah Moffitt	Barratt
"	26	Jeremiah Woodrow	to	Clarissa Everett	Duke
"	26	Jonathan P. Burns	to	Jane Alexander	McKee
"	27	William Aiken	to	Margaret Jackson	Magraw
"	27	George Davis	to	Mary Smith	Duke
"	27	Daniel M. Jilton	to	Amelia Tyson	Griffith
"	28	Peter Pearson	to	Rebecca Simpers	Griffith
	1832				
Jan.	5	John Bouchell	to	Hannah Bayard	Rees
"	6	Charles Boulden, N. C., Co, Del	to	Mary H. Thomas, Cecil Co., Md.	Rees
"	14	Robert Murphy	to	Elizabeth Jackson	Goforth
"	16	William Taylor	to	Eliza Margaret Thomas	Rees
"	18	William Keatly	to	Rachel Culbertson	Barratt
"	21	John D. F. Brown	to	Martha J. Humphries	McCarroll
"	24	Samuel Thompson	to	Allice Calvert	Griffith
"	30	Mark Arthurs	to	Araminta Maulden	Barratt
Feb.	2	Thomas Giles	to	Mary Hemphill	Barratt
"	4	William M. Townsend	to	Sarah Galbraith	Magraw
"	7	Richard Rutter	to	Elizabeth Jackson	Magraw

		MAN		WOMAN	MINISTER
"	21	James Ewing	to	Martha Barnes	Griffith
"	23	Aquilla Jones	to	Esther Bates	Magraw
	1831				
Feb.	1	William Lynch	to	Lydia Ann Baker	Goforth
"	1	Roger Mayner	to	Ann Veach	Hodson
"	7	Ely Cameron	to	Sarah Brooks	Griffith
"	8	William Hudson	to	Mary Ann Borcham	Duke
"	15	William Watson	to	Maria McClenahan	Mahan
"	17	James Evans Cooper?	to	Sarah Brown	Magraw
"	22	James Boyd	to	Eliza Bailey	Goforth
"	22	Mark Brown	to	Lydia E. Brown	Griffith
Mar.	9	Thomas Caton	to	Mary Galloway	Hodson
"	21	John Boulden, N. C. C., Del.	to	Eliza Boulden, Cec. Co., Md.	Duke
"	23	Norris Levis	to	Eliza Kirk	Duke
"	25	David Lockart	to	Adriann Hammersmith	Magraw
"	26	William Ferguson	to	Susan Thompson	Magraw
"	26	Thompson Leonard	to	Lydia Bryan	Duke
Apr.	5	William Brickley	to	Margaret McMullen	Duke
"	5	Henry S. Stites	to	Harriet Stump	Duke
"	5	Reece Merritt	to	Ann Elizabeth McGee	Duke
"	19	James Alexander	to	Amy Simpers	Barrett
"	25	Solomon Blake	to	Mary Lynch	Griffith
"	30	Charles T. Cloud	to	Julianna Pouder. Bal., Md.	Duke
	1832				
Feb.	29	Samuel Boreland	to	Nancy Owens	Magraw
"	29	George Haines	to	Jane Jones	Griffith
Mar.	6	John D. Wherry	to	Ann Eliza Biles	Duke
"	6	William W. Wilson	to	Eliza Ann Price	Duke
"	6	Samuel Buckwith	to	Eliza Smith	Smith
"	10	George Alden	to	Hannah Matthias	Duke
Apr.	2	John H. Bolton	to	Catharine P. Ruley	Duke
"	3	William Boyd, Ches. Co., Pa.	to	Sarah Mahan, Cecil Co., Md.	Duke
"	4	Justus Dunbar	to	Sarah Ann Boulden	Barnes
"	7	George M. Cole, Cecil Co., Md.	to	Ann Eliza Johnson, Har. Co., Md.	Webster
"	11	Amos Ewing	to	Mary Steel	Magraw
"	11	William Brown	to	Charlotte Carter	Duke
"	17	Jonathan McVey	to	Frances Taylor	Magraw
"	26	Passmore McVey	to	Jane McKinney	Barratt
May	1	Joshua Richardson	to	Mary Ann Scott	Duke
"	3	William McClay	to	Lydia Peterson	Duke
"	9	William Rutter	to	Sarah Jane Pennington	Barratt
"	15	Albert R. Teague	to	Eliza M. Williamson	Griffith
"	26	Cornelius McLean, Jr., Bal. Co.	to	George Anna E. Gale	Higby
"	28	James R. Reynolds	to	Jane Moore	Duke
June	11	Henry Burnes	to	Hannah McVey	Duke
"	20	Caleb Reed, Kent Co., Md.	to	Julia Ann Cox, Cecil Co., Md.	Duke
July	16	John Markee	to	Sarah Ann Harding	Duke
"	25	David Thompson	to	Elizabeth Ann McJilton	McCarroll
"	28	John Wright	to	Mary Ann Clifton	Torbert
Aug.	1	James Fury	to	Hannah Ann Cowan	Duke
"	7	Jedediah Hayes	to	Hannah Knight	Duke
"	8	Thomas Ball, N. Y. State	to	Ann M. Giles	Benson
"	25	Silas H. Watson, Ch. Co., Pa.	to	Ruth Ann Alden	Duke
"	29	Ebenezer Mayberry	to	Ann Foster	Goforth
Sept.	3	Dr.Jas. S.Naudain, N.C.Co.Del.	to	Ann E. Blackiston	Duke
"	4	George C. Weaver	to	Martha Gill	Mahan
"	12	Timothy N. Terrell	to	Harriet C. Andrews	Rees
"	12	Benjamin Ferguson	to	Harriet Ann Cooper	Magraw
"	19	Lewis Wright	to	Eliza Jane Brown	Duke
"	19	James Carter	to	Sarah Owens	Goforth

		MAN		WOMAN	MINISTER
"	27	Abraham Clark	to	Naomi Stewart	Mahan
"	29	William Hackett	to	Ann Eliza Ford	Duke
Oct.	3	Peregrine F. Lloyd	to	Jane Mercer	Duke
"	5	Isaac B. Jester	to	Rebecca Stradley	Duke
"	15	William F. Savin	to	Eliza Margaretta?	Goforth
"	16	George E. Woolley	to	Mary Ann Turner	McCarroll
"	22	John T. Simpers	to	Mary Boulden	Mahan
"	25	Arthur Beatty	to	Mary Davis	Goforth
"	25	Caleb Emmons	to	Eleanor Ann Kyle	Reese
Nov.	1	James T. Hayden	to	Ann Mayson	Duke
"	7	William D. Hackett	to	Martha Ann Morgan	Duke
"	13	Robert James Duhamell	to	Amelia Ann Patterson	Duke
"	20	Benjamin McWee	to	Mary Ann Riker	McCarroll
"	21	James L. Maxwell	to	Jane M. McCullough	Magraw
"	28	Joshua Hyland	to	Elizabeth W. Crouch	Torbert
Dec.	3	William Beatty	to	Caroline Maffitt	McCarroll
"	5	Henry Woodrow	to	Margaret Hindman	Magraw
"	10	William Price	to	Temperance King	Duke
"	20	James Merritt	to	Elizabeth Johnson	Benson
"	21	John Benjamin	to	Charlotte Owens	Goforth
"	24	Peter Ross	to	Elizabeth Wiley	Magraw
	1833				
Jan.	2	William Campbell	to	Jane Davidson	Wilson
"	2	William Sherer	to	Ruth Ann Brown	Graham
"	3	William Scott	to	Mary Short	Benson
"	5	Samuel Hindman	to	Jane Eleanor Tosh	Magraw
"	7	Philip Jackson	to	Mary Jackson	Goforth
"	9	Richard Groves	to	Ann Henderson	Duke
"	22	Stephen Hyland of Stephen	to	Mary Jane Maulden	Duke
"	26	James Ford	to	Temperance E. Myers	Duke
"	26	James Knight	to	Lepora Cordes	Smith
"	28	Nicholas George	to	Araminta Hyland	Duke
"	28	Thomas White	to	Susan E. White	Goforth
"	29	William Conlyn	to	Jane Rebecca Kimble	Torbert
"	29	Bayard Tatman	to	Eleanor Cunningham	Torbert
"	31	Samuel McCullough	to	Jane Ann Beard	Wilson
Feb.	5	Jacob Woolehand	to	Elizabeth Taylor	Duke
"	8	Nevin Orr	to	Isabella Galbraith	Goforth
"	13	Peregrine F. Lloyd	to	Rebecca Price	McKenney
"	13	Robert Lewis	to	Mary Grey	Duke
"	14	Robert Pennington	to	Mary Segars?	Benson
"	14	Henry H. Gilpin	to	Margaret Ricketts	Duke
"	23	James Hepbron	to	Sarah Jane Morgan	Duke
Mar.	1	Ebenezer D. McClennahan	to	Margaret Megredy	McCarroll
"	9	William Robinson	to	Eliza Saterfield	McKenney
"	20	Absalom Oldham	to	Henrietta M. White	McCarroll
"	21	Nathan Dolby	to	Isabella Maxwell	Magraw
"	25	John Graham	to	Elizabeth Love	Magraw
Apr.	4	William Philips	to	Mary Smith	Magraw
"	6	John Davis	to	Rebecca Sample	Benson
"	11	John Shafer	to	Caroline Spence	Barratt
"	18	Abraham Taylor	to	Mary L. Pearce	Duke
May	1	James H. L. Drummond	to	Maria Spence	Mahan
"	7	Henry Carman	to	Elizabeth Price	Duke
"	14	John Miller	to	Mary Mackey	Hagany
"	22	Henry Kimble	to	Martha Cunningham	Hagany
"	28	John McClain	to	Easter Dupelle	Duke
June	5	Stephen Hodgson	to	Araminta Ferguson	Wilson
"	18	Joel Bryan	to	Frances Andrews	Rees
"	25	Caleb Reynolds	to	Mary Simpson	Duke
"	26	John Cunningham	to	Margaret Whitelock	Goforth

MAN			WOMAN	MINISTER
July	8	Thomas S. Reed	to Mahala Morris	Barratt
"	24	William McOrea	to Mary Slack	Duke
"	29	Hazelit Owens	to Adeline J. Benjamin	Griffith
Aug.	17	Thomas Rogers	to Jane McGaughlin	Mahan
"	21	John Kidd	to Ann Boyd	Goforth
"	22	John T. West	to Araminta Boyse	Barratt
"	24	Andrew J. Gilbreath	to Jane Gaily	Goforth
"	29	William (Barwick?)	to Mary Ann Mears	Duke
Sept.	14	James H. Reily	to Cassy Mercer	McKinney
"	14	George Turner	to Caroline N. Devor?	Duke
"	24	Stephen Woodrow	to Alice Cook	Guiber
"	26	George Davis	to Mary Young	Barratt
"	27	John H. McCartney	to Eliza Woodrow	Guiber
Oct.	2	Francis A. Ellis	to Eliza Ann Howard	Hagany
"	2	Charles K. Manly	to Rachel Howard	Hagany
"	7	Andrew Orr	to Isabella Morgan	Goforth
"	14	Clinton J. White	to Barbara H. Dennison	Goforth
"	14	Henry Jackson	to Ann Gorrell	Goforth
"	21	John Archer	to Ann D. Savin	Goforth
"	23	Nathan Brumfield	to Elizabeth Lowe	Duke
Nov.	2	James H. Benson	to Louisa Severson	Duke
"	19	Green Williams	to Sarah Edmundson	Duke
"	27	William McCullough	to Martha A. McCullough	Magraw
"	28	James Veal	to Elizabeth Biddle	Duke
Dec.	3	James Wesley Duaule?	to Mary Richardson	Barratt
"	10	James Jackson	to Margaret Craig	Goforth
"	10	John Wesly Buckwith	to Eliza Ann Robinson	Duke
"	10	William W. McCullough	to Lucy Haines	Duke
"	11	Daniel Killy	to Sarah Ellen Clark	Barratt
"	16	Cyrus H. Jacobs	to Jane W. Mackall	Duke
"	16	George W. Cannon	to Sarah Reese	Duke
"	24	John Ewing	to Mary Jane Philips	Duke
"	28	Thomas Price	to Margaret Ann Price	Duke
"	30	William B. Giles	to Mary Wells	Goforth
1834				
Jan.	4	Victor Jackson	to Sarah Brumfield	Goforth
"	7	Alexander Greenwood	to Catharine Purnell	Duke
"	7	Henry L. Gaw	to Millicent Wingate	Hagany
"	8	Thomas Lake	to Mary Ann Hays	Barratt
"	13	Lambert W. Biddle	to Ann T. Slayter	McKinney
"	14	John Richardson	to Jane Logan	Duke
"	22	Samuel Stradley	to Lucretia Stradley	Duke
"	27	James Conlyn	to Ellen Cosden	Duke
"	27	John K. Walmsley	to Sarah Dalster	McKinney
"	27	Aaron Keech	to Julian A. Death	Goforth
"	29	John Mauldin	to Sophia T. Simpers	Wolley
"	29	Alexander Brown	to Mary Walker	Goforth
"	30	Jacob Scott	to Ellen Johnson	Hammil
Feb.	10	Joseph W. Abrams	to Susan Reynolds	Duke
"	12	Johnson Hyland	to Rachel Cochran	Barratt
"	12	Alexander Wilson	to Catharine Mauldin	Barratt
"	12	John Ramsey	to Hannah Ginna	Magraw
"	27	Charles H. Crouch	to Caroline May	Davis
"	27	John Conelkin	to Rebecca Henshaw	Duke
Mar.	5	Arthur Morrison	to Susan Pennington	Duke
"	11	John Craig	to Catharine Jackson	Goforth
"	12	Richardson Plummer	to Susan Ann Coulson	Duke
"	12	Isaac Wilson	to Letitia W. Jones	Davis
"	14	Simon Baker	to Mana Galloway	Duke
"	19	Thomas Janney	to Rachel Blake	Duke
"	20	Seth Stewart	to Hannah Johnson	Hagany

	MAN		WOMAN	MINISTER
" 29	Thomas Kelly	to	Sarah Rutter	Duke
Apr. 1	James Lyon	to	Maria Taylor	Goforth
" 10	Moses Gallaher	to	Lydia Ann Farnley	Wilson
" 16	James Kirkpatrick	to	Martha Owens	Hammil
" 17	Joseph Gurlie	to	Emily Taylor	Magraw
May 13	Benjamin W. Thornton	to	Rachel Layton	Goforth
" 13	Francis B. Crookshank	to	Mary E. Mitchell	McKenney
June 1	Wiliam Broadwell	to	Susannah I. Woolston	Smith
" 2	Thomas Crawford	to	Eliza Cowan	Duke
" 2	Isaac A. Lum	to	Mary B. Beaston	Morris
" 18	Howard Morris	to	Mary A. Kirk	Barratt
May 21	William Crow	to	Susan Rider	Cropper
July 9	Nathan McVey	to	Jane Logan	Griffith
" 16	Thomas K. Stephens	to	Juliana V. Wilson	McKinney
" 28	Edward Evans	to	Ellen Kimble	Hammil
Sept. 3	Amos Cameron	to	Emeline Brown	Stork
" 5	John Wroth	to	Araminta M. Morgan	McKinney
" 8	John Brook	to	Ann Gall	Goforth
" 17	Stephen Smith	to	Jane Eliza Gordon	Hammil
" 22	Thomas Neville	to	Sarah Sophia Pearce	Morris
" 29	William Conley	to	Eliza Jane White	McKinney
Oct. 3	Thomas Crookshanks	to	Sarah Comegys	Sharp
" 7	Evan Morgan	to	Ann Strawbridge	Stork
" 11	Enos T. Wood	to	Francina McCauley	Wilson
" 15	John Epp	to	Elizabeth Gritz	Goforth
" 16	Robert Lutton	to	Margaret Ramsey	Hammil
" 20	John Tyson	to	Mary McDowell	Hammil
" 28	John Walker	to	Eliza Noble	Griffith
" 29	Richard Hall	to	Elizabeth K. Berry	Griffith
Nov. 1	Arthur M. Strout	to	Susanna W. Thompson	Griffith
" 8	John Rutter	to	Catharine Keatly	Griffith
" 10	Ephrain P. Lowe	to	Jane Roach	Barratt
" 13	William Richards	to	Louise Jane Baynard	Duke
" 19	Albun Price	to	Mary E. Cannon	Davis
" 26	James McCauley	to	Sarah Beard	Wilson
" 27	Otho Nowland	to	Eliza Warburton	Sorin
Dec. 3	John Rutter	to	Elizabeth Jackson	Griffith
" 6	George Boulden	to	Louise Biddle	Spry
" 9	Isaac Wardell	to	Ann Logan	Griffith
" 15	Stephen H. Ford	to	Maria S. Dawson	Duke
" 17	Jesse Tatman	to	Mary Stubbs	Smith
" 17	John Stump	to	Mary A. Mitchell	Hammil
" 20	James Nickle	to	Hannah Allen	Magraw
" 22	Benjamin W. Jones	to	Nancy Cowan	Duke
" 24	Josiah Hall	to	Elmira Ford	Sharp
" 24	Damuel H. Freeman	to	Harriet Thomas	Morris
" 30	James Gillespie	to	Elizabeth Craig	Griffith
" 31	Ebenezer Alden	to	Caroline Owens	Duke
1835				
Jan. 2	Jacob Fleck	to	Cumford Hudson	Duke
Sept. 17	Robert Ross	to	Elizabeth Mahan	Warburton
" 19	Jno. Walmsley	to	Aramintha Dowling	Coleman
" 26	Samuel Tosh	to	Mary Jane Wiley	Magraw
" 26	John Tuffree	to	Mary Ann Maria Cropper	Wilson
Oct. 7	Jose Updegrave	to	Laney Miller	Woolley
" 13	Jas. Raisin	to	Jane Robinson	Morrison
" 14	John Martin	to	Rosanna Silk	Duke
" 14	John Brown	to	Rachel Maria Tosh	Duke
" 15	Jesse Simpers	to	Mary Ann Simpers	Morrison
" 16	Cyprus Colmerry	to	Elizabeth Bennett	Barratt
" 28	John P. Lockard	to	Ann McKenney	Barrett

	MAN		WOMAN	MINISTER
Nov. 25	John Owens	to	Martha Jane Black	Finney
Dec. 14	Joseph Scott	to	Lydia Abbott	Houston
" 16	Thomas Simpers	to	Mary Moyle?	Barrett
" 16	George J. Beaston	to	Susan Mitchell	Coleman
" 18	Francis Russum	to	Francina Dennis	Coleman
" 19	Wm. Vinsinger	to	Levinia Ann Hill	Hammil
" 19	John Conekin	to	Elizabeth Duncan	Houston
" 22	Gueensberry Purnell	to	Mary McGredy	Houston
" 28	Daniel Clendenin	to	Rebecca Horton	Finney
" 28	Wm. Reed	to	Rebecca Lusby	Morrison
1836				
Jan. 5	Thomas West	to	Ann McCullough	Potts
" 20	John James Moore	to	Sarah R. Arrants	Barrett
" 26	Samuel Logan	to	Sarah Reed	Megready
Feb. 2	Geo. H. Joyce	to	Maria Louise Chapman	Williams
" 2	Richard Burnett	to	Jane Hart	Barrett
" 3	Caleb Edmundson	to	Eliza M. Boulden	Houston
" 3	Thomas Edmundson	to	Eliza Janney	Houston
" 12	John Brumfield	to	Ellen C. Gibson	Potts
" 29	Frederick H. Mitchell	to	Mary Walkins	Potts
Mar. 2	John W. Alexander	to	Eliza J. Benjamin	Wilson
" 2	Stearns Bullins	to	Elmira Barrett	Barrett
" 12	Elisha Atkinson	to	Eliz. Mahoney	Wilson
" 26	Richard Roach	to	Patty Lake?	Barrett
" 29	Levi Lotman	to	Majory Foster	Wilson
Apr. 9	James Wilson	to	Letitia Thompson	Megredy
" 14	Rouce Coe?	to	Rachel Smith	Morris
" 28	Andrew W. Alexander	to	Harret Aldridge	Potts
" 29	Robert W. Gilmore	to	Adeline White	Hickey
May 10	Eli White	to	Sarah Megredy	Crouch
June 4	Joseph Mewson	to	Emily Alexander	Potts
" 6	William Roe	to	Mary Jane Roe	Morrison
" 8	Wm. P. Morgan	to	Ann Jane Lee	Potts
" 28	John Wesley Freeman	to	Araminta Johnson	Potts
July 2	Edw. B. Lewis	to	Margaret A. Gottier	Duke
" 22	John J. Dillahunt	to	Maria Greenwood	Smith
" 30	Elijah Moore	to	Eliz. Huff	Stephenson
Aug. 2	Samuel Watkins	to	Harriet McMullin	Megredy
" 4	Thos. Osborne	to	Adalina? White	Megredy
" 25	James Bulin	to	Mary Ann Bailey	Duke
" 25	John Boulden	to	Rachel Simpers	Wilson
" 26	Joseph Brumfield	to	Jane Rutter	Duke
" 30	James Jones	to	Ann McDowell	Lane
Sept. 1	Amos Cummings	to	Eliza Hundlen	Potts
" 12	Wm. Reed	to	Amy McVey	Lane
" 20	Fagan Earnest	to	Martha A. Mitchell	Morrison
1835				
Jan. 3	David White	to	Millicent A. Cozier	Spry
" 6	Thomas Stradley	to	Penance Ruley	Duke
" 7	Ezekial Thompson	to	Elizabeth Aiken	Griffith
" 10	Joseph Coale	to	Sarah Ann Watson	Griffith
" 19	Israel Snow	to	Ann Craig	Griffith
" 24	Robert Faulkner	to	Elizabeth Price	Duke
" 27	Wm. Z. Etherington	to	Ann Eliz. Davis	Duke
Feb. 1	Charles Buckworth	to	Elizabeth Orr	Duke
" 2	Wilder Harris	to	Allice McMullin	Smith
" 4	Robert Aiken	to	Mary Jackson	Griffith
" 12	Philip C. Plummer	to	Mary E. Robinson	Morris
" 12	Jno. N. Baldwin	to	Eliza J. Anderson	Duke
" 18	Wm. Tyson	to	Eliza Poe	Griffith

		MAN		WOMAN	MINISTER
"	21	Daniel J. McCauley	to	Sarah Miller	Reed
"	26	William Kirk	to	Jane Williams	Griffith
Mar.	2	John Pennington	to	Jane Mitchell	Spry
"	5	Mills Rickards	to	Mary Stoney	Duke
"	7	Wm. P. Mahan	to	Ann Spence	Wilson
"	7	Joseph Hannah	to	Jane Marshall	Magraw
"	11	Benj. Miller	to	Lidia M. Simpson	Duke
"	11	Wm. Rock	to	Melinda Perry	Griffith
"	11	John Cannon	to	Francis Kirk	Griffith
"	23	Isaac Cordray	to	Ann M. Rickards	Morris
"	24	Henry P. Bennett	to	Ellen J. Scott	Duke
"	24	Benj. Walmsley	to	Sarah Ann Ward	Smith
"	25	Jno. B Hagany	to	Caroline S. Ford	Smith
Apr.	7	Jos. T. Brown	to	Milliscent Simpers	Wolley
"	9	William Moss	to	Joannah Jennings	Barrett
"	13	John Marnes	to	Jane Maffitt	Duke
"	14	David Wherry	to	Sarah Ann Alexander	Duke
"	16	Isaac Clark	to	Sarah Bellville	Hamill
"	18	Edwin D. Ford	to	Rosetta H. Lusby	Duke
"	29	David Cathers	to	Charlotte Cooley	Magraw
May	2	John W. Jackson	to	Sarah Alexander	Crane
"	6	Jacob Biddle	to	Elizabeth Marcus	Duke
"	13	Robert Hayes, Jr.	to	Alethea Money	Coleman
"	19	Wm. C. Glenn	to	Martha E. Sewell	Johns
"	20	Hugh Hamilton	to	Sarah Donaho	Cramer
"	23	Richard Davis	to	Martha Ann Mars	Barrett
June	1	Robert Thackery	to	Sarah Ann Knotts	Houston
"	9	Wm. B. Terbit	to	Hannah Lynch	Houston
"	13	Elmer Falls	to	Emily Riddle	Cramer
"	27	Robert Walmsley	to	Mary Sister	Coleman
"	30	Geo. H. Armstrong	to	Mary Ann Clark	Barrett
"	30	Wm. H. Nowland	to	Eliza Stephens	Morrison
July	4	Henry Richards	to	May Moore	Magraw
"	4	Joseph Tuffree	to	Mary Ann Woolston	Smoth
"	13	James Scott	to	Mary Garrett	Hammill
"	19	Jno. Wesley Taylor	to	Mary Black	Coleman
"	20	John Barnes	to	Jane Nickle	Magraw
"	27	Levi Smith	to	Isabella Burnite	Barrett
Sept.	3	Edw. Kelly	to	Rebecca Cunningham	Potts
"	9	James Ruley	to	Elizabeth Whitelock	Houston
"	14	Jno. Wright	to	Carlotta Ralston	Houston
"	15	Wm. D. Spence	to	Eliza J. Dunn	Wilson
"	15	Benj. P. Fowler	to	Mary Jane Maffitt	Hammill
1836					
July	30	Elijah Moore	to	Elizabeth Huff	Rev. Mr. W. Stephenson
Aug.	2	Samuel Matkins	to	Harriet McMullin	Rev. Mr. W. Megredy
"	4	Theodore Osborne	to	Adaliza White	Rev. Mr. W. Megredy
"	25	James Berlin	to	Mary Ann Bailey	Rev. Mr. Wm. Duke
"	25	John Boulden	to	Rachel Simpers	Rev. Mr. Wm. Wilson
"	26	Joseph Brumfield	to	Jane Rutter	Rev. Mr. Wm. Duke
"	30	James Jones	to	Ann McDowell	Rev. Mr. W. Lane
Sept.	1	Amos Cummings	to	Eliza Handlen	Rev. Mr. W. Potts
"	12	William Reed	to	Ann McVery	Rev. Mr. W. Lane
"	20	Lagan Earnest	to	Martha Ann Mitchell	Rev. Mr. W. Morrison
Oct.	3	Nicholas Golden	to	Abrigail Jane Brady	Rev. Mr. H. Williams
"	6	Parker Bernard	to	Ann Carlisle	Rev. Mr. Wm. Morris
"	6	Horatic N. Sherwood	to	Mary Ann Hunter	Rev. Mr. W. Williams
"	11	Hasson Lynch	to	Rachel Johnson	Rev. Mr. W. Wilson
"	15	John McVey	to	Hester Ann Blake	Rev. Mr. W. Davis
"	15	Levy Boulden	to	Mary Elizabeth Benneat	Rev. Mr. W. Potts
"	27	Richard James Marcus	to	Mary Girvin	Rev. Mr. Wm. Potts

		MAN		WOMAN	MINISTER
"	27	Joseph W. Cochran	to	Eliza Robinson	Rev. Mr. Wm. Potts
"	30	John S. Inskip	to	Martha Jane Foster	Rev. Mr. Wm. Potts
Nov.	21	Edward H. Hyland	to	Mary Clark	Rev. Mr. Wm. Potts
"	23	John E. Brown	to	Ann W. Robb	Rev. Mr. Wm. Potts
Dec.	5	William Hulton	to	Ann Bennett	Rev. Mr. W. Morris
"	6	Robert Cantwell	to	Mary E. Brown	Rev. Mr. W. Potts
"	10	George Pennington	to	Sarah Flintham	Rev. Mr. W. Duke
"	13	Thomas Gainor	to	Mary Barnett	Rev. Mr. W. Duke
"	13	Thomas L. VanDyke	to	Elizabeth Cochran	Rev. Mr. W. Duke
"	14	John Caulk	to	Cornelia Brown	Rev. Mr. W. Potts
"	15	James Whitelock	to	Susan Price	Rev. Mr. W. Potts
"	15	John W. Tarburton	to	Eliz. Van Digrift	Rev. Mr. W. Potts
"	19	James Cormer	to	Sarah Ann Turner	Rev. Mr. W. Barratt
"	22	Christopeh Price	to	Emily Perry	Rev. Mr. W. Wooley
"	24	Bebron Benson	to	Ann Price	Rev. Mr. W. Reed
	1837				
Jan.	4	William Biggs	to	Ann Helens	Rev. Mr. W. Smith
"	5	David Jenniss	to	Jane Brookings	Rev. Mr. W. Rider
"	23	William B. Donaldson	to	Juliana Donaldson	Rev. Mr. W. Smith
"	24	William Logue	to	Margaret Ann Simmons	Rev. Mr. W. Smith
"	24	Robert N. Hindman	to	Rachel Maria Swisher	Rev. Mr. M. Burris
Feb.	8	John E. Thomas	to	Matilda Jones	Rev. Mr. W. Potts
"	8	J. Heckart	to	Angeline Gilmore	Rev. Mr. W. Potts
"	14	Alexander Anderson	to	Louisa Vansant	Rev. Mr. W. Reed
"	20	William Bartley	to	Ann Davis	Rev. Mr. W. Morris
"	21	Richard Leverson	to	Helen Johnson	Rev. Mr. W. Barratt
"	21	Thomas Howard, Jr.	to	Ann Ash	Rev. Mr. W. Hamil
"	24	Isaac Crouch	to	Margaret Buchanan	Rev. Mr. W. Potts
"	27	Williams Huids	to	Rachel Kirkpatrick	Rev. Mr. Barratt
Mar.	7	Samuel Hessey	to	Sarah Biggs	Rev. Mr. Smith
"	11	Stephen Biddle	to	Deborah Compt	Rev. Mr. Morris
"	20	James H. Willard	to	Mary Bryan	Rev. Mr. Morris
"	22	John Jester	to	Hannah Updegrove	Rev. Mr. Potts
"	23	John Davis	to	Margaret Wallis	Rev. Mr. Potts
"	24	Edmund Physick	to	Sarah Black	Rev. Mr. Potts
"	28	Joseph W. Smith	to	Sarah Ann Guthrie	Rev. Mr. Wilson
"	29	James H. George	to	Harriett Ann Hyland	Rev. Mr. Barratt
"	30	William Williams	to	Ann Smith	Rev. Mr. Wilson
	1836				
Oct.	2	Nicholas Golden	to	Abegail J. Brady	Williams
"	6	Parker Bernard	to	Ann Carlislie	Morris
"	6	Horatio N. Sherwood	to	Mary Ann Hunter	Williams
"	11	Hasson Lynch	to	Rachel Johnson	Wilson
"	15	John McVey	to	Hester Ann Blake	Davis
"	15	Levy Boulden	to	Mary Elizabeth Bennett	Potts
"	27	Richard James Marcus	to	Mary Girvin	Potts
"	27	Joseph W. Cochran	to	Eliza Robinson	Potts
"	30	John S. Inskip	to	Martha Jane Foster	Potts
Nov.	21	Edward H. Hyland	to	Mary Clark	Potts
"	23	John E. Brown	to	Ann W. Robb	Potts
Dec.	5	William Hulton	to	Ann Bennett	Morris
"	6	Robert Cantwell	to	Mary E. Brown	Potts
"	10	George Pennington	to	Sarah Flintham	Duke
"	13	Thomas Gainor	to	Mary Barnett	Duke
"	13	Thomas L. VanDyke	to	Elizabeth Cochran	Duke
"	14	John Caulk	to	Cornelia Brown	Potts
"	15	James Whitelock	to	Susan Price	Potts
"	15	John W. Tarburton	to	Eliz. S. Van Digrift	Potts
"	19	James Cormer	to	Sarah Ann Turner	Barrett
"	22	Christopher Price	to	Emily Terry	Wooley
"	24	Hebron Benson	to	Ann Price	Reed

	MAN		WOMAN	MINISTER
1837				
Jan. 4	William Biggs	to	Ann Helens	Smith
" 5	David Jenness	to	Jane Brookings	Rider
" 23	William B. Donaldson	to	Juliana Donaldson	Smith
" 24	William Logue	to	Margaret Ann Simmons	Smith
" 24	Robert N. Hindman	to	Rachel Maria Swisher	Burris
Feb. 8	John E. Thomas	to	Matilda Jones	Potts
" 8	J. Heckart	to	Angeline Gilmore	Potts
" 14	Alexander Anderson	to	Louisa Vansant	Reed
" 20	William Bartley	to	Ann Davis	Morris
" 21	Richard Severson	to	Helen Johnson	Barratt
" 21	Thomas Howard, Jr.	to	Ann Ash	Hamil
" 24	Isaac Crouch	to	Margaret Buchanan	Potts
" 27	Williams Huids (Hinds)?	to	Rachel Kirkpatrick	Barratt
Mar. 7	Samuel Hessey	to	Sarah Biggs	Smith
" 11	Stephen Biddle	to	Deborah Compt	Morris
" 20	James H. Willard	to	Mary Bryan	Morris
" 22	John Jester	to	Hannah Updegrove	Potts
" 23	John Davis	to	Margaret Wallis	Potts
" 24	Edmund Physick	to	Sarah Black	Potts
" 28	Joseph W. Smith	to	Miss Sarah Ann Guthrie	Wilson
" 29	James H. George	to	Harriett Ann Hyland	Barratt
" 30	William Williams	to	Ann Smith	Wilson
Apr. 5	John Markee	to	Margaret A. Pluck	Potts
" 6	William Holland	to	Catherine Armstrong	Jordan
" 11	Robert Thompson	to	Jane Orr	Burrows
" 13	James Cooper	to	Phoebe Ann Thompson	Barratt
" 21	Justus Alexander	to	Rebecca Reynolds	Barratt
May 13	William Physick	to	Rebecca Whitelock	Grace
June 5	Arthur Dyke	to	Eliza Ann Walker	Morris
" 8	Jeremiah Cox	to	Susan Kirk	Morris
" 8	Samuel Green	to	Mary Eadea?	Morris
" 13	James Campbell	to	Elizabeth Clark	Kennard
" 14	John Thomas Huggins	to	Sarah Oldham	Barratt
" 15	Samuel Whitelock	to	Elizabeth Bell	Grace
" 22	James Mansfield	to	Mrs. Mary R. Garritson	Peck
July 11	Firman Layman	to	Elizabeth Ann Conway	Morris
" 12	Frederick Slagle	to	Mary Jane Johnson	Barratt
" 26	William Shelly	to	Elizabeth Bruce	Grace
Aug. 1	Thomas C. Cazier	to	Maria L. Ward	Farland
" 22	Lewis Jones	to	Ann Patten	Parks
Sept. 5	William Hassan	to	Elizabeth Burnight	Kennard
" 21	Thomas Wilson	to	Emily Thomas	Barratt
" 23	John Barratt	to	Hannah Simpers	Barratt
" 27	William Boyd	to	Sarah White	Greenbanks
Oct. 19	John Murphy	to	Jane Lane	Kennard
" 25	Eli Pearson	to	Elizabeth Foster	Barratt
" 28	William S. Hesse	to	Louisa Hayes	Pickett
" 31	Andrew Fisher	to	Caroline Yeamans	Burrows
" 31	Thomas Kennard	to	Elizabeth Riker?	Burrows
Nov. 7	John W. Gallahan	to	Maria Boice	Farland
" 8	Samuel Phillips	to	Susan Thomas	Barratt
" 9	James H. Jamar	to	Vilotta R. Scott	Farland
" 13	Thomas P. Abrams	to	Mary Owens	Duke
Dec. 9	Francis King	to	Deborah Mears	Greenbanks
" 28	James Shockley	to	Ann Elizabeth Clark	Morrison
1838				
Jan. 1	Joseph Tyson	to	Mary Abrahams	Wooley
" 1	Lewis Littaway	to	Sarah Cunningham	**Morris**
" 2	Nicholas Lum	to	Ann Zane	Barratt
" 6	Isaac H. R. Cox	to	Elizabeth Lee	Pickett

		MAN		WOMAN	MINISTER
"	8	Frisby Tull	to	Charlotte Brown	Farland
"	8	James Sweeny	to	Margaret Alexander	Russell
"	15	Thomas J. Cochran	to	Elizabeth Colmary	Farland
"	15	Thomas Cunningham	to	Mary Ann Fulton	Farland
"	15	Francis B. Gottier	to	Alicia Moore	Kennard
"	16	William C. Blackiston	to	Eliz. Tomlinson	Greenbanks
"	16	Samuel Tippett	to	Sarah Moore	Pickett
"	18	James Matthews	to	Leah Moody	Farland
"	24	Robert A. Landeris?	to	Mary Russell	Goldsborough
"	24	John R. Abrams	to	M. Chandlee	Wooley
"	29	Joseph W. Veazey	to	Margaret Manley	Farland
'	30	William Marshall	to	Rebecca Bayley	Greenbanks
"	31	Benjamin Reed	to	Rebecca Harrington	Pickett
Feb.	7	John Williams	to	Rebecca Ann Irwin	Dun
"	12	Joseph Benjamin	to	Mary Ann Johnson	Kennard
"	13	William Calvert	to	Louisa Bennett	Kennard
"	14	David T. Aspril	to	Caroline E. Lighter	Brown
"	16	Samuel Grace	to	Ann Goforth	Wooley
"	26	Edward Wilkins	to	Deborah Jones	Kennard
"	28	Elisha Mahanny	to	Rebecca Ann Weaver	Parkins
Mar.	1	John White	to	Rachel Phillips	Kennard
	1837				
Apr.	5	John Markey	to	Margaret A. Pluck	Mr. Potts
"	6	William Halland	to	Catharine Armstrong	Mr. Jordan
"	11	Robert Thompson	to	Jane Orr	Mr. Burrows
"	13	James Cooper	to	Phebe Ann Thompson	Mr. Barratt
"	21	Justus Alexander	to	Rebecca Reynolds	Mr. Barratt
May	13	William Physick	to	Rebecca Whitelock	Mr. Grace
June	5	Arthur Dyke	to	Eliza Ann Wacku	Mr. Morris
"	8	Jeremiah Cox	to	Susan Kirk	Mr. Morris
"	8	Lemuel Green	to	Mary Eadea	Mr. Morris
"	13	James Campbell	to	Elizabeth Clark	Mr. Kennard
"	14	John Thomas Huggins	to	Sarah Oldham	Mr. Barratt
"	15	Samuel Whitelock	to	Elizabeth Bell	Mr. Grace
"	22	James Mansfield	to	Mrs. Mary R. Garritson	Mr. Peck
July	11	Firman Layman	to	Elizabeth Ann Conway	Mr. Morris
"	12	Frederick Slagle	to	Mary Jane Johnson	Mr. Barratt
"	26	William Sheely	to	Elizabeth Bruce	Mr. Grace
Aug.	1	Thomas C. (Cazier?)	to	Maria L. Ward	Mr. Farland
"	22	Lewis Jones	to	Ann Patten	Mr. Parks
Sept.	5	William Hassan	to	Elizabeth Burnight	Mr. Kennard
"	21	Thomas Wilson	to	Emily Thomas	Mr. Barratt
"	23	John Barratt	to	Hannah Simpers	Mr. Barratt
"	27	William Boyd	to	Sarah White	Mr. Greenbanks
Oct.	19	John Murphy	to	Jane Lane	Mr. Kennard
"	25	Eli Pearson	to	Elizabeth Foster	Mr. Barratt
"	28	William L. Hesse	to	Louisa Hayes	Mr. Pickett
"	31	Andrew Fishu	to	Caroline Yeomans	Mr. Burrows
"	31	Thomas Kennard	to	Elizabeth Riku	Mr. Burrows
Nov.	7	John W. Gallahan	to	Maria Boice	Rev. Mr. W. Farland
"	8	Samuel Phillips	to	Susan Thomas	Rev. Mr. Barratt
"	9	James H. Jamar	to	Vilotta R. Scott	Rev. Mr. W. Farland
"	13	Thomas T. Abrams	to	Mary Owens	Rev. Mr. Duke
Dec.	9	Francis King	to	Deborah Mears	Rev. Mr. Greenbanks
"	28	James Shockley	to	Ann Elizabeth Clark	Rev. Mr. Morrison
	1838				
Jan.	1	Joseph Tyson	to	Mary Abrahams	Rev. Mr. Wooley
"	1	Lewis Littaway	to	Sarah Cunningham	Rev. Mr. Morris
"	2	Nicholas Lum	to	Ann Zane	Rev. Mr. Barratt
"	6	Isaac H. R. Cox	to	Elizabeth Lee	Rev. Mr. Pickett

		MAN		WOMAN	MINISTER
"	8	Frisby True	to	Charlotte Brown	Rev. Mr. W. Farland
"	8	James Sweeny	to	Margaret Alexander	Rev. Mr. Russell
"	15	Thomas J. Cochran	to	Elizabeth Colnmary	Rev. Mr. W. Farland
"	15	Thomas Cunningham	to	Mary Ann Talton	Rev. Mr. W. Farland
"	15	Francis B. Gottier	to	Alicia Moore	Rev. Mr. Kennard
"	16	William C. Blackiston	to	Eliz. Tomlinson	Rev. Mr. Greenbanks
"	16	Samuel Tippett	to	Sarah Moore	Rev. Mr. Pickett
"	18	James Matthews	to	Leah Moody	Rev. Mr. W. Farland
"	24	Robert R. Landeric	to	Mary Russell	Rev. Mr. Golsborough
"	24	John R. Abrams	to	M. Chandler	Rev. Mr. Wooley
"	29	Joseph W. Veazey	to	Margaret Manley	Rev. Mr. W. Farland
"	30	William Marshall	to	Rebecca Bayley	Rev. Mr. Greenbanks
"	31	Benjamin Reed	to	Rebecca Harrington	Rev. Mr. Pickett
Feb.	7	John Williams	to	Rebecca Ann Irwin	Rev. Mr. Dun
"	12	Joseph Benjamin	to	Mary Ann Johnson	Rev. Mr. Kennard
"	13	William Calvert	to	Louisa Bennett	Rev. Mr. Kennard
"	14	David Aspril	to	Caroline E. Lightner	Rev. Mr. Brown
"	16	Samuel Grace	to	Ann Goforth	Rev. Mr. Wooley
"	26	Edward Wilkins	to	Deborah Jones	Rev. Mr. Kennard
"	28	Elisha Mahanny	to	Rebecca Ann Weaver	Rev. Mr. Parkins
Mar.	1	John White	to	Rachel Phillips	Rev. Mr. Kennard
"	3	William W. Tipton	to	Harriet Ramsey	Rev. Mr. Parkins
"	5	Jeremiah Foard	to	Sophia Maulden	Rev. Mr. Kennard
"	6	Reuben D. Jamar	to	Ann Rebecca Ford	Rev. Mr. W. Farland
"	15	John Mears	to	Eliza Hudson	Rev. Mr. Morris
"	20	Sampson Lum	to	Mary Crouch	Rev. Mr. Barratt
"	20	James Matthews	to	Mary Weaver	Rev. Mr. W. Farland
"	22	James K. Burnite	to	Martha C. Hyland	Rev. Mr. W. Farland
"	24	James Tosh	to	Eliza Hindman	Rev. Mr. Burris
"	26	Thomas T. Benjamin	to	Mary A. Jackson	Rev. Mr. Grace
"	29	Thomas Thackery	to	Sarah Matthews	Rev. Mr. W. Farland
"	29	Andrew Camblin	to	Leah Moody	Rev. Mr. W. Farland
Apr.	4	Benjamin C. Cowan	to	Jane Taylor	Rev. Mr. McFarland
May	24	Joshua Bradley	to	Margaret Cameron	Rev. Mr. Burrows
"	25	Yadock Veach	to	Mary Ann Evans	Rev. Mr. Hagany
"	26	Caleb K. Burgoine	to	Elizabeth Lidley	Rev. Mr. Hagany
"	30	Joseph Benson	to	Mary Roberts	Rev. Mr. Pickett
"	30	Joseph Briggs	to	Rebecca Pennington	Rev. Mr. Pickett
June	7	William Cameron	to	Jane Maxwell	Rev. Mr. Burrows
"	7	Richard Miller	to	Sarah Jane Grant	Rev. Mr. Barratt
"	25	James Getty	to	Rebecca Ann Burnite	Rev. Mr. Kennard
July	24	William Richardson	to	Jane Calvert	Rev. Mr. Kennard
"	24	William Moore	to	Mary Ann Thorton	Rev. Mr. Grason
"	26	John Haines	to	Rebecca Biddle	Rev. Mr. Kennard
Aug.	19	Thomas Neal	to	Catherine Tomlinson	Rev. Mr. Greenbank
Sept.	3	Joseph S. Cranmer	to	Sarah Hamilton	Rev. Mr. Duke
"	10	James Bailey	to	Sarah M. Robinson	Rev. Mr. Duke
"	19	William R. Mahanny	to	Harriet Mahanny	Rev. Mr. Budd
"	19	James Girvin	to	Ann Taylor	Rev. Mr. Hagany
"	27	Oliver Killingtonworth	to	Elizabeth Waters	Rev. Mr. Greenbank
Oct.	1	Robert White	to	Mary Ann McVey	Rev. Mr. Hagany
"	1	John T. Gallalier	to	Sarah Morrison	Rev. Mr. Wilson
"	2	John B. Pennington	to	Ann Mercer	Rev. Mr. Hagany
"	3	William Spence	to	Jane Gilpin	Rev. Mr. Greenbank
"	6	Joseph McCrea	to	Rebecca Jamison	Rev. Mr. Hagany
"	8	Harry K. Reynolds	to	Ann E. Davidson	Rev. Mr. Kennard
"	8	John Wilson	to	Adaline Gilmore	Rev. Mr. Greenbank
"	15	Thomas A. Biddle	to	Jane L. Wolcott	Rev. Mr. Young
Nov.	5	Frances Keatley	to	Emily Barnett	Rev. Mr. Barratt
"	10	William Stradley	to	Frances Carroll	Rev. Mr. Pickett
"	12	William D. Mercer	to	Margaret S. Biddle	Rev. Mr. Piggott

		MAN		WOMAN	MINISTER
"	22	Thomas Knotts	to	Elizabeth Pattison	Rev. Mr. Hagany
Dec.	11	Thomas Lusby	to	Mary E. Lusby	Rev. Mr. King
"	17	Samuel Moffett	to	Victorine Johnson	Rev. Mr. Hagany
"	19	John J. Alexander	to	Mary A. Rollings	Rev. Mr. Burrows
"	20	Thomas Logan	to	Isabella Jones	Rev. Mr. Inskip
"	22	John W. Lynch	to	Mary M. Hirons	Rev. Mr. Piggott
"	26	William R. Biddle	to	Ann Ruley	Rev. Mr. Piggott
	1839				
Jan.	1	James W. Morgan	to	Rebecca Ann Hayes	Rev. Mr. Piggott
"	1	Samuel Tyson	to	Harriet Gorrell	Rev. Mr. Wooley
"	2	William Jague	to	Rachel Lurtz	Rev. Mr. Smith
"	9	William Manley	to	Frances Kirk	Rev. Mr. Barrett
"	11	Samuel Evans	to	Mary B. Phillips	Rev. Mr. McIntire
"	14	Joseph Craddock	to	Helena A. Green	Rev. Mr. King
"	16	Nicholas Lloyd	to	Catherine Stephens	Rev. Mr. Smith
"	19	Samuel Reagraves	to	Ann Elizabeth Colley	Rev. Mr. Smith
"	23	David Hagan	to	Milcah Lowe	Rev. Mr. King
"	25	William H. Snowden	to	Miss Lydia M. Carter	Rev. Mr. Miller
"	25	Elisha Foster	to	Elizabeth A. Evans	Rev. Mr. Barrett
"	25	Caleb Edmondson	to	Eliza Jane Campbell	Rev. Mr. Hoffman
"	29	Sylvester Williams	to	Rebecca Ash	Rev. Mr. Hagany
"	30	Nathaniel Gilmore	to	Hannah Brumfield	Rev. Mr. Greenbank
"	31	John W. Stradley	to	Mary Walmsley	Rev. Mr. Piggott
Feb.	2	John Tosh	to	Jemima McCormick	Rev. Mr. Burrows
"	11	Wharton Register	to	Susan Ann Spence	Rev. Mr. Piggott
"	16	John Armour	to	Ruth Anna Jenkings	Rev. Mr. Burrows
"	20	Joseph Scarborough	to	Sarah Williams	Rev. Mr. Wilson
"	25	William Rutter	to	Ann Maria Whittall	Rev. Mr. Grace
Mar.	6	Benjamin Croncer	to	Rachel Stoops	Rev. Mr. Barrett
"	14	Joseph Pennock	to	Phoebe Ann Ferguson	Rev. Mr. Miller
"	18	Victor Craig	to	Margaret Eliza Gibson	Rev. Mr. Grace
"	20	John McCall	to	Sarah Anderson	Rev. Mr. Barrett
"	26	Daniel Stull	to	Mary Ann Smith	Rev. Mr. Kennard
Apr.	1	Richard Wingate	to	Sarah Robinson	Rev. Mr. Farland
	1838				
Mar.	3	William W. Tipton	to	Harriet Ramsey	Parkins
"	5	Jeremiah Foard	to	Sophia Maulden	Kennard
"	6	Reuben D. Jamar	to	Ann Rebecca Ford	Farland
"	15	John Mears	to	Eliza Hudson	Morris
"	20	Sampson Lum	to	Mary Crouch	Barratt
"	20	James Matthews	to	Mary Weaver	Farland
"	22	James K. Burnite	to	Martha C. Hyland	Farland
"	24	James Tosh	to	Eliza Hindman	Burris
"	26	Thomas T. Benjamin	to	Mary A. Jackson	Grace
"	29	Thomas Thackery	to	Sarah Matthews	Farland
"	29	Andrew Camblin	to	Leah Moody	Farland
Apr.	4	Benjamin C. Cowan	to	Jane Taylor	McFarland
May	24	Joshua Bradley	to	Margaret Cameron	Burrows
"	25	Zadock Veach	to	Mary Ann Evans	Hagany
"	26	Caleb K. Burgoine	to	Elizabeth A. Lilley	Haggany
"	30	Joseph Benson	to	Mary Roberts	Pickett
"	30	Joseph Briggs	to	Rebecca Pennington	Pickett
June	7	William Cameron	to	Jane Maxwell	Burrows
"	7	Richard Miller	to	Sarah Jane Grant	Barratt
"	25	James Getty	to	Rebecca Ann Burnite	Kennard
July	24	William Richardson	to	Jane Calvert	Kennard
"	24	William Moore	to	Mary Ann Thorton	Grason
"	26	John Haines	to	Rebecca Biddle	Kennard
Aug.	19	Thomas Neal	to	Catherine Tomlinson	Greenbank

MAN			WOMAN	MINISTER
Sept.	3	Joseph S. Cranmer	to Sarah Hamilton	Duke
"	10	James Bailey	to Sarah M. Robinson	Duke
"	19	William R. Mahanny	to Harriet Mahanny	Budd
"	19	James Girvin	to Ann Taylor	Hagany
"	27	Oliver Killingsworth	to Elizabeth Waters	Greenbank
Oct.	1	Robert White	to Mary Ann McVey	Hagany
"	1	John T. Gallalier	to Sarah Morrison	Wilson
"	2	John B. Pennington	to Ann Mercer	Hagany
"	3	William Spence	to Jane Gilpin	Greenbank
"	6	Joseph McCrea	to Rebecca Jamison	Hagany
"	8	Harry K. Reynolds	to Ann E. Davidson	Kennard
"	8	John Wilson	to Adaline Gilmore	Greenbank
"	15	Thomas A. Biddle	to Jane L. Wolcott	Young
Nov.	5	Frances Keatley	to Emily Barnett	Barratt
"	10	William Stradley	to Frances Carroll	Pickett
"	12	William D. Mercer	to Margaret S. Biddle	Piggott
"	22	Thomas Knotts	to Elizabeth Pattison	Hagany
Dec.	11	Thomas Lusby	to Mary E. Lusby	King
"	17	Samuel Moffett	to Victorine Johnson	Hagany
"	19	John J. Alexander	to Mary A. Rollings	Burrows
"	20	Thomas Logan	to Isabella Jones	Inskip
"	22	John W. Lynch	to Mary M. Hirons	Piggott
"	26	William R. Biddle	to Ann Ruley	Piggott
1839				
Jan.	1	James W. Morgan	to Rebecca Ann Hayes	Piggott
"	1	Samuel Tyson	to Harriet Gorrell	Wooley
"	2	William M. Hayes	to Rachel Lurtz	Smith
"	9	William Manley	to Frances Kirk	Barrett
"	11	Samuel Evans	to Mary B. Phillips	McIntire
"	14	Joseph Craddock	to Helena A. Green	King
"	16	Nicholas Lloyd	to Catherine Stephens	Smith
"	19	Samuel Redgraves	to Ann Elizabeth Colley	Smith
"	23	David Hagan	to Milcah Lowe	King
"	25	William H. Snowden	to Miss Lydia M. Carter	Miller
"	25	Elisha Foster	to Elizabeth A. Evans	Barrett
"	29	Sylvester Williams	to Rebecca Ash	Hagany
"	25	Caleb Edmondson	to Eliza Jane Campbell	Hoffman
"	30	Nathaniel K. Gilmore	to Hannah Brumfield	Greenbank
"	31	John W. Stradley	to Mary Walmsley	Piggott
Feb.	2	John Tosh	to Jemima McCormick	Burrows
"	11	Wharton Register	to Susan Ann Spence	Piggott
"	16	John Armour	to Ruth Ann Jenkings	Burrows
"	20	Joseph Scarborough	to Sarah Williams	Wilson
"	25	William Rutter	to Ann Maria Whittall	Grace
Mar.	6	Benjamin Crouch	to Rachel Stoops	Barrett
"	14	Joseph Pennock	to Phoebe Ann Ferguson	Miller
"	18	Victor Craig	to Margaret Eliza Gibson	Grace
"	20	John McCall	to Sarah Anderson	Barrett
"	26	Daniel Stull	to Mary Ann Smith	Kennard
Apr.	1	Richard Wingate	to Sarah Robinson	Farland
"	4	Fredus Aldridge	to Eliza Jane Grant	Kennard
"	20	Thomas Wood	to Temperance Ann Shivery	Hagany
May	2	George W. Moore	to Elizabeth Simmons	MacIntire
"	7	William Stalcup	to Eliza Ann Hitchcock	Hagany
"	14	John Clark	to Harriet P. Colmerry	Foulks
"	14	John Riddell of Wm.	to Rachel Ewing	Hoopman
"	14	Diedrick H. Black	to Eliza Jane Tyson	McIntire
"	20	William Scotten	to Martha Spence	Miller
"	20	Benjamin B. Chambers	to Mary Jane Fowler	Pierson
"	24	James Stalcup	to Rebecca Matthews	Hagany
"	31	Richard Lee	to Nancy Galaher	Wiggin

	MAN		WOMAN	MINISTER
June 5	Thomas Hines	to	Mary Bennett	Barrett
" 14	Benjamin B. Sweet	to	Hetty Ann Humphries	Pierson
" 18	Josiah Borum	to	Amelia Robinson	Hagany
" 20	John Ward	to	Mary Richardson	MacIntire
" 22	John Cunningham	to	Margaret Jackson	Young
" 28	Joseph McMullen	to	Sarah Ann Owens	Hagany
Aug. 2	George W. Hasson	to	Mary Ann Whittaker	Grace
" 7	George W. Thompson	to	Sarah Ann Tarring	Diggins
Sept. 2	George Wash. Richardson	to	Agnes Jackson	Grace
" 12	William Warden	to	Mary Ann Gibson	Pierson
" 19	Soverighn Andrews	to	Eliza Mumford	Hagany
" 21	Thomas Logan	to	Mary Baker	Grace
" 23	James Orr	to	Caroline Davis	Wiggins
" 25	Wm. P. Green	to	Elizabeth A. Craddock	King
" 26	Benjamin M. Ruley	to	Sarah E. Severson	Hagany
Oct. 1	Thomas J. Davidson	to	Martha Gallaher	Wilson
" 14	Alfred B. Thomas	to	Jane A. Shields	King
" 16	John F. Coulson	to	Margaret Tosh	Wiggins
Nov. 2	Samuel Campbell	to	Sarah Ann Reynolds	Hoopman
" 9	Joseph Chick	to	Martha Boies	Barratt
" 13	Joseph Carter	to	Elizabeth Harrigan	Woolley
" 25	James Whittaker	to	Ann Maria Jones	Mason
Dec. 10	Henry Bosie	to	Mlinda Hamer	Barrows
" 26	Charles W. Jackson	to	Georgiana Gorrell?	Grace
" 26	Samuel Gay, Jr.	to	Mary Ann Blumfield	Burrows
" 26	Israel Alexander	to	Catherine McClure	Barratt
" 28	Joseph T. Terrell	to	Lydia Ann McCauley	Miller
" 30	George W. Craig	to	Ann Elizabeth Moore	Piggatt
" 30	Joseph Lambson	to	Susan Green	Hagany
1840				
Jan. 2	Richard Keatley	to	Mary Jones	Purson
" 8	John McClure	to	Mary E. Crouch	Barratt
" 22	Peter Mariner	to	Ann McGerr	Hagany
Feb. 4	Jacob Johnson	to	Caroline Brown	Hagany
" 5	Samuel Gillespie	to	Mary McVey	Burrows
" 6	Elias P. Barneby	to	DonMaria Money	Piggatt
" 13	Ebenezer W. Nowland	to	Phoebe Ann Smith	Burrows
Mar. 11	Richard L. Simpers	to	Rachel Wood	Hagany
Apr. 11	John C. Cochran	to	Ann Buckworth	Fouchs
" 18	Joshua Ash	to	Rebecca Wallace	McIntyre
" 20	Jonathan Zanes	to	Mary Wood	Kennard
May 4	George W. Wells	to	Elizabeth Hutton	McIntyre
" 5	Reese Mahan	to	Elizabeth Garrett	Warburton
" 6	Sanders McCullough	to	Sarah Maria Rowland	Burroughs
" 7	Thomas Sturgeon	to	Martha Ann Redgraves	Barroll
" 13	David Tucker	to	Grisella Lynch	Torbut
" 20	Josiah McClenahan	to	Margaret Walker	Grace
June 1	Michail Hauge	to	Alice A. Barnwell	Piggatt

Marriages Omitted When Copy Was Made

DATE	MAN		WOMAN	MINISTER
1777, Nov.,	Benjamin Sluyter	to	Thompson	Rev. Mr. Thompson
1779, July 10,	Robert Hart	to	Ann Hyland	
1780, Jan. 18,	Edward Burris	to	Eleanor McMullin	
1780, July 9,	Justis Brown?	to	Grace Palmer?	Rev. Mr. Thompson
1781, Aug. 1,	Robert Ware	to	Jane Cunningham	
1784, Nov. 19,	William Ward	to	Ann Veasey	Rev. Mr. Thompson
1786, Dec. 21,	John Kinkead	to	Frances Dorsus Hamilton	
1787, Jan. 25,	Hyland Gears	to	Mary Beavins	Rev. Mr. Couden
1788, Jan. 7,	Joseph Nevens	to	Sarah Alexander	
1795, Apr. 2,	Adam Short	to	Ann Mary Johnson	Rev. Mr. Duke
1796, May 24,	Lewis Fight	to	Rachel Todd	
1798, Aug. 21,	John White	to	Mary Williams	Rev. Mr. Cosden
1800, Dec. 23,	Robert Ratliff?	to	Ann Husler	
1801, June 4,	Jethro Barr	to	Eliza Kirkpatrick	
1804, Dec. 14,	William Smith	to	Margaret Brooks	
1805, Nov. 19,	Doctor Richard L. Savin	to	Julian N. Veazey	
1806, April 10,	John Price	to	Elizabeth Simpers	
1808, Aug. 18,	George Mercer	to	Sarah Evenston	
1813, Feb. 3,	Frances Johnson	to	Mary Milburn	
1813, Mar. 27,	Wm. Wainick	to	Sarah Taylor	
1815, Feb. 14,	James Jarvis	to	Sina Lerett	Rev. Mr. Duke
1821, Jan. 25,	William Biddle	to	Catherine Williams	
1821, June 20,	James Todd?	to	Ariminta McCartney	
1822, Mar. 18,	John Lusby?	to	Hannah Evans	
1824, Sept. 13,	James Marnes	to	Lavenia Oldham	
1833, Sept. 12,	James Wilson	to	Lavenia Green	
1835, Sept. 28,	James White	to	Ann R. Cameron	
1835, Dec. 22,	Joseph S. Wingate	to	Mary Ann Little	
Dec. 9,	John Alexander	to	Ann Eliza Thomas	

THE SCOTTISH ALEXANDERS

First William the Norman, then William his son,
Henry, Stephen, and Henry, then Richard and John,
Next Henry the third, Edward one, two and three
And again after Richard, three Henries we see:
Two Edwards, the third Richard, if one rightly guess,
Two Henries, sixth Edward, Queen Mary, Queen Bess?
Next James the Scot, then Charles whom they slew,
But received after Cromwell another Charles too:
Then James called the Second ascended the throne,
Then William and Mary together came on:
'Till Anne, Georges four and fourth William all past,
Victoria, seventh Edward, the fifth George, the last.

INDEX

A

Name	Page
Andrewson, John	1
Andrews, James	2
Arrants, Herman	3
Armstrong, Robert	4
Arrants, William	4
Allen, John	6
Alexander, Edward	8
Aldridge, Samuel	8
Allieson, John	9
Adam, John	9
Ash, George	9
Adair, Joseph	10
Anderson, Abraham	10
Alexander, Justine	11
Archibald, David	11
Abrahams, Peter	12
Arbuckle, Joseph	13
Arnold, David	14
Freadus, Aldridge	16
Alexander, William, Esq.	16
Archer, Robert H.	25
Anderson, Andrew	19
Anderson, Saumel	20
Aikin, Samuel	21
Alexander, Alexander	21
Aikens, James	21
Allen, James	22
Alexander, Benjamin	22
Allman, John	23
Abbot, William Freeman	24
Alexander, David	24
Arnerica, John	33
Arrants, John	33
Abrams, John	33
Alexander, Ephraim	34
Abbot, Benjamin	35
Alexander, Alexander	35
Arrants, Joseph	35
Alexander, Andrew	35
Arrants, James	36
Anderson, Samuel	36
Aldridge, Samuel	26
Alexander, Israel	26
Alexander, Matthew	27
Armstrong, John	27
Aldridge, Freadus	28
Anderson, James	29
Anderson, John	30
Ash, Joseph	30
Allen, Mathias	30
Alexander, Henry	31
Ash, Jacob	31
Arthur, Mark	32
Anderson, John, Jr.	32
Alexander, James	17
Alfond, John	17
Abbot, Jacob Freeman	17
Alexander, Mark	18
Ash, George	18
Alexander, James	18
Altzee, John	18
Allman, Isaac	18
Atwell, Benjamin	38
Alexander, William	38
Adams, John	39
Alexander, Edward	40
Alexander, William	40
Anderson, Adam	41
Alexander, Andrew	41
Atwell, Benjamin	41
Austin, David	41
Alexander, Andrew	42
Atwell, Benjamin	42
Austin, David	42
Alcorne, George	43
Aldridge, Thomas	43
Abbot, William F.	43
Ashton, Daniel	43
Alcorn, George	44
Aldridge, Thomas	44
Abbot, William F.	44
Ashton, Daniel	44
Alden, Joshua	44
Akison?, Henry	44
Alden, Joshua	45
Akison?, Henry	45
Atkinson, Samuel C.	46
Alexander, David	46
Alexander, Joseph	46
Adams, John	46
Alexander, Joseph	48
Allen, Hammond	48
Aslip, Benjamin M.	48
Alexander, James	49
Ash, John	50
Atkinson, Frances	51
Anderson, John C.	51
Abrahams, Richard	52
Armstrong, Robert	52
Anderson, James	52

	Page		Page
Aldridge, John	52	Alexander, Andrew W.	61
Archibald, Robert	52	Aikin, Robert	61
Alexander, James	52	Armstrong, George H.	62
Alerton, Robert	52	Anderson, Alexander	63
Anderson, John	52	Alexander, Justus	64
Alexander, Arthur	53	Abrahams, Thomas P.	64
Aikin, William	56	Abrahams, John R.	65
Arthurs, Mark	56	Aspril, David I.	65
Anderson, Allen	56	Alexander, John J.	67
Alexander, James	57	Armour, John	67
Alden, George	57	Aldridge, Fredus	68
Archer, John	59	Andrews, Soverighn	69
Abrahams, Joseph W.	59	Alexander, Israel	69
Alden, Ebenezer	60		
Alexander, John W.	61	Ash, Joshua	69
Atkinson, Elisha	61	Alexander, John	70

B

	Page		Page
Boggs, Archibald	1	Bevins, Thomas	7
Booth, William	1	Bell, James	7
Bateman, Rheuben	1	Beedle, Samuel	7
Beedle, Spencer	1	Bouldin, James	7
Brown, William	1	Belme, Isaac	7
Bulteal, Henry	1	Beaston, William	8
Bond, Samuel	1	Bowen, Jonathan	8
Biles, Robert	2	Bevins, James	8
Boyed, John	2	Bevins, James	8
Bolding, John	2	Brumfield, Francis	8
Baylay, James	2	Bristow, Samuel	8
Bayard, Samuel	2	Batten, James	9
Brown, John	2	Boyd, Hugh	9
Blake, Solomon	2	Beard, Alexander	10
Barckley, James	2	Ballard, Jonathan	10
Bowen, Richard	3	Brown, John	10
Beaty, Samuel	3	Byard, Samuel, Jr.	10
Bird, Thomas	3	Briscoe, Joseph	10
Benjamin, John	3	Beam, Nathan	10
Brown, William	3	Beetle, Samuel	10
Barrington, Richard	3	Bennett, Henry	10
Bateman, William	3	Burran, John	10
Burris, Edward	4	Bond, Abel	11
Boys, Alexander	4	Briscoe, Peregrine	12
Baxley, James	4	Biddle, Jacob	13
Bayard, Benjamin	4	Brooks, John	13
Brison, William	5	Bunting, Charles S.	13
Brackley, Jehockim	5	Bryan, Andrew	13
Barrett, Samuel	5	Bristow, John	13
Barnes, James	5	Bing, Oliver	13
Boulden, Noble	6	Bryan, Michael	13
Beaston, William	6	Brumfield, Edward	14
Bristow, John	6	Bateman, William	14
Beedle, Andrew	6	Baker, Jeremiah	14
Biggs, Richard	6	Bennett, John	14
Bailey, John	6	Bargoe, Andrew	15
Beedle, Augustine	6	Brookings, Richard	15
Bond, Richard, Jr.	6	Beedle, Thomas	15
Broom, Abraham	6	Biddle, Tobias	15
Barr, Robert	6	Bowen, Isaac	15
Bennett, Philip	6	Burrows, Edward	15
Beedle, Thomas	7	Burgayne, James	15

Name	Page	Name	Page
Biddle, Peregrine	15	Brumfield, William	24
Barnaby, Benjamin	16	Buckworth, Charles	24
Beedle, Samuel	16	Batten, Hezekiah	16
Beeks, William	16	Boggs, Barzzelly?	16
Bostick, Hezekiah	31	Boyer, Peregrine	16
Baker, John	31	Benjamin, George	25
Burke, Nathaniel	31	Bryson, Richard	25
Booth, Daniel	31	Briscoe, Peregrine	25
Brown, Hugh	31	Biddle, Ramond	25
Beedle, Augustine	32	Biggs, Joseph	25
Biddle, John	32	Boyce, Andrew	26
Bell, John	17	Barnes, John	26
Boozer, John	17	Bennett, Joshua	26
Beasten, Charles	17	Boulden, Nathan	26
Benson, Benjamin	17	Boyd, John	26
Bair, William	17	Bayard, Stephen	27
Boulden, John	17	Black, Charles F.	27
Black, Philip	18	Buckworth, Samuel	27
Bolden, Haunen	18	Boldin, John	27
Bolden, Richard	18	Brown, John	27
Beasten, Zebulon	18	Burke, Edmund	27
Bryson, John	18	Black, Jacob	28
Biddle, Levi	19	Blackistone, James	28
Bunting, Charles J.	19	Burd, John	28
Beaston, Charles	19	Brown, Hugh	28
Boree?, Samuel	19	Bowland, Abraham	28
Bartley, Barney	19	Brown, Joseph	28
Burns, Thomas	19	Booth, John	28
Buchanan, William	19	Biddle, Abraham	28
Bowlay, John	20	Burke, John	29
Beedle, Spencer	20	Barnett, John	29
Banan, George,	20	Bricks?. Christopher	29
Boyd, David	20	Brown, David	30
Benson, James	20	Beetle, Isaac	30
Barton, Philip A.	20	Buckworth, Charles	30
Bell, Thomas	20	Black, John N.	30
Bracther, Richard	20	Burnite, Samuel	30
Bivens, Charles T.	21	Bayham, William	30
Brown, Joseph	21	Biddle, Noble	31
Bolton, Joseph	21	Boulden?, James	31
Boulden, Reuben	21	Beaston, George	31
Bricison, Thomas	21	Buchanan, John	33
Beeks, John	22	Brown, Edmund	33
Beasten, Richard	22	Barroll?, Solomon	33
Bouldin, Nathan	22	Burnsides, Thomas	34
Bowen, Joseph	22	Booth, Henry	34
Beetle, Raymond	22	Badger, Charles, Jr.	34
Bayard, Joseph	22	Beetle, Thomas	34
Black, Robert	22	Boulden, Andrew	35
Burgoin, Caron	22	Brison, Thomas	35
Berry, James	22	Bennett, George	35
Bryan, John	22	Bennett, Enoch	35
Boulden, William	23	Bennett, Henry	35
Boyer, Thomas	23	Brady, Philip	35
Bateman, Jacob	23	Biddle, Frisby L.	35
Biddle, Isaac	23	Biddle, Thomas	35
Burllin, Samuel	24	Beetle, Tobias	35
Boulton, Joseph	24	Burkins, Jacob	35
Boulden, Joseph	24	Bailey, Floyd	35
Beaston, Charles	24	Brian, Joseph	35
Brumfield, Daniel	24	Biddle, Tobias	36
Blake, Nathan	24	Barnet, John	36
Bryan, Andrew	24	Brown, Allen	36

	Page		Page
Baker, Henry	37	Brown, William	48
Bohemer?, George	37	Boggs, James H.	48
Brumfield, William	37	Bristow, William	48
Boyd, Richard	37	Brumfield, James	48
Biggs, William	37	Bailey, Edward T.	49
Badger, Charles	37	Barnes, James	49
Bristow, Richard	38	Brickley, Jehorceium	49
Beetle, Lamuel	38	Biddle, John H.	49
Britanham, Thomas	38	Biddle, Uphres	49
Bayard, Stephen	38	Barrett, Andrew	49
Barnard, Parker	39	Bryan, Thomas	49
Boyd, Alexander	39	Boulton, William	50
Brown, Isaih	39	Bailey, Edward T.	50
Burris, John	39	Boulden, Richard	50
Brickley, John	39	Briley, Samuel	50
Ball, Henry	39	Buenes, Samuel	50
Badders, Sam	40	Bristow, Lewis	50
Brickley, Jehoiacim	40	Broughton, Henry B.	50
Benjamin, Isaac	40	Baker Jeremiah	50
Bowers, Benjamin	40	Boyd, Hugh	51
Bates, John	40	Brown, William J.	51
Boyd, Hugh	41	Brumfield, William	51
Boyd, Alexander	41	Bennett, William	51
Brisban, Henry	41	Boyd, Frances	52
Briscoe, John	41	Brown, William	52
Biddle, Andrew	41	Bostick, Samuel	52
Boyd, Hugh	42	Burden, Samuel	52
Boyd, Alexander	42	Barrett, Andrew	52
Brisban, Henry	42	Brickley, John	53
Briscoe, John	42	Brickley, Andrew	54
Biddle, Andrew	42	Burk, John	54
Blunkshawl?, Joseph	43	Brookings, Charles	54
Bowen, Benjamin	43	Bullen, Harrison T.	54
Bristow, William	43	Biddle, George	54
Bateman, Richard	43	Boulden, Thomas	54
Butler, James	43	Bouchelle, Thomas	54
Brown, Elisha	43	Bennett, Rudulph	54
Blunkshawl, Joseph	43	Black, George W.	54
Bowen, Benjamin	43	Baldwin, John	54
Bristow, William	44	Burnes, Henry	57
Bateman, Richard	44	Ball, Thomas	57
Butler, James	44	Blake, Soloman	57
Brown, Elisha	44	Bolton, John H.	57
Betts, Franklin	44	Beatty, Arthur	58
Barrett, Andrew	44	Beatty, William	58
Baker, James	44	Benjamin, John	58
Betts, Franklin	45	Bryan, Joel	58
Barrett, Andrew	45	(Barwick)?, William	59
Baker, James	45	Brumfield, Nathan	59
Barclay, Thomas	46	Benson, James H.	59
Beans, Jonathan	46	Buckwith, John Wesley	59
Beattie, Samuel, Jr.	46	Biddle, Lambert W.	59
Brown, James	46	Brown, Alexander	59
Boulden, Thomas	46	Baker, Simon	59
Burrows, John	46	Broadwell, William	60
Blake, Soloman	47	Boulden, George	60
Barclay, John	48	Brown, John	60
Bowdon, James	48	Brook, John	60
Biggs, Benjamin	48	Beaston, George J.	61
Burnite, David	48	Burnett, Richard	61
Bacum, James	48	Brumfield, John	61
Biddle, Spencer	48	Bullins, Stearns	61
Boulden, Samuel	48	Bulin, James	61

	Page		Page
Boulden, John	61	Bailey, James	66
Brumfield, Joseph	61	Biddle, Thomas A.	66
Buckworth, Charles	61	Biddle, William R.	67
Baldwin, John U.	61	Black, Diedrick H.	68
Bennett, Henry P.	62	Borum, Josiah	69
Brown, Joseph T.	62	Brown, Edmund	54
Biddle, Jacob	62	Brown, James	55
Barnes, John	62	Bruce, Charlie	55
Berlin, James	62	Barwick, John R.	55
Boulden, John	62	Brown, John	55
Brumfield, Joseph	62	Biddle, Raselan	55
Bernard, Parker	62	Bailey, Lloyd	55
Boulden, Levy	62	Bristow, William	56
Brown, John E.	63	Boyd, Enoch	56
Benson, Bebron	63	Boulden, Levi	56
Biggs, William	63	Burns, Jonathan P.	56
Bartley, William	63	Bouchelle, John	56
Biddle, Stephen	63	Boulden, Charles (N.C.Co.,Del.)	56
Bernard, Parker	63	Brown. John D. F.	56
Boulden, Levy	63	Boyd, James	57
Boulden, Nicholas	63	Brown, Mark	57
Biggs, William	64	Boulden, John (N.C.Co.,Del.)	57
Bartley, William	64	Brickley, William	57
Biddle, Stephen	64	Borland, Samuel	57
Barrett, John	64	Buckwith, Samuel	57
Boyd, William	64	Boyd, William (ChesterCo.,Pa.)	
Blackiston, William C.	65	Brown, William	57
Benjamin, Joseph	65	Bosie, Henry	69
Burnite, James K.	66	Barnaby, Elias P.	69
Benjamin, Thomas T.	66	Burris, Edward	70
Bradley, Joshua	66	Brown, Justus	70
Burgoyne, Caleb K.	66	Barr, Jethro	70
Benson, Joseph	66	Biddle, William	70
Briggs, Joseph	66		

C

	Page		Page
Cunningham, John	1	Crangle, James	4
Crouch, John	1	Collings, Jeremiah	4
Comegyes, Jessey	1	Cooper, John	4
Clements, Fergus	1	Cosgrove, Michael	4
Cother, George	1	Crage, George	4
Conner, James	1	Crouch, James	5
Cather, Robert	1	Carr, John	5
Craig, John	1	Comagys, William	5
Carpenter, Valentine	1	Crouch, Thomas	5
Campbell, Lliander	1	Crouch, John	5
Criswell, James	1	Cazier, Abraham	6
Crocket, Samuel	1	Carr, John	6
Cook, William	2	Cooper, Thomas	6
Coulter, Samuel	2	Chappell, John	6
Curtis, Francis, Esq.	2	Clark, Gideon	6
Cromwell, John	2	Cole, Elijah	7
Corcoa, John	3	Craig, John	7
Campbell, George Harvey	3	Conner, Thomas	7
Campbell, James	3	Cox, Benjamin	7
Coulson, Thomas, Jr.	3	Calvert, Robert	7
Carroll, Joseph	3	Cowardin, James	7
Crow, Andrew	4	Campble, Robert	8
Cummins, Timothy	4	Cazier, Abraham	8

Name	Page	Name	Page
Crouch, Edward	8	Christie, James	26
Creswell, Robert	8	Cameron, William	26
Campbell, Samuel	8	Cameron, Matthew	26
Craig, James	8	Cummings, James	26
Coudon, Samuel	8	Culvertson, John	18
Callender, John	8	Cunningham, Joseph	19
Caruthers, John	9	Crouch, Thomas	19
Campbell, John	9	Cantley, William	19
Casten, Andrew	9	Cannon?, John	20
Currier, Elijah	9	Crouch, Robert	20
Cooke, John	9	Culvertson, David	20
Cunningham, David	10	Comegys, William	20
Cosden, Jeremiah	10	Crouch, John	21
Cox, Peregrin	10	Cummings, David	21
Currier, Jonathan	10	Culiy, George	21
Craig, Alexander	10	Cook, Robert	21
Crouch, Robert	10	Cox, Emery	21
Cossett?, Nathaniel	10	Coppin, John	22
Caldwell, Robert	10	Craige, Benjamin	22
Conner, Morton	10	Collins, Patrick	22
Couch, William	10	Cleaver, Nathaniel	22
Chick, Peregrine	11	Cunningham, David	22
Crouch, John Daw	11	Cashner, John	23
Ceal, Nicholas	11	Coale, John	23
Carty, John	11	Cameron, James	23
Chambers, John	12	Cannon, Moses	23
Cather, William	12	Cannon, Moses	26
Cord, William	12	Carruthers, John	26
Crouch, John	12	Colmary, James H.	27
Chandley, John	12	Coudon, Samuel	27
Cooper, Nathaniel	12	Cox, Thomas	27
Crouch, William	12	Chalk, Joseph	27
Cochran, William	12	Crofford, Joseph	28
Campbell, John	13	Carson, Robert	28
Coale, William	13	Carley, Charles	28
Cuddick, Daniel	13	Churchman, Ezra	28
Cazier, John	13	Craig, Benjamin	28
Campbell, William	14	Clark, William	28
Cosden, Alphonse	14	Cook, James	29
Cunningham, Joseph	14	Cannady, Moses	29
Croscon, Daniel	14	Calloway, John	29
Collins, Peter	14	Crouch, Edward	29
Clayton, Richard	14	Cox, Elias	29
Crawford, John	14	Craddoche, Benedict	29
Counsel, Samuel	14	Creswell, John	30
Chew, Nathaniel	15	Cork?, Thomas	30
Craig, Nathaniel	15	Cox, Peregrine	30
Craig, William	15	Curl, William	30
Chandlee, John	15	Cummings, Joseph	31
Chandler, Frances Bellow	15	Cather, Robert	31
Crookshanks, John, Jr.	15	Cunningham, David	31
Creswell, Robert	15	Conrad, John	31
Cully, Levi	15	Childs, Levi	31
Chambers, Nicholas	16	Craig, William, Jr.	31
Cay?, Alexander	16	Coudon, Joseph	32
Clark, Thomas	16	Clark, John	32
Cameron, Robert	16	Clark, Henry	32
Clark, Thomas	25	Coudon, Thomas W.	32
Creswell, John	25	Craig, James M.	32
Culvertson, Thomas	25	Chesney, James	32
Comby, William	25	Cloney, James	17
Cochran, John	25	Crozier, Thomas	17
Couson, James	25	Claypool, Septimus	17

	Page		Page
Opsden, Benjamin	17	Coudon, Joseph	44
Comegys, John	17	Chamberlaine, Joel	45
Carson, Robert	17	Carter, Robert	46
Coale, Samuel	17	Carruthers, John L.	46
Carpenter, John	18	Coale, Philip	46
Crow, William	18	Churchman, David	46
Cosden, Edward	18	Cummings, James	46
Clark, John	23	Cox, Noble	46
Clark, Charles	24	Carter, Cloud	46
Cloud, Enoch	24	Crowle?, Alexander	46
Calhoun, Thomas	33	Crouch, Samuel	46
Currin?, Jeremiah	33	Chandlee, Sydney	46
Cosgrove, Hugh	33	Craig, Richard	47
Cross, Andrew	33	Calvert, John	47
Coulson, Eli	33	Calvert, Thomas	47
Cooper, John	34	Cameron, William	47
Clark, George	34	Craig, James	47
Carter, John	34	Cameron, Thomas W.	47
Conrad, Jacob	34	Carpenter, William	47
Conway, William	34	Copes, John	47
Cosgrove, William	34	Coolin, William	48
Craig, Levi	35	Cruikshanks, John	48
Cameron, Robert	35	Cameron, John	48
Cook, Jason	35	Clayton, Thomas	48
Chamberlain, Henry	36	Cloud, Enoch	48
Chambey?, James	36	Clark, John	48
Cilloney, Alphonse	36	Crokshanks, John	48
Clausen, William	36	Comegys, Alphonso	49
Connelly, John	36	Carll, James	49
Carol, James	36	Carter, John D.	49
Crow?, Andrew	37	Crothers, James	49
Carretson, William	37	Campbell, John B.	49
Currier, James	37	Cameron, John	50
Craig, Levi	37	Cummings, Samuel	50
Clark, Stephen	38	Cooper, John	51
Curry, William	38	Campbell, William	51
Carratt, James L.	38	Caldwell, John	51
Cully, Thomas	38	Clark, Samuel	51
Collins, Lawrence	39	Cooley, Corbin	51
Crawford, James	39	Craig, Philip	51
Clendenin, Samuel	39	Crouch, John F.	51
Cullough, Samuel M.	40	Cameron, John Thomas	51
Coleman, Henry E.	40	Colmery, William	51
Chilson, Waters	40	Crouch, Samuel	51
Crouch, Stephen	40	Clendennin, Arthur	52
Cannon, Moses N.	40	Chambers, Benjamin B.	52
Carroll, Thomas	40	Cantwell, John	52
Cray, John	40	Conegan, John	52
Collis, John	41	Conlin, William	52
Coolie, John	41	Cazier, John	52
Crookishanky?, Reece	41	Campbell, John	52
Cooper, John	41	Clark, Arthur	53
Currier, Victor	41	Cray, Samuel	53
Cochran, George W.	41	Cameron, William	54
Crookishanky?, Reece	42	Curry, Alexander	54
Cooper, John	42	Clayland, Samuel R. (Kent)	54
Currier, Victor	42	Cox, Benjamin	54
Cochran, George W.	42	Cleaver, John	55
Cameron, John C.	43	Cloud, Caleb W.	56
Carpenter, Richard	43	Carter, Joseph	56
Coudon, Joseph	43	Clark, Nicholas	56
Cameron, John C.	44	Currier, Richard	56
Carpenter, Richard	44	Crouch, James	56

	Page		Page
Chesbrough, Isaac M. (Bal. Co.)	56	Caulk, John	63
Cameron, Eli	57	Cormer, James	63
Cooper?, John Evans	57	Crouch, Isaac	63
Caton, Thomas	57	Cochran, Joseph W.	63
Cloud, Charles T.	57	Cantwell, Robert	63
Cole, George M. (Cecil Co., Md.)	57	Caulk, John	63
Carter, James	57	Cormer, James	63
Cole, George M.	57	Crouch, Isaac	64
Clark, Abraham	58	Cooper, James	64
Campbell, William	58	Cox, Jeremiah	64
Conlyn, William	58	Cazier, Thomas C.	64
Carman, Henry	58	Cox, Isaac H. R.	64
Cunningham, John	58	Campbell, James	64
Cannon, George W.	59	Cochran, Thomas J.	65
Conlyn, James	59	Cunningham, Thomas	65
Crouch, Charles H.	59	Calvert, William	65
Craig, John	59	Cooper, James	65
Conelkin, John	59	Cox, Jeremiah	65
Crookshank, Frances B.	60	Campbell, James	65
Crawford, Thomas	60	(Cazier), Thomas C.	65
Crow, William	60	Camblin, Andrew	66
Cameron, Amos	60	Cowan, Benjamin C.	66
Conley, William	60	Cameron, William	66
Crookshank, Thomas	60	Cranmer, Joseph S.	66
Colmerry, Cyprus	60	Croncer, Benjamin	67
Conekin, John	61	Craig, Victor	67
Clendennin, Daniel	61	Craddock. Joseph	67
Coe?, Rouce	61	Clark, John	68
Cummings, Amos	61	Chambers, Benjamin B.	68
Coale, Joseph	61	Cunningham, John	69
Cannon, John	62	Coulson, John F.	69
Cordray, Isaac	62	Campbell, Samuel	69
Clark, Isaac	62	Chick, Joseph	69
Cathers, David	62	Carter, Joseph	69
Cummings, Amos	62	Craig, George W.	69
Cochran, John W.	63	Cochran, John C.	69
Cantwell, Robert	63		

D

	Page		Page
Dempsey, Denis	1	Davis, John	16
Dougherty, Aelxander	2	Dennis, John	16
Dawson, William	4	Donaldson, Robert	25
Davis, James	4	Donathy, John	25
Daugherty, James	5	Davis, Richard L. Dr.	25
Devine, Peter	5	Davis, John	26
Dennis, John	6	Derickson, Zacharias	26
Davis, John	6	Devenport, John	28
Dawkins, Greenbury	7	Damsell, William	29
Dickey, Joseph	7	Devlin, John	29
Dawson, Nathaniel	8	Dysart, James	29
Douglas, James	9	Davis, William	29
Dobson, Adam	9	Davidson, William	29
Durgin, John	10	Dixon, Jonas	29
Davis, Richard	10	Dennis, Benjamin	29
Dougherty, Edmund	10	Death, Randal	30
Duffey, John	11	Dixon, George	30
Dobson, George	11	Dixon, John	31
Donal, John	13	Dixon, Thomas	31
Duke, William Rev.	13	Dowland, Hezekiah	32
Davis, Joseph	14	Davis, Joseph	32

	Page		Page
Davis, David Dr.	32	Davidson, Robert	45
Davis, Joseph	32	Davis, Samuel	47
Davis, William	18	Davidson, Edward	47
Dickey, David	22	Davis, Morris	47
Deween, William	23	Daily, George	48
Davidson, George	24	Davis, Wm. H.	49
Dennison, Simon	24	Davis, Stephen	50
Davis, George	33	Davidson, George	50
Death, John	33	Dennison, William	51
Davis, Noble	34	Dupellee, Antorie	52
Devlin, Owen	35	Dean, Richard	53
Deer, Thomas	35	Dennison, William	54
Davis, John	35	Deal, George	54
Davidson, John	36	Denney, John	54
Denny, John	37	Dechan, Samuel (N. Cas., Del.)	55
Davis, Joseph	37	Davis, James	56
Davis, Benjamin M.	37	Davis, Samuel	56
Davidson, Robert	37	Davis, George	56
Dorsey, William E.	38	Dunbar, Justus	57
Dacey, William	39	Duhamell, Robert James	58
Dixon, Thomas	40	Drummond, James H. L.	58
Dorsey, William E.	40	Dolby, Nathan	58
Davis, William	40	Davis, John	58
Dougherty, Patrick	4J	Davis, George	59
Dennison, Joseph	43	Duaule?, James Wesley	59
Dougherty, Patrick	44	Dillahunt, John J.	61
Dennison, Joseph	44	Davis, Richard	61
Donohoe, Stephen	44	Donaldson, William B.	62
Donaldson, William	45	Davis, John	63
Donohoe, Stephen	45	Dyke, Arthur	64
Dorr, Leonard	45	Davidson, Thomas J.	69
Donaldson, William	45		

E

	Page		Page
Etherington, John	2	Etherington, John W.	26
Evans, Amos	3	Ethrington, Joseph	28
Edge, William	3	Everon, George	28
Ely, Maland	3	Egner, Jacob	28
Everson, Evert	5	Etherington, John	28
Epson, Thomas	5	Egner, Mathias	31
Evans, James, Jr.	6	Ewing, Elihu	32
Ewing, Amos	6	Elliott, Henry	32
Etherington, Bartholemew	6	Eliason, Ebenezer	18
Ewing, Robert	6	Evans, William	18
Etherington, Spencer	8	Ellis, William C., Dr.	19
Eagon, Solomon	9	Ewing, William	20
Ewing, Patrick	9	Ewing, Putnam	20
Evans, Richard	10	Eliason, Elizah	21
Ewing, John	11	Evans, John, Jr.	21
Eliason, Elijah	12	Evans, Israel	22
Ellsbury, Fredrick	12	Evans, James	22
Ewing, Robert	13	Etherington, Spencer	23
Edwards, Veazey	14	Egan, Andrew	24
Empson, Cornelius	14	Evans, John	24
Evans, Thomas	14	Edmunson, David	33
Egner, Peter	15	Evans, Robert	33
Egner, John	15	Evans, James	34
England, Jacob	16	Ehillipy, (Phillips)?, Levin	37
Etherington, John	25	Eainter?, Jacob	37

	Page		Page
Etherington, William	38	Evans, Joel	56
Ewing, Samuel	39	Ellis, Rowland	56
Ewing, Joh nL.	40	Ewing, James	57
Egan, Andrew	41	Ewing, Amos	57
Egan, Andrew	42	Emmons, Caleb	58
Ewing, Patrick	46	Ellis Francis A.	59
Evans, John	46	Ewing, John	59
Evans, John	46	Evans, Edward	60
Egner, Jacob	46	Epp, John	60
Evans, Levi H.	48	Edmundson, Caleb	61
Evans, Jesse	49	Edmundson, Thomas	61
Eliason, Jeremiah	49	Earnest, Fagin	61
Evans, Thomas	51	Etherington, William Z.	61
Edmundson, William	52	Earnest, Lagan	62
Elliott, Benjamin	53	Evans, Samuel	67
Evans, George	53	Edmundson, Caleb	67

F

	Page		Page
Ferguson, Thomas	2	Foard, William	32
Fisher, John	3	Fox, Gilbert	17
Forrester, George M.	3	Fulton, James	17
Foster, Francis	3	Foster, Thomas	17
Field, William	4	Ferguson, John	18
Foster, James	4	Fox, Philip	19
Fagan, James	5	Foard, Charles	19
Foster, William	6	Ford, Thomas	20
Farris, William	8	Ford, Charles	20
Ford, Hezekiah	8	Faytor?, John	21
Finley, John	8	Ford, William	21
Fulton, John	9	Fulton, David	22
Ford, Richard	10	Ferguson, Thomas	23
Foard, George, Jr.	10	Fowler, Henry	23
Frem ,Joseph	11	Ford, Levi G.	24
Fulton, James	11	Frances Macey	24
Foster, William	11	Ford, William	24
Ford, James	12	Ford, Lambert	24
Fowler, George	12	Foster, Isaac	24
Fulton, William	12	Foster, Nathan	24
Feddis, Jonothan	13	Frank Nicholas	33
Fitcher, John	13	Farr, David M.	34
Foster, Jesse	14	Fatman, James	34
Farias, James	14	Fisher, John	35
Fulton, David	14	Foster, George	37
Fisher, John	15	Freeman, Samuel H.	37
Fordain, John	15	Fulton, David	38
Fullam, Walter	15	Flintham, Richard	38
Fox, Philip	16	Fulton, George	38
Frazirr, James	16	Fee, Robert W.	38
Ferguson, William	16	Foster, Thomas	39
Ford, Joseph	16	Fee, Robert W.	40
Farris, William	16	Flintham, Richard	40
Foard, Josiah	16	Ford, George	41
Foard, John	25	Ford, George	42
Foy, Patrick	25	Foster, Harmon	43
Ferguson, Hugh T.	26	Foster, Harmon	44
Fulton, Hugh	28	Foster, Jesse	44
Fulton, James	28	Foster, James	44
Foard, John	29	Fritt?, Baker	45
Farrow, Nathan	30	Foster, Jesse	45
Fox, John	31	Foster, James	45

	Page		Page
Fisher, John	45	Ford, James	55
Frist, Baker	45	Fisher, Samuel	55
Fairbank, James	45	Finnegan, Patricious	55
Faris, James	45	Fillingame, Richard	56
Fisher, Thomas	46	Ferguson, William	56
Ford, John	47	Ferguson, William	57
Ford, Richard	47	Ferguson, Benjamin	57
Foard, George	48	Fury, James	57
Freeman, Samuel	49	Ford, James	58
Fillingame, John	49	Ford, Stephen H.	60
Ford, John	49	Freeman, Damuel	60
Flinn, Morris	50	Fleck, Jacob	60
Freize, Noah	50	Freeman, John Wesley	61
Ferguson, William	50	Faulkner, Robert	61
Forman?, James	50	Ford, Edwin D.	62
Ferry, John O.	51	Falls, Elmer	62
Ford, Edward B.	51	Fowler, Benjamin P.	62
Foard, John	53	Fisher, Andrew	64
Foard, Hezikiah, Jr.	54	Foard, Jeremiah	66
Foster, Harmon	54	Foster, Elisha	67
Foster, Thomas, J.	54	Fight, Lewis	70

G

	Page		Page
Grear, Isaac	1	Griffith, David	15
Gibson, William	2	Gonce, Rudolph	16
Gonce, Daniel	2	Gordon, Empson	16
George, John	3	Gillespie, George	25
Gallaher, Thomas	3	Guytor, Clement	25
Graw, William	3	Graham, Zachariah B.	26
Gorrole, Thomas	3	Griffith, John	26
Gilchrist, Robert	3	Gillespie, George	26
Greiner, George	4	George Sampson	27
George, Sidney	4	Gainor, Barnaby	27
Gibson, Robert	5	Gonell, John	27
Gearvis, Ephraim	5	George, Stephen	28
Griffee, John	5	Grimes, Joseph T.	29
Glasford, Harry	5	Gillespie, James	30
Glasgow, Robert	6	Gilmore, David	30
Grimes, William	6	Gatts, Samuel	31
Gilmoure, Samuel	8	Grievy, Edward	31
George, Joshua	8	Greenwood, Jonathan	31
Ginna, John	8	Gillespie, Frances	32
Gibony, Alexander	9	Gilpin, John	17
Galoway. John	9	Gillespie, James	17
Grace, William	10	Gribbon, Henry	18
Grant, John	10	Gaddiss, William	18
George, Sidney	10	Gay, Samuel	18
Grant, James	10	Groome, John Dr.	19
Gatchell, Jacob	10	Garrett, William	19
Groves, Jacob	11	George, John	19
Greig, William	11	Gillespie, John	19
Gillespie, Daniel	11	Gottier, John	19
Grant, Hugh	12	Gray, John	19
Griffeth, James	12	Guy, William	20
Geers, Benjamin Benson	13	Gracie, Edward	20
Gordon, Andrew	13	Groves, William	20
Gears, John	14	Gatchell, David	20
Gillmore, David	14	Gonce, Rudolph	20
Glasgow, Jonothan	14	Gordon, Andrew	21

	Page		Page
Graham, Peter	21	Gillespie, Robert	51
Gatchell, Elisha	21	Gibson, William	51
George, John	22	Goleober?, Francis	51
Goodwin, Peter	23	Gamble, John	52
Greenwood, Peregrine	24	Grace, William	52
Gray, Zachary	24	Gillespie, Daniel	53
Galaher, William	33	Grady, Robert	53
Griffee, Richard	33	Green, William	53
Grist, William	33	Gilmore, David	53
Gibson, Joshua	33	Gatchell, Henry E.	53
Genness, Samuel	33	Grant, George	53
Grace, Alexander	34	Garrett, Thomas	53
Garrett, Thomas	35	Gallaher, John	53
Galloway, Robert	35	Gibson, Joseph	53
Gorrell, James	35	Greer, Joseph	54
Greenwald?, Joshua	36	Gary, Robert	54
Grace, William	36	Grant, George	54
Garrett, John	36	Gillespie, Samuel	54
Goforth, John	37	Gillespie, Jonathan	54
Grant, John	37	George, Nicholas	55
Gillespie, James	37	Graham, John H.	55
George, John, Jr.	38	Griffee, Richard	55
Gamble, John	38	Gillespie, William	55
Gifford, William	39	Gordon, Francis	55
Gorrell, William	39	Grant, William	55
Galbraith, James	39	Giles, Thomas	56
Grant, Joseph	40	Graham, William E. G.	56
George, John Jr.	40	Groves, Richard	58
Grubb, Joseph	40	George, Nicholas	58
George, John Sr.	41	Gilpin, Henry H.	58
George, John, Sr.	42	Graham, John	58
Gibson, Andrew	42	Gilbreath, Andrew J.	59
Garrett, Samuel	43	Giles, William B.	59
Gibson, Andrew	43	Gaw, Henry L.	59
Garet, Samuel	44	Greenwood, Alexander	59
Grant, Joseph	44	Gurlie, Joseph	60
Girvan, John	44	Gillespie, James	60
Gamble, John	44	Gallaher, Moses	60
Gamble, John	45	Gilmore, Robert W.	61
Garvin, John	45	Glenn, William C.	62
Grant, Joseph	45	Golden, Nicholas	62
Garrett, William	46	Gainor, Thomas	63
Grace, John	47	George, James H.	63
Graham, William	47	George, James H.	63
Gonce, George	47	Green, Samuel	64
Gillespie, Samuel	48	Gallahan, John W.	64
Gothris?, John	48	Gottier, Francis B.	65
Garrison, Andrew	49	Grace, Samuel	65
Gilmore, David	49	Green, Lemuel	65
Gallaway, John	49	Getty, James	66
Gilpin, Isaac H.	50	Girvin, James	66
Grant, Seborn	50	Gallalier, John T.	66
George, Joseph	50	Gilmore, Nathaniel	67
Gibbs, Edward B.	50	Green, William P.	69
Grant, William	50	Gay, Samuel, Jr.	69
Glenn, Elias B.	50	Gillespie, Samuel	69
Glean, John	50	Gears, Hyland	70
Gottier, Frances B.	51		

H

	Page		Page
Heroston, William	1	Hinchman, Adam	13
Hugg, William	1	Hey, Robert	13
Hill, John	1	Hiller, Frederick	13
Hukill, Peter	1	Hersey, Benjamin	14
Hollingsworth, Henry	1	Heath, Richard Key	14
Hayes, Richard	1	Hartshorn, Benjamin	14
Hopkins, Robert	1	Holden, Isaac	14
Harwood, Robert	1	Hendrickson, Hyland	14
Horn, Thomas	2	Hall, Richard	15
Hauson, Thomas	2	Hall, Andrew	15
Hooper, Isaac	2	Hall, Isaac	15
Hylan, Isaac	3	Hyer, Lewis	15
Hart, Robert	3	Hasson, John	15
Hollihan, John	3	Hossinger, Peter	15
Hoery, Vachel	4	Hinckey, Charles	16
Hukill, James	4	Hodgson, William	16
Hall, William	4	Higgins, David	16
Hukill, Jess	4	Hitchcock, John	25
Hamelton, Robert	4	Hessey, Harthsel	25
Hoyt, Thomas	4	Harris?, Joseph	25
Hall, Richard	5	Hollingsworth, William	25
Hair, Stephen	5	Hendrickson, Joseph	25
Hamilton, John, Jr.	5	Hyland, John	26
Humphrey, William	5	Hamilton, William	26
Hugg, Benjamin	6	Harlan, Joshua	28
Hendrick, Phillip Anto	4	Harlan, Lewis	29
Howell, William	7	Hemptton, Samuel	29
Hodgson, Richard	7	Hukill, William	29
Hynson, Peregrine	7	Hayes, Robert	29
Hutchman, William	7	Hyland, Nicholas	19
Hamm?, Noble (Harmon)	8	Howard, Thomas	19
Hartshorne, John	9	Hindman, Robert	19
Hall, Andrew	9	Hicks, John	19
Holt, Abraham	9	Hildwal, Robert	19
Harding, Reuben	9	Harding, Peter	19
Holladay, John	9	Hedency, George	19
Hairs, David	9	Harkness, Samuel	20
Hall, John	9	Hollen, John	20
Hughes, Andrew	9	Hayes, William	20
Harvey, Archibald	9	He'mstarff, William	21
Holmstoaff, William	9	Holt, Joseph	21
Hodgeson, Jonathan	9	Harvey, Francis	21
Hottham, Spencer	10	Husband, Harmon	21
Hill, David	10	Haltham, Jesse	21
Hill, George	10	Howard, John	22
Hemphill, Joseph	10	Hague, Michael	22
Hincky, Charles	10	Hall, Richard	22
Hukill, John	10	Hanna, Edward	22
Harris, Nathan	10	Hasson, John	22
Homes, William	11	Hyland, Jacob	22
Hood, Samuel	11	Henderson, John	29
Howard, William	11	Hyland, Sampson G.	29
Henry, James	11	Hyland, Thomas	29
Huddabuck, John	11	Hellough, John	30
Haywood, Robert	12	Hasson, Alexander	30
Huston, William	12	Hayes, James	30
Hill, James	12	Hayes, Joel	30
Henderson, David	12	Harry John	30
Hukill, Henry	12	Hitchcock, Robert	31
Hyland, Samuel George	13	Hyland, Johnson	31

	Page		Page
Henderson, John	32	Henderson, Frisby	41
Hill, Richard	32	Hitchcock, Elisha J.	41
Hendrickson, Peregrine	32	Hitchcock, Elisa J.	42
Hyland, Nicholas C. of Edward	32	Henderson, Frisby	42
Daveris, David	32	Henderson, Andrew	43
Harlan, Joseph	17	Hayes, Manlove	43
Hanson, Nathan	17	Hayes, George	43
Hindman, John	18	Henderson, Andrew F.	43
Harkness, Samuel	18	Hayes, Manlove	44
Hartley, Charles William	18	Hayes, George	44
Hendrickson, Joseph	18	Hurlock, Ebenezer	44
Hukill, Richard	18	Hukill, William	45
Hayes, Henny	22	Hart, James	45
Hamill, Roger	23	Hurlock, Ebenezer	45
Hodgson, Arnold	23	Hall, Peter	46
Hyland, Samson G.	23	Holt, Isaac	46
Harlan, Joseph	23	Holden, Cogle	46
Howell, Enos	23	Hutton, William	47
Hill, Samuel	23	Hornes, John	47
Holt, Jesse	23	Hall, Robert	47
Holt, Jesse	24	Hill, James	47
Hukill, Richard	24	Holton, Thomas	47
Handy, George D.	24	Hannah, Samuel	48
Hyland, Stephen	33	Hayes, George	48
Hawkins, Reuben	33	Hall, Jesse	48
Harris, John	33	Howard, George	48
Huett, Samuel	33	Hevelow, Roderick	48
Hendrick, Dan	33	Hayes, James	49
Horner, James	34	Hamab?, Stephen	49
Hogg, Samuel	34	Hill, Levi	49
Huttan, John	34	Herbert, James B.	50
Haveim, Stephen	34	Hall, Joseph	50
Holt, Andrew	34	Heath, John	50
Harding, Philip	34	Holland, Thomas	50
Hart, Robert	35	Harris, Samuel	51
Holliday, Jesse	35	Hogg, William	51
Hyland, Joshua	35	Hutson, William	51
Hudson, James	35	Hayes, Samuel	51
Hyland, Nicholas	35	Howard, Jacob C.	52
Hinds, George	36	Hollingsworth, William	52
Hughes, Edward	37	Hall, Samuel	53
Hackett, William	37	Harlan, Joseph	53
Hudson, Joseph	37	Hayes, Robert	53
Harlan, Lewis	37	Howard, Samuel	53
Hard, Abraham	37	Huggins, Andrew	54
Hudson, Joshua	38	Hogg, Robert E.	54
Hamilton, James	38	Hasson, Samuel	55
Hemhill, James	38	Henderson, John	55
Harvey, Andrew	38	Harvey, John	55
Holliday, John	38	Hyland, Stephen of W.	55
Hanan, John	39	Hayes, Thomas	55
Hart, Nicholas	39	Holden, Jacob	55
Hall, Lewis	39	Hollace, George D.	55
Hays, William	39	Holt, John W.	56
Hill, Elijah	39	Hudson, Richard	56
Hueston, John	40	Hayes, John	56
Humphreys, Charlie	40	Hacket, Joseph	56
Hudson, Joshua	40	Hayes, John	56
Hamilton, James	40	Hudson, William	57
Hewitt, William	41	Haines, George	57
Hewitt, Jacob R.	41	Hayes, Jedediah	57
Hewite, William	41	Hackett, William	58
Hewite, Jacob R.	41	Hayden, James T.	58

	Page		Page
Hackett, William D.	58	Howard, Thomas, Jr.	63
Hyland, Joshua	58	Huids, Williams	63
Hindman, Samuel	58	Hessey, Samuel	63
Hyland, Stephen of Stephen	58	Heckart, J.	63
Hepbron, James	58	Huids, (Hinds?) William	64
Hodgson, Stephen	58	Holland, William	64
Hyland, Johnson	59	Huggins, John Thomas	64
Hall, Richard	60	Hassan, William	64
Hall, Josiah	60	Hesse, William S.	64
Harris, Wilder	61	Hessey, Samuel	64
Hannah, Joseph	62	Haines, John	66
Hagany, John B.	62	Hagan, David	67
Hamilton, Hugh	62	Hinds, Thomas	69
Hayes, Robert, Jr.	62	Hasson, George W.	69
Hyland, Edward H.	63		
Hulton, William	63	Hague, Michael	69
Hindman, Robert N.	63	Hart, Robert	70

I

	Page		Page
Irvine, Christopher	3	Israels, Peter	20
Ireland, Nathan	8	Ireland, Nathan	21
Irwin, Robert	12	Iler, John O.	36
Israel, Isaac	16	Iler, Edward	42
Irvine, Jesse	28	Iler, Edward	43
Ireland, John	30	Irvin, James	45
Israel, John	32	Inskip, John S.	63

J

	Page		Page
Johnson, Elisha	1	Jackson, Thomas	32
Jones, William	2	Joyce, Joseph	17
Jobe, Morrico	2	Jackson, Tilghman	18
Jeneas, Elias	3	Janes, Thomas	19
Jennings, Jacob	5	Johnson, Samuel	19
Jones, William	6	Jones, Isaac	20
Jackson, John	6	Jones, Noleto	20
Johannah, Lewis	7	Johnson, Levi	20
Jones, Thomas	7	Johnson, Robert	21
Jefferys, William	8	Jackson, Edward	21
James, John	10	Janney, James	23
Jacob, Thomas	10	Jones, Thomas	33
Jaquet, Jesse	12	Johnson, John	33
Jones, Jacob	13	Jones, John	33
Johnson, Simon	15	Jarekind, John	33
Jackson, James	16	Jones, James	34
Johns, Brinton	25	Jenkins, Philip	35
Johnson, John	26	Johnson, James	35
Junior, John Ward	26	Johnson, John M.	35
Johnson, Jonathan	27	Jackson, John	35
Johnson, Josiah	27	Jones, Richard	36
Jones, Edwarr I.	27	Joennans?, John	36
Johnson, John	28	Johnson, Jethro	36
Jackson, Hugh	28	Jones, Robert	36
Jennings, John	29	Jones, John	36
Johnston, John	30	Johnson, Samuel	36
Joyce, Joshua	30	Jones, Thomas	38
Jester, James	32	James, William	38

	Page		Page
Jones John Ward	38	Jackson, John	52
Jackson, Robert	38	Jamar, Henry	52
Jones, John	38	Johnson, Benjamin F.	55
Janney, Jesse	40	Johnson, William	55
James, William	40	Johnson, John A.	55
Jackson, James	40	Jackson, Samuel	56
Johnson, William	41	Jilton, Daniel N.	56
Janney, Eli	41	Jones, Aquilla	57
Jamison, William	41	Jester, Isaac B.	58
Johnson, William	42	Jackson, Philip	58
Janney, Eli	42	Jackson, Henry	59
Jamison, William	42	Jackson, James	59
Johnson, John	43	Jacob, Cyrus H.	59
Jones, Charles	43	Jackson, Victor	59
Johnson, John	44	Janney, Thomas	59
Jones, Charles	44	Jones, Benjamin W.	60
James, John	45	Joyce, George H.	61
Jackson Samuel	45	Jones, James	61
Jones, Hugh	45	Jackson, John W.	62
Janney, John	46	Jones, James	62
Jackson, William	46	Jenniss, David	63
Jones, Phineas	46	Jester, John	63
Johnson, Samuel	47	Jenness, David	64
Jack, William	48	Jester, John	64
Jarvis, Francis	48	Jones, Lewis	64
Jester, Outoix?	48	Jamar, James H.	64
Jones, William	49	Jamar, Reuben D.	66
Jackson, Edward	49	Jague, William	67
Jordon, John	50	Jackson, Charles W.	69
Jennis, David	50	Johnson, Jacob	69
Johnson, Isaac	50	Jarvis, James	70

K

	Page		Page
Kirk, Garrett	1	Kankey, Stephen	15
Knight, John	1	Kirkpatrick, John	16
Kennedy, Phillip	2	Knight, George	16
Kilpatrick, Samuel	2	King, Matthew	17
Kenb?, Thomas	2	Kidd, James	17
Kidman, S. James	2	Kearn, John	18
Kirk. John	2	Kile, John	18
Knox, Robert	3	Kankey, Zebulon	18
Killon?, William	5	King, John, Dr.	18
Kirk, James	6	Kirk, John	19
Kinney, William	7	Kirk, Elisha	19
Keinksly, Samuel	7	Kirkpatrick, Robert	19
Kirk, Abner	8	Keatley, Richard	21
Kirk, Felix	8	Kirk, John	22
Kirk, Elijah	9	Keathly, Henr	22
Kankley, Harmon	9	Klinton, John W.	25
Keysen, James	10	Kelly, Thomas	26
Kirk, John	10	Kearns, John	27
Kelly, Thomas	11	Knight, Emmor	27
Kelly, Ebenezer	11	Kirk, Abner	28
Kirk, Levi	12	Keene, Manley	30
Keathley, William	12	Kerr, Robert	31
Kidd, John	12	Kepling, Richard H.	31
Kimball, Titenleades	14	Kelley, Charles	31
Knight, Reuben H.	14	Keathley, Jonathan	32
Keatley, Thomas	14	Killiman, John	32
Kirkpatrick, Samuel	15	Knight, Thomas	33

	Page		Page
Kirk, Allen	34	Kelly, Hugh	53
Kirk, Levi	34	Kirk, Levi	54
Kidd, George	34	Keeler, Richard	54
Kirk, John	35	Kirk, Alexander	54
Knock, Benjamin	36	Keatly, John	55
Kerr, Samuel	38	Knight, John T.	55
Kenhead, George	38	Knapp, Ambrose	56
Kerr, Robert	39	Keatley, William	56
Kerr, Samuel	40	Knight, James	58
Knight, William	41	Kimble, Henry	58
Knight, William	42	Kidd, John	59
Kirk, George W.	45	Killy, Daniel	59
Kirk, George W.	45	Keech, Aaron	59
Kilgor, William	46	Kelly, Thomas	60
Keatley, Henry	46	Kirkpatrick, James	60
Kirk, Rowille	47	Kirk, William	62
King, William	49	Kelly, Edward	62
King, Hugh	49	King, Francis	64
Keetley, Joseph	52	Kennard, Thomas	65
Keetley, William	52	Killingtonworth, Oliver	66
Kidd, Andrew	52	Keatley, Francis	66
Kinkead, John	53	Knotts, Thomas	67
Keath, John	53	Keatley, Richard	69
Kidd, James T.	53	Kinkead, John	70
Keeck, Aaron	53		

L

	Page		Page
Layhua, John	1	Lowry, James	12
Lewis, Richard	2	Leavey, Moses, Esq.	12
Lark, Joseph	2	Logue, William	15
Lasly, George	2	Lasselle, William	15
Ladd, Samuel	4	Leviason, Haines	16
Lusby, William	4	Lackey, Thomas	16
Lockerman, Vincent	5	Lyons, Bartholomew	16
Lauferty, Jackson	5	Leech, Thomas	25
Livingston, Alexander	5	Lynch, Peregrine L.	25
Latham, Aaron	5	Lomax, James	25
Linton, William	5	Lusby, John	25
Lasley, John	5	Lochard, Robert	26
Little, James	5	Linton, John	26
Lewite, Robert	6	Lum, Jacob	26
Lyon, Robert	5	Logan, William	26
Lee, John	5	Lochtan, Nathan	27
Lynch, John	5	Lusby, Robert	27
Lyons, Bartholomew	5	Lowe, Henry	27
Leather, William	7	Lancaster, Sinclair	27
Lowrey, William	7	Lum, Michael	27
Lowrey, Elijah	7	Lorte, Isaac	28
Lackland, Jeremiah	7	Lusby, William	28
Lisby?, Thomas	7	Leech, Robert	28
Lewis, Robert Veasey	8	Leech, William	30
Lynch, John	8	Lewis, Thomas	30
Loag, William	8	Langdon, Peter	31
Labesvine?, John	9	Louhan, John	31
Latham, Robert	10	Lightner, George W., Esq.	32
Lashu, John	11	Luster, Edward	32
Longe, Ephraim	12	Lloyd, Frisby P.	32
Lacky, Thomas	12	Lockerman, John	17
Lloyd, Frisby	12	Lucus, Abraham	17

	Page		Page
Leslie, Jeremiah Larkin	18	Lowery, James	51
Lobes?, Daniel	19	Lusby, William	52
Lewis, Edward	20	Lusby, Gideon	52
Lake, James	21	Landces, George	52
Little, John	22	Lotman, Nicholas	52
Lowrey, James	22	Little, Christopher	52
Logan, Thomas	23	Lockard, John	53
Latman?, Jacob	23	Logan, Hazlet	53
Lancaster, Isaac	23	Lloyd, Peregrine F.	53
Low, William	23	Lynch, Hasson	53
Lum, Isaac	24	Little, Adam	54
Little, Christopher	24	Lancaster, Joh n	54
Lewis, Thomas	33	Logan, William	55
Lester, Edward	34	Lake, Reuben	55
Lynch, John	34	Lottman, Lavi	55
Logan, Robert	34	Leavis?, William	55
Lum, John	35	Lewis, William	56
Lusby, Nioholas	35	Little, John	56
Lusby, John of Thomas	36	Lynch, William	57
Lynch, Andrew	37	Levis, Norris	57
Little, Samuel	37	Lockard, David	57
Lackland, Nathan	37	Leonard, Thompson	57
Lusby, John	37	Lloyd, Peregrine F.	58
Lee, Elicy?	38	Lloyd, Peregrine F.	58
Leslie, George	39	Lewis, Robert	58
Luning, Philip	39	Lake, Thomas	59
Lightmer, John	41	Lyon, James	60
Lynch, James	41	Lum, Isaac A.	60
Landsborough, William	41	Lutton, Robert	60
Lourey, John	41	Lowe, Ephraim P.	60
Lusby, Robert A. C.	42	Lockard, John P.	60
Lightner, John	42	Logan, Samuel	61
Lynch, James	42	Lotman, Levi	61
Landsborough, William	42	Lewis, Edward B.	61
Lowery, John	42	Lynch, Hasson	62
Lusby, Robert C.	42	Logue, William	63
Lowe, Thomas	43	Leverson, Richard	63
Langdon, Giles T.	43	Logue, William	63
Lowe, Thomas	44	Layman, Firman	64
Langdon, Giles S.	44	Littaway, Lewis	64
Linden, James	44	Lum, Nicholas	64
Linden, James	45	Landeris?, Robert A.	65
Lister, Edward	46	Lum, Sampson	66
Logue, James	46	Lusby, Thomas	67
Latham, Enoch	46	Logan, Thomas	67
Little, William	49	Lynch, John W.	67
Lunney, James	49	Lloyd, Nicholas	67
Little William	50	Lee, Richard	68
Lewis, George	50	Logan, Thomas	69
Logan, Samuel	50	Lambson, Joseph	69
Lake, Reuben	51	Lusby?, John	70
Lowey, William	51		

M

	Page		Page
McCutcheon, John	1	McBride, James	2
Morris, Samuel	1	Miller, William	2
McCloud, John	1	Moss, Joseph	2
McKinley, Charles	1	Miller, John	2
McIntier, Archable	2	McTwilley, James	2

	Page		Page
McGowne, Hackery	2	Maffitt, Charles	12
McToy, John	2	Mullet, Peter	12
McMun, Alexander	2	McCorkal, James	12
Manley, Teasey	2	McBride, James	13
Meray, John	3	Makin, John	13
McCullough, James	3	Matthews, John	13
Moloney, Morie	3	Manley, William	13
Metcalf, Curtis	3	McNail, Aaron	13
Marquis, John, Jr.	3	Mehaffey, Rowland	13
Mercer, James	3	McCullough, Samuel	13
Morrow, Robert	3	McIntire, William	14
Mackey, William	3	MaGee, James	14
Mackey, John	3	Mercer, John	14
McKeney, Brice	3	McCoy, William	14
McKeown, John	4	McClure, James	14
Miller, Henry, Jr.	4	McHaffey, Edward	15
Mofill?, Thomas	4	Milligan, John	15
Matherman, John	4	Mercer, Edward	15
McCauley, Robert	4	Miller, Thomas	15
McClay, John	5	Mercer, James	15
McCollum, James	5	McClure, James	15
McCollan, Samuel	5	McCreary, Wililam	15
Martin, John	5	McClure, Richard	15
McCleland, Nathaniel	6	McCracken, John	15
Money, Isaac	6	Meloney, Lantz	16
Mahaffey, Hugh	6	McCullough, William	16
Mitchell, Edward	6	McNeil, John	16
Mackey, James	6	McKenney, Benjamin	16
Marquiss, Samuel	6	McCrea, Samuel	16
Mackey, James	6	Mansfield, Richard	16
Montgomery, Dr. John H.	7	Miles, Peter	16
Milburn, Nicholas	7	McGrath, William	16
Meekins, Joshua	7	Murphy, Owen	25
McClain, Andrew	7	Money, Jesse	25
McCoy, John	7	Matthews, Thomas	25
Marquis, David	7	Munnigan, James W.	25
Mauldin, William	8	McCauley, Henry	26
McDowell, Thomas	8	Morgan, James	26
McDowell, William	8	McCray, Elijah	26
McGill, Samuel	8	McVey, Benjamin	26
Moore, Pasmore (Meve)?	8	McCoy, John	27
McCormick, Robert	8	McClenahan, John	27
McVey, John	8	Maslin, John	27
McGinnas, James	9	Morrison, Alexander	27
Miller, Lewis	9	Miller, Henry	27
Manley, John	9	McVey, Jamy?	27
Miller, Richard	9	Mather, George	27
McKinsey, Benjamin	10	McCray, Charles	28
Montgomery, Samuel	10	McCauley, John	28
Moody, Alexander	10	Moody, Thomas	28
Montgomery, Hugh	10	Moore, William	28
McDonnell, Alexander	10	Mackey, Thomas	28
McElwee, Samuel	10	McCormick, James	28
Morrison, Alexander	11	McKinney ———	29
Manley, Nicholas G.	11	McVey, Nathan	29
McVeigh, Edward	11	Mercer, James	29
Moore, John	11	Moore, Isaac	29
Manley, James	11	McCoy, Samuel	30
Manley, John	11	McGowan, John	31
McDowell, William	11	McCoy, Hugh	31
Manley?, James	11	Mackey, William	31
McCoy, Henry	11	McLaughlin, David	31
McCrea, David	12	Marshall, Joseph	31

	Page		Page
Mahan, Stephen	31	McDowell, James	34
Milligan, William	32	Marple, Able	33
McClure, Christopher	32	Miller, Richard	35
McGregor, James	32	Morgan, William	35
Morgan, William	32	McCay, Benjamin	35
Matthews, James	32	McIntire, Thomas	35
McIntire, Thomas	32	Miller, William	35
Moore, William	17	M'Corkle, Archibald	36
McDermott, Charles	17	Maxwell, Charley	36
McCauley, Dennis	17	Merritt, John S.	36
Moans?, William	17	Murray, Charles	36
Maxwell, James	17	McIntire, Andrew	36
Miller, William, Dr.	17	McKenney, Samuel	36
Moody, Robert	17	Meekings, Benjamin	36
Meekens, Joshua	18	McCullough, James	36
Maston, Joseph	18	Matthews, James	36
Marrs, Samuel	18	Mingling, Isaac	37
Milligan, William	18	McLaughlin, Robert	37
McCoy, John	18	Mackey, William	37
McKinsey, Benjamin K.	19	McKenney, Daniel	37
Money, William	19	Mahan, William	37
Marshall, Henry	19	McCauley, James	37
McCracken, John	20	McGreedy, Enoch	37
Morgan, Evan	20	McClung, William	37
Miller, Thomas, Sr.	20	McCullough, Alexander	37
Manley, James	20	Megredy, Daniel	37
Moffett, John S.	20	McCraig, John	37
Millard?, James	20	Marus, Samuel	38
McCluser, Jonas	21	Matthews, William	38
McCreary, Joseph	21	Manley, John	38
McKay, Samuel	21	McKinsey, Benjamin	38
McCracken, James	23	Maxwell, John	39
McKelnay, William	23	McMullen, James	39
Melvolin?, Thomas	24	McDowell, James	39
McCullough, John	24	McIntire, John	39
Milburn, William	24	Mauldin, Zebulon	39
McIntosh, James	24	McKinney, John	39
McLaughlin, Thomas	24	McCray, Robert	40
McDowell, Samuel	24	Milburn, Levi	40
McKinney, Peter	24	Milburn, Benjamin	40
McKenney, Benjamin	33	MacKeunan, Hector	40
McCann, William	33	Matthews, William	40
McDonald, Cornelius	33	Mitchell, Abraham D.	40
McCoy, John	33	McKinney, John	40
McMullen, Thomas	19	Money, Alphonso	41
Miller, Thomas	22	Manley, William	41
Morford, Samuel	22	Money, Alphonso	41
McCracken, William	23	Marcus, John	41
Mitchell, John	23	Miller, Henry D.	41
Mahan, Richard	23	Mercer, John	41
Mullen, John	23	Miles, Amos	41
Mahan, Thomas	23	McClary, John	41
Morrison, George	23	Marcus, John	42
McCullough, Samuel	34	Miller, Henry D.	42
Morgan, Thomas H.	34	Miles, Amos	42
MaGaraty, James	34	Mercer, John	42
Marshall, John	34	McKinney, Stephen	42
Mauldin, Benjamin	34	Maklum, Robert	42
Meyers, William	84	McClary, John	42
Meyers, John	34	McCauley, Daniel	43
Marshall, Williams	34	Miller, Thomas	43
Morgan, James	34	Mahan, John	43
McCullough, Andrew	34	Moore, Harvey?	43

Name	Page
Macklum, Robert	43
McBride, William	43
McKay, James	43
McCauley, Daniel	44
Miller, Thomas	44
Mahan, John	44
Moore, Harvey	44
McBride, William	44
Miller, Samuel A.	44
Mathias, Joseph	45
Miller, Samuel R.	45
Mathias, Joseph	45
Moore, James G.	45
Manlove, John	45
Marnes, Able	45
McClary, Joseph	45
McCracken, James	46
Mahan, James E.	46
Moore, David	46
Millegan, Michael	46
McClelland, James W.	46
Miller, James	46
Montgomery, William	46
Miller, James	46
Mahan, George	46
Masten, Hezekiah	46
Martin, James	47
McMullan, Samuel	47
McWearles?, Robert	47
Moore, John	47
McCreary, Samuel	47
McIntire, Samuel	47
McCulser, John	47
McKnitt, Robert	47
Maller, Alexander	48
McGee, James	48
Mullin, Daniel	48
Murphy, John C.	48
McCrea, Jesse	48
Moore, Washington Edward	48
Maulden, Benjamin	49
Marnes, James	49
McKinsey, Benjamin	49
McKinsey, Tobias	49
Mercer, Benjamin	49
McCreary, Thomas	49
Miller, Joseph W.	50
McCrea, John	50
McNitt, James	50
McClay, Isaac	50
Maffitt, William H.	50
Murphy, Patrick	50
McGee, John	50
McCauley, Daniel M., Jr.	50
Marnes, Hugh	51
McMillan, Robert	51
McNeal, John	51
Mulholland, James	51
Mullen, Barney	51
Maxwell, Samuel	51
Moffitt, Thomas	51
McCue, Andrew	51
McCord, John	51
Maxwell, Allen	52
Marnes, Andrew	52
Morrow, James	52
Moore, George H.	52
Marcee, Joseph	52
Moore, Richard	52
Marshall, John	52
Martin, Henry	53
McIntire, John	53
Moore, William	53
McGee, Sylvester	53
McCall, John W.	53
McGilton, John F.	53
McKey, Lewis	54
Murphey, Nicholas	54
McCullough, John	54
Mercer, James N.	54
Morgan, John W.	54
Moore, William R.	54
McCracken, John	54
Morgan, Evan	55
Miller, Joseph	55
McCreary, John	55
Moore, Elijah	55
McConkey, Hugh, Jr., (Lan., Pa.)	56
McVey, James	56
Mathias, Jones	56
Murphy, Robert	56
Mayner, Roger	57
Merritt, Reece	57
McVey, Jonothan	57
McVey, Passmore	57
McClay, William	57
MeLean, Cornelius, Jr., (Bal., Co.)	57
Markee, John	57
Mayberry Ebenezer	57
McWee, Benjamin	58
Maxwell, James L.	58
Merritt, James	58
McCullough, Samuel	58
McClenahan, Ebenezer D.	58
Miller, John	58
McClain, John	58
McCrea, William	59
McCartney, John H.	59
Manley, Charles K.	59
McCullough, William	59
McCullough, William W.	59
Mauldin, John	59
Morrison, Arthur	59
Morris, Howard	60
McVey, Nathan	60
Morgan, Evan	60
McCauley, James	60
Martin, John	60
Moore, John James	61
Mitchell, Fredrick H.	61
Mewson, Joseph	61
Morgan, William P.	61
Moore, Elijah	61
McCauley, Daniel J.	62
Mahan, William P.	62
Miller, Benjamin	62

	Page		Page
Moss, William	62	McCrea, Joseph	66
Marnes, John	62	Mercer, William D.	66
Moore, Elijah	62	Morgan, James W.	67
Matkins, Samuel	62	Manley, William	67
McVey, John	62	Moffitt, Samuel	67
Marcus, Richard James	62	McCall, John	67
McVey, John	63	Moore, George W.	68
Marcus, Richard James	63	McMullan, Joseph	69
Markee, John	64	McClure, John	69
Mansfield, James	64	Mariner, Peter	69
Murphy, John	64	McCullough, Henry	30
Matthews, James	65	Miller, Thomas	30
Marshall, William	65	McCullough, Sanders	69
Mahany, Elisha	65	McClenahan, Josiah	69
Mears, John	66	Mahan, Reese	69
Miller, Richard	66		
Moore, William	66	;Mercer, George	70
Mahaney, William R.	66	Marnes, James	70

N

	Page		Page
Nowland, Gilbert	1	Nowland, Isaac	42
Neal, George	3	Nesbit, Samuel, Jr.	46
Nesbitt, Robert	3	Nesbitt, John	47
Nowland, James	4	NesBitt, Robert, Jr.	48
North (Worth?,) James	4	Norris, William	49
Newill, James	5	Nesbitt, Robert, Jr.	50
Neighy, Samuel	7	Nowland, Alfred C.	51
Nesbitt, Alexander	8	Noland, John	52
Nesbitt, Jonathan	8	Newland, Charles	52
Nowland, John	9	Niblock, John	52
Nevens, Joseph	9	Nicholas, Samuel	53
Nesbitt, Moses	13	Nowland, Benoni	54
Norris, Daniel	15	Nowland, Alfred	55
Nowland, Dennis James	15	Nichol, Andrew	55
Nuomee?, Michael	25	Nowland, Lambert D.	55
Newton, John	25	Naudain, Dr. James S. (N.C.C.,Dl.)	57
Nowland, James A.	29	Neville, Thomas	60
Nowland, James, Jr.	32	Nowland, Otho	60
Nowland, Sylvester	20	Nickle, James	60
Nixon, James	23	Nowland, William H.	62
Nickle, William	41	Neal, Thomas	66
Nickle, William	41	Nowland, Ebenezer W.	69
Nowland, Isaac	42	Nevens, Joseph	70

O

	Page		Page
Ore, John	4	O'Neal, Bernan	30
Orick, James	6	O'Donald, James	32
Owens, Stephen	7	Oldham, Jacob	17
Oar, Charles	7	Oglevas, John	17
O'Neal, John	9	Odonald, James	18
Oldham, Zebulon	13	Orr, Thomas	19
Oldham, Joseph	14	Owens, Stephen	19
Oldham, Levi	25	Owens, Benjamin	23
O'Hara, Edward	27	Owens, Samuel	24
Oldham, John	27	O'Donald, Daniel	24
Owens, Thomas	29	Owens, Stephen	24

	Page		Page
Oldham, Cyrus	33	Oldham, George W.	51
Orr, James	34	Onley, Patrick	52
Owens, Fredus	36	Orr, Nevin	58
Owens, Nathan	40	Oldham, Absalem	58
Otterson, Samuel	42	Owens, Hazelit	59
Otterson, Samuel	43	Orr, Andrew	59
Oldham, Elisha	44	Owens, John	61
Oldham, Elisha	45	Osborne, Thomas	61
Owens, Frances	46	Osborne, Theodore	62
Owens, Frances	51	Orr, James	69

P

	Page		Page
Phillips, Nathan	1	Penington, Edward	13
Pettit, Jacob	1	Price, Benjamin	13
Penington, Drake William	1	Parker, Joseph	13
Porter, Jesse	1	Price, Ephraim	15
Perry, James	1	Penington, Robert	15
Perry, Lewin	2	Pennington, William C.	16
Parsley, Edward	2	Phillips, Edward	16
Price, Lewis	3	Parkerson, Richard	16
Pearce, William	3	Piper, John	25
Pennington, John	3	Price, Benjamin	16
Phillips, Stephens	4	Philips, Isaac	27
Patterson, William	4	Postle, John	27
Pierce, (Price)? Jesse	4	Pearson, David	27
Phillips, John	4	Phillips, James	27
Piner, Nathaniel	4	Phillips, Samuel	28
Pearce, William	4	Pennington, Benjamin	28
Price, Andrew	4	Price, Nicholas	28
Pennington, Anthony	4	Plummer, Philip	28
Patterson, James	5	Pearson, Charles	29
Pennington, Joseph	5	Price, William	29
Parker?, William	5	Pearce, Joshua	29
Parizot, Nicholas	5	Patterson, Hugh	29
Price, Noble	5	Porter, James, Jr.	17
Pennington, Henry	5	Price, Hyland	17
Phillips, Nicholas	6	Pryor, Thomas	18
Pearce, Harry	6	Price, Spencer	18
Pearce, Henry	6	Price, John Hyland	18
Pennington, John	6	Pennington, Benedict	18
Pearce, Henry	8	Pearson, Nathan	18
Price, Thomas	8	Penington, Hyland Biddle	18
Price, Ephraim	8	Price, Thomas	19
Pippen, Samuel	8	Penington, Edward	19
Penington, John	10	Partridge, James	20
Partridge, Frances	10	Putts, William	20
Parker, Robert	12	Prower, John	20
Peterson, Henry	12	Patterson, William	20
Pugh, Humphrey	14	Pearce, Henry	20
Patterson, Moses	7	Price, Jacob	21
Pearce, Thomas	7	Porter, Edward	21
Price, Edward	7	Porter, Johnson	21
Patton, David	9	Patten, Thomas	21
Pennington, Robert	9	Peerie, John	14
Price, Edward	9	Porter, James B.	26
Pennington, Samuel	10	Porter, John	26
Parsley, Edward	10	Partridge, James	26
Pearce, Benjamin	11	Price, George	26
Patton, Thomas	11	Patterson, Alexander	26
Philips, Joseph	13	Puntney, John	30

	Page		Page
Phillips, Joseph	30	Price, Andrew	46
Phillips, Harmon	30	Patten William	46
Price, Benjamin	31	Purdy, William	47
Pennington, Thomas	31	Price, George W.	47
Penington, William	31	Price, Andrew	47
Palmer, John	31	Patterson, William	47
Penington, Henry	31	Perry, John	47
Parker, Isaac	32	Phillips, Joseph	47
Patterson, Henry	32	Penington, Edward	47
Patcher, Jonathan	32	Peters, John	48
Price, Benjamin	32	Price, William C.	48
Pennington, Joseph	17	Peters, William	48
Price, John	17	Pugh, James	48
Polke, James	17	Price, James A.	48
Prockton, Nathan	22	Price, William	48
Price, Thomas	22	Pearce, William	48
Pearce, William	22	Penington, Asasiah	49
Penington, Thomas	22	Price, Ambrose	49
Pennington, James	22	Patterson, Hugh	49
Pearce, William	23	Price, John V.	49
Pearce, Benjamin	23	Pennington, Abraham F.	50
Pearce, John	24	Procter, James	51
Polloch, Joseph	24	Pennington, James	51
Price, Samuel	24	Pitt, John B.	51
Price, Hyland	24	Paunell, William	52
Penington, Richard	24	Pritchard, James	52
Pennington, Benjamin	24	Price, John H.	53
Price, John	33	Price, Morgan	53
Pattison, William	34	Parker, Charles	53
Price, Nicholas	36	Price, John R.	54
Palmer, Levy	36	Price, Lewis	54
Palmer, Nickolas	36	Pearce, George R.	54
Patterson, William	36	Pearce, Edward	54
Price, Fredus	36	Pryor, William Henry	55
Pennington, Henry	36	Pantry, John	55
Porter, John J.	37	Powley, John E.	55
Penington, John	37	Perry, Samuel	56
Purnell, Greenbury	37	Pennington, Noble	56
Pierce, William H.	37	Price, Noble	56
Penington, John H.	37	Price, Jacob	56
Penington, Hyland J.	38	Pearce, Matthew C.	56
Penington, Robert	38	Pearson, Peter	56
Penington, John A.	39	Paunel,? William	56
Price, George	39	Price, William	58
Perry, William	40	Pennington, Robert	58
Penington, Elias	41	Phillips, William	58
Pugh, Joseph	41	Price, Thomas	59
Penington, Elias	42	Plummer, Richardson	59
Pugh, Joseph	42	Price, Albun	60
Price, Benjamin	43	Purnell, Greenbury	61
Price, David H.	43	Plummer, Philip C.	61
Pearce, Davidson D.	43	Pennington, John	61
Polk, John	43	Pennington, George	63
Price, Benjamin	43	Price, Christopher	63
Price, David H.	43	Physick, Edmund	63
Pearce, Davidson C.	44	Physick, William	64
Pope, John	44	Pearson, Eli	64
Penington, Elias	44	Phillips, Samuel	64
Penington, Elizas	45	Pennington, John B.	66
Price, William	45	Price, John	70
Penington, William C.	45	Pennock, Joseph	67
Peters, Joseph	46		

96

Q

	Page		Page
Quinsley, Levi	27	Quinley, Andrew	40
Quigley, Thomas	18		

R

	Page		Page
Ross, Frances	1	Robinson, John	16
Ross, Adam	1	Rawlings, James	16
Roberts, John	1	Rutter, John	16
Roberts, John	2	Reeley, William	16
Ryan, John	2	Ratcliff, Robert	25
Reynolds, John	2	Ricketts, William	25
Rich, Stephen	3	Ricketts, George	26
Reik, James	3	Roach, Elihu	26
Ramsey, Thomas	3	Rawlings, John	26
Russell, Thomas	3	Roberts, John	28
Rowland, Robert	4	Roach, Ira	28
Rogers, Elisha	4	Radley, William	30
Robinson, John	5	Roach, Thomas	31
Roberts, Morgan John	5	Robnat, Richard	32
Ricketts, John Thomas	5	Richardson, Joseph	32
Roberts, Robert	6	Ramsey, James	32
Reason, Joseph	6	Ruley, Benjamin	15
Robinet, Richard	6	Reynolds, William	27
Richardson, William	6	Ramsey, Samuel	27
Rutter, Isaac	7	Roach, John	27
Reese, George	7	Reynolds, Rubin	27
Roberts, Lewis	7	Reeves, William	29
Ruley, Seth	7	Rutter, Samuel	29
Rhea, George	8	Redman, William	29
Redgraves, Isaac	8	Rolliston, Charles	29
Ratliffe,? Robert	8	Remington, George	29
Rogers, Elijah	9	Rob, John	29
Russell, John	9	Ryland, Joshua	29
Richardson, Thomas	10	Runk, John	29
Roach, James	10	Richardson, Wm. G.	30
Ricketts, Reuben	10	Ryland, Fredy	30
Reed, John	10	Robinson, David	30
Ramsey, Nathaniel	11	Rutter, Moses	32
Reynolds, William	11	Riley, Benjamin	32
Rudulph, John	11	Robinson, John	32
Ryland, Peter	12	Ramsey, Charles	32
Rowbuck, William	12	Ruth Mathias	17
Robinett, James	12	Robins, James Bowdoin	17
Ramsey, James	12	Reily, Samuel	17
Reynolds, Joshua	12	Roberts, Thomas	20
Rutter, Joshua	13	Richardson, William	20
Roach, James	13	Rich, William	21
Ryland, Thomas	13	Roach, Thomas	21
Ruley, John	13	Rice, William	22
Reynolds, Francis	13	Ross, Moses	23
Rosback, Christopher	13	Rutter, Thomas	23
Rawlings, John	14	Richardson, John	23
Reagan, Hugh	14	Robinson, Fredus	23
Ricketts, John	14	Robinson, Thomas	23
Riggs, Daniel	14	Robinson, Aldridge	23
Reason, Joseph	6	Reed, Caleb	23
Richardson, William	6	Ruley, Michael	23
Roach, James	6	Roth, Samuel	33
Roberson, William	16	Robertson, William	33

	Page		Page
Ray, Jonothan	33	Roswell, Joseph	49
Roliston, William	33	Rutter, Thomas	49
Robinson, Richard	33	Rumsey, Moses	50
Rigs, Andrew	32	Ramsey, Andrew	50
Roach, Howard	32	Robertson, Robert	50
Rock, John	17	Reynolds, Benjamin	51
Reynolds, William	18	Robinson, Isaac	51
Redgrave, Isaac	18	Rutter, John	52
Rice, George	18	Roch, Frances	52
Rea, George	19	Riddle, Umphrey	52
Richardson, Daniel	19	Rielly, Michel	52
Roach, Philip	19	Roberts, Thomas A.	53
Richard, Aquillo	19	Ravick, John	53
Rigan, James	19	Robinson, William	53
Richardson, Joseph	24	Reece, Thomas	54
Russell, Thomas	24	Rider, William	54
Rudolph, Tobias	33	Reed, George	54
Richardson, William	34	Robinson, William	54
Redgrave, James	35	Rutter, James W.	55
Rutter, Charles	35	Reed, William	55
Robinson, William	35	Roberts, John	55
Rutter, Charles	35	Ruley, James	55
Roch, George	36	Ricketts, Joseph	56
Rowe, Thomas	36	Richie, Robert (N. Y. State)	56
Ricketts, Thomas	36	Rutter, Richard	56
Ryland, Joseph	37	Richardson, Joshua	57
Rutter, Charles	37	Rutter, William	57
Reynolds, Elisha	37	Reynolds, James R.	57
Reynolds, Elijah	37	Ross, Peter	58
Riggs, Daniel	38	Robinson, William	58
Rutter, Samuel	38	Reynolds, Caleb	58
Ruple, William	38	Reed, Thomas S.	59
Roberts, Samuel	39	Rogers, Thomas	59
Rayhnor, Dan	39	Reily, James H.	59
Ramsey, William	39	Richardson, John	59
Riddle, James	40	Ramsey, John	59
Rutter, Samuel	40	Rutter, John	60
Reynolds, Warren?	40	Richards, William	60
Richards, John	41	Rutter, John	60
Rarrick, John	41	Ross, Robert	60
Riggs, Andrew	41	Raisin, James	60
Russell, John	41	Russum, Francis	61
Richard, John	42	Reed, William	61
Ranick, John	42	Roach, Richard	61
Riggs, Andrew	42	Roe, William	61
Russell, John	42	Reed, William	61
Ryan, Joseph P.	43	Rickards, Wills	62
Reed, William	43	Rock, William	62
Richardson, Henry	43	Richards, Henry	62
Ryan, Joseph P.	43	Ruley, James	62
Richardson, Henry	44	Reed, William	62
Roach, James	46	Reed, Benjamin	65
Ryland, John	47	Richardson, William	66
Richardson, Joseph	47	Reynolds, Harry K.	66
Roddis, Isaac	47	Reagraves, Samuel	67
Raughley, John	47	Register, Wharton	67
Richardson, William C.	47	Rutter, William	67
Ryan, John P.	48	Riddle, John of William	68
Roberson, Tylus	48	Richardson, George Washington	69
Ruby, John	48	Ruley, Benjamin M.	69
Russell, James	49	Ratliff,? Robert	70
Reynolds, Isaac	49		

S

	Page		Page
Steel, James	1	Simcoe, George	14
Sheperd, John	1	Scott, John	14
Stoops, John	1	Severson, Hance	14
Stoops, William	1	Simpers, William	14
Sproutt, William	1	Sherer, James	15
Simpers, George	1	Swan, Robert	15
Severson, Benjamin	2	Smith, William	15
Smith, Michael	2	Sutton, David	16
Sandobersey, Richard	2	Stuart, James	16
Sulvan, John	2	Spencer, Nicholas	16
Stephens, Thomas	2	Steel, Hugh	16
Spear, James	3	Suppile, Henry	16
Sears, William	4	Smith, Joseph	25
Sappington, Benjamin	4	Smith, William	25
Sutton, Stephen	4	Scott, James	25
Stewart, William	5	Short, Jonathan	25
Sterrett, John	5	Sc—y, Augustine	25
Stoops, Philip	5	Stalkep, or Kup Andrew	25
Simpers, Jacob	5	Simpson, George	25
Smith, John	6	Songwell, Walter	26
Smith, Nathan	6	Shields, John M.	26
Simpson, Alexander	6	Smith, Benjamin	26
Sutton, John C.	7	Sewell, Lambert	26
Sears, John	7	Scott, Thomas	26
Savin, Edward	7	Stephenson, John	26
Simpson, Thomas	7	Smith, Fisher	26
Sappington, Benjamin	7	Sparrowgrove, John	26
Silvester, Benjamin	7	Slicer, John Thomas	26
Shields, William	7	Scott, Alexander	20
Stump, John	7	Smith, James	20
Smith, Robert	7	Slagle, Thomas	20
Smith, Anthony	8	Slagle, Thomas	20
Scott, John	8	Shattuck, Levi	21
Severson, Benjamin	8	Sloan, James	21
Simpers, Richard	8	Steele, James	21
Sappington, Thomas P.	8	Sprorten, Thomas	21
Stevenson, James	9	Sluyter, Benjamin	21
Simpers, John	9	Scoll, (Scotten) Abner?	21
Spencer, Henry	9	Savin, Richard, Sr.	22
Sutton, Robert	9	Smith, Thomas	22
Springer, James	10	Stokes, Edward	22
Shaw, Thomas	10	Severson, Peregrine	22
Simms, James	11	Smiley, Robert	22
Savin, William	11	Sappington, John	22
Springer, Joseph	11	Shepherd, William	22
Sharp, William	11	Sluyter, Harry	23
Severson, Thomas	11	Sterling, Isaac	23
Smiley, William	12	Scott, John	24
Savin, Edward	12	Smith, William	24
Short, John	12	Simpers, Thomas	27
Simms, Robert	12	Smith, John	27
Simm, James	12	Spence, John	27
Swesey, David	12	Stevenson, James	27
Steel, Allen	13	Sturgeon, Alexander	27
Springer, Peter	13	Slaughter, William	27
Smith, John Wheeler	13	Sappington, Thomas P.	27
Savin, Peregrine	13	Smith, Andrew	27
Smith, Robert	13	Spence, Henry	28
Sulivan, John	13	Smith, John	28
Smith, Frances	13	Simpers, Henry	28
Swesey, Amos	14	Smith, George	28

	Page		Page
Scott, Thomas	28	Stubbs, Eli	43
Short, Adam	28	Severson, Samuel	43
Scott, Moses	29	Slack, Amos	43
Simpson, Richard	29	Stevens, Adam	43
Stephens, Jacob	29	Sappington, Asbury	43
Sewell, James	29	Stubbs, Eli	44
Stephens, Thomas	29	Severson, Samuel	44
Smith, William	30	Slack, Amos	44
Stewart, Robert A.	30	Stevens, Adam	44
Stewart, William	30	Sappington, Asbury	44
Simpers, Thomas	30	Stebbings, George	44
Stalcup, John	30	Smith, Thomas W.	45
Scott, John	30	Stebbings, George	45
Shaw, Thomas	31	Smith, Thomas W.	45
Shaw, John	31	Sterling Ephraim	45
Sappington, John	31	Short, Jeremiah	46
Shirkey, James	31	Sutton, Robert	46
Smith, Joshua	31	Simpers, Jesse	46
Simmons, Laurence	31	Sumplin, James	46
Seo,? George	32	Simpers, John	46
Short, David	32	Simpson, Henry B.	47
Stephens, Jacob	32	Severson, Hance	47
Steele, Thomas	17	Sneakinburgh, John	47
Sullivan, Henry	17	Sampson, John	47
Sewell, Wm. E.	17	Stites, Henry S.	47
Short, John	18	Spence, William	47
Springer, David	18	Segars, Frances	47
Standley, Robert	19	Siles, Owin	48
Short, David	19	Scarborough, Joseph	48
Stall, Joseph	19	Sargeant, Benjamin	48
Stedham, Henry	24	Sample, Samuel C.	48
Sorret, Joseph	24	Scott, Moses	49
Smith, Henry James	33	Shockley, Levin	49
Sutton, John	33	Sumption, John	49
Shank, Jacob	34	Stanton, William	49
Simmons, Elisha	34	Stewart, Joseph Henry	49
Short, William	35	Satterfield, John M.	49
Scott, John	35	Smith, Eber	50
Stradley, Thomas	35	Simpers, Nathaniel	50
Swift, Richard	36	Sumption, Joseph	50
Swift, Richard	36	Strawbridge, Joseph	50
Simpson, Ebenezer	36	Short, John	51
Smith, Robert F.	36	Smith, Nicholas	51
Simpers, Jonothan	37	Slack, Amos	51
Scott, James	37	Steigal, William	51
Simco, William	37	Smith, James	52
Standley, George	38	Severson, Samuel	52
Simpers, Richard	38	Shannon, George	53
Smith, Cornelius	38	Simpers, Henry G.	53
Simpers, Richard	38	Smith, Samuel	53
Scarborough, John	38	Steele, Jeremiah	53
St—, John	39	Scarborough, Watson	54
Simco, William	39	Skerven, Thomas W.	54
Simpers, John	39	Stoops, Joseph T.	54
Stoops, Augustus	39	Steel, Caleb	54
Smith, Samuel	40	Simpers, David	54
Simpers, Richard	40	Segers, Reuben	54
Smith, Cornelius	40	Simpers, William	54
Smith, Richard	40	Simpers, John E.	55
Smith, William	40	Slack, John, (Balto., Md.)	55
Steel, David	41	Severson, Samuel	55
Simpers, William	41	Sidwell, Isaac U.	55
Steele David	42	Simmons, James	56
Simpers, William	42	Steel, John	56

	Page		Page
Staples, Samuel W.	56	Severson, Richard	64
Stites, Henry S.	57	Slagle, Fredrick	64
Savin, William F.	58	Shelley, William	64
Simpers, John T.	58	Shockley, James	64
Sherer, William	58	Smith, Joseph W.	64
Scott, William	58	Sweeney, James	65
Shafer, John	58	Shelby, William	65
Stradley, Samuel	59	Sweeney, James	66
Scott, Jacob	59	Spence, William	66
Stewart, Seth	59	Stradley, William	66
Stephens, Thomas K.	60	Snowden, William H.	67
Smith, Stephen	60	Stradley, John W.	67
Strout, Arthur M.	60	Scarborough, Joseph	67
Stump, John	60	Stull, Daniel	67
Simpers, Jesse	60	Stalcup, William	68
Scott, Joseph	61	Scotten, William	68
Simpers, Thomas	61	Stalcup, James	68
Stradley, Thomas	61	Sweet, Benjamin	69
Snow, Israel	61	Simpers, Richard L.	69
Scott, James	62	Sturgeon, Thomas	69
Smith, Levi	62	Sluyter, Benjamin	70
Spence, William D.	62	Short, Adam	70
Sherwood, Horatio N.	62	Smith, Richard	70
Smith, Joseph W.	63	Savin, Dr. Richard L.	70
Sherwood, Horatio N.	63		

T

	Page		Page
Thackery, James	1	Tyson, Jonah	31
Trew, James	1	Todd, Edward	31
Thomas, William	1	Tyson, Thomas	32
Taler, Walter	2	Thompson, John D.	17
Thomas, Richard	2	Tyson, John	17
Two Lee,? Ephraim	3	Taylor, William	18
Trimble, Thomas	3	Tull, David	20
Teague, Luke	4	Tipton, Nathaniel	20
Taylor, Thomas	5	Thompson, John	20
Turner, Isaac	5	Thompson, Ingry	20
Thackery, William	5	Tigard, Peter	20
Terry, William	5	Turner, George	21
Theason, John	6	Tyson, Benjamin	21
Taylor, Moses	8	Tyson, Nathan	21
Taylor, William	9	Thompson, John	21
Tarnly,? John	10	Thomas, Benjamin	22
Todd, William	11	Taylor, Isaac	23
Thompson, James	11	Thomas, Lewis	24
Thompson, John	11	Taylor, Thomas	33
Todd, Lancelott	11	Taylor, John	34
Thomas, Edward	11	Taylor, John	35
Thomas, Isaac	12	Taylor, Thomas	35
Turner, Andrew	13	Thomas, Joseph	35
Taggart, Alexander	14	Thomas, Benjamin	36
Tilden, Edward	15	Todd, John	36
Templin, James	15	Tyson, Jacob	36
Thompson, William	15	Tyson, Isaac	38
Tolan, John H.	16	Tyson, Mathias	38
Thackery, John	25	Turner, John	38
Tyson, Nathan	27	Tyson, Levi	38
Turner, George	27	Terry, Tazea?	38
Thompson, John	29	Thompson, James	39
Tosh, William	30	Thomas, William	39

	Page		Page
Thomas, Lewis	39	Thompson, Samuel	56
Tyson, Matthias	40	Townsend, William N.	56
Turner, John	40	Turner, John D. (N. Cas. Co., Del.)	56
Thompson, William	40	Teague, Albert R.	57
Taylor, John L.	41	Thompson, David	57
Thomas, Thomas	42	Terrell, Timothy M.	57
Taylor, John S.	42	Tatman, Bayard	58
Thomas, Thomas S.	42	Taylor, Abraham	58
Taylor, Ferdinand	43	Turner, George	59
Tatman, John	43	Thornton, Benjamin W.	60
Taylor, Isaac	43	Tyson, John	60
Taylor, Ferdinand	44	Tatman, Jesse	60
Tatman, John	44	Tosh, Samuel	60
Tayolr, Isaac	44	Tuffree, John	60
Torbert, William	44	Thompson, Ezekiel	61
Torbert, William	45	Tyson, William	61
Thompson, John	45	Thackery, Robert	62
Todd, James	46	Tuffree, Joseph	62
Tyson, Nathan	47	Terbit, William B.	62
Thomas, Samuel	48	Taylor, John Wesley	62
Thompson, Samuel	49	Tarburton, John W.	63
Thompson, Andrew	49	Thomas, John E.	63
Taylor, Samuel	50	Thompson, Robert	64
Terry, Myron	51	Tyson, Joseph	64
Templeman, Henry	52	Tull, Frisby	65
Thompson, William	53	Tippett, Samuel	65
Taylor, Thomas	53	True, Frisby	66
Todd, Levi	53	Tipton, William W.	66
Trimble, Isaac	53	Thackery, Thomas	66
Thomas, Alfred B.	54	Tosh, James	66
Thomas, Richard	55	Tyson, Samuel	67
Taylor, David	55	Tosh, John	67
Thompson, John	56	Thompson, George W.	69
Taylor, Reuben	56	Thomas, Alfred B.	69
Tigna, John	56	Tucker, David	69
Tamany, William	56	Terrell, Joseph T.	69
Taylor, William	56	Todd,? James	70

U

	Page		Page
Underwood, John	11	Updegrave, Jose	60
Updegrove, Jesse	39		

V

	Page		Page
Veasey, William	2	Vallindan, John	29
Vanhorn, Jacob	3	Vandegrift, John	31
Vansant, Garrett,	4	Vansant, Nathan	31
Veasey, Noble	4	Veazey, Noble	32
Veasey, Thomas Brooks	4	Vaunce, James	32
Veasey, Ezekiel	5	Veitch,? Charles	19
Veasey, William	5	Vanhorn, Dennis	20
Veal, Pearce	13	Vansant, Cornelius	22
Veazey, Edward Henry	14	Veasey, Lambert	24
Veazey, James	15	Veazey, Thomas	33
Vansant, Daniel	15	Varriluden, Jacob	34
Vandagrift, Nicholas	25	Veazey, John Dr.	35
Veazey, Stephen	25	Vansant, Daniel	36
Veazey, Joseph	28	Vandegrift, Christopher	38

	Page		Page
Veazey, Thomas B.	39	Venort, John	51
Veitch, John	39	Virtue, Robert	52
Veazy, Benjamin	40	Vandever, Benjamin	53
Vint, John	40	Vandegrift, Nicholas	55
Vansant, Joshua	43	Veal, James	59
Vansant, Joshua	43	Vinsinger, William	61
Vinhekle, Charles C.	46	VanDyke, Thomas L.	63
Veazey, Edward	47	Veazey, Joseph W.	65
Vandegrift, John	48	Veach, Yadock	66
Virtue, John	49		

W

	Page		Page
Wood, Jacob	1	White, Solomon	13
Watch, John	1	Works, William	13
Watt, John	1	Wallace, Joseph	13
Wroth, James	2	Wills, Joshua	13
Work, Alexander	2	Woolsey, George	14
Ward, William	2	Ward, Joshua	14
White, Seward	3	Wardell, John	14
Work, William	3	Whann, William	14
Wood, John	3	Wilcox, Isaac	14
Whittam, William	3	Wheeler, John	15
Wallace, Robert	3	Wilson, James	25
Whitaker, Ralph	4	Wilkinson, Adam	25
Walsh, George	4	Watson, Isaac D.	25
Walmsley, Benjamin	4	Willox, Andrew	25
Walmsley, Robert	4	Watson, Thomas	25
Ward, John	5	Wilson, Robert	26
Wallace, David	5	Wimble, John	26
White, Abner	5	Watts, Ebenezer	26
Ward, William	6	White, Joseph	27
Willy, William	7	Welsh, William	27
Williams, Archibald	7	Whann, David	27
Williams, Robert	7	Woodall, William	28
Ward, John	7	Wilkinson, Robert	19
Wallace, Adam	8	Williams, Thomas	20
Willy, Allen	8	Wilson, Benjamin	20
Waters, Wilson	8	Wright, John	20
Wilson, Andrew	8	White, Frederick	20
Walmsley, Robert, Jr.	8	Whartz, Richard	20
Williams, John	8	Walmsley, George	21
Wilson, Andrew	9	Whan, William	21
Winchester, William	9	Watkins, Gassaway	21
Wagner, Joseph	9	Wilkinson, Adam	21
Werkfield, George	9	Walker, Joseph	21
Walmsley, Thomas Kimball	10	Wilcox, William	21
Wrothwell, Joseph	10	Wallace, John	22
Willson, Levi	11	Winstandley, William	22
Walmsley, Thomas	11	Willson, George	22
Willey, James	11	Wappleton, Thomas	22
White, Jonothan	11	Williams, John	23
Walmsley, Robert Coudon	11	Winchester, William	23
Willson, William	12	Wright, Robert	23
White, David	12	Walsh, Robert	23
Willson, Joseph	12	Willson, James	23
Walmsley, Thomas	12	Wilson, Alexander	23
Wingate, Edward	12	Williams, Thomas	28
Walmsley, Thomas	12	Ward, Peregrine	29
Ward, William, Sr.	12	Warden, William	69
Whittam, William	13	Whitaker, James	69
Wilson, Frances	13	Wells, George W.	69

	Page		Page
Wirt, Samuel	29	Wells, Ebenezer	42
Willson, Samuel	29	Wright, Daniel	42
Wall, David	29	Watson, Abraham	42
Ward, William	30	Williams, Robert	42
Watson, Robert	30	Wimble, Joseph	43
Wingate, James	30	Winate, Peter	43
Whiteside, Thomas	30	Wimble, Joseph	44
Winchester, William	31	Wingate, Peter	44
Walker, William	31	Wilson, George	44
Wilson, George	32	Wilson Andrew	44
Wilson, William	32	Wilson, George	45
Wilson, Jacob	32	Wilson, Andrew	45
Wingate, Edward	18	Work, Henry	46
Williams, Abraham	18	Williams, Samuel	47
Williams, Robert	18	Walmsley, George	47
Williams, Joseph	18	Whitelock, Edward	48
Wallace, Samuel	18	Williamson, Samuel	48
Wingate, Thomas	19	White, Nicholas	48
Williams, Alexander	19	Watson, John	49
Wallace, James	19	Wilson, George	49
Wilcox, Jacob	19	White, John	49
Wood, John	23	Wilson, William W.	57
Waggener, William	24	Wright, John	57
Wilson, Jacob	24	Watson, Silas (H. Ches. Co., Pa.)	57
White, Thomas H.	24	Weaver, George C.	57
Weight, James P.	33	Wright, Lewis	57
Whitelock, John	33	Wooley, George E.	58
Whitelock, John	33	Woodrow, Henry	58
Williamsm, Jesse	33	Woolehand, Jacob	58
Watson, Thomas	33	White, Thomas	58
Williams, Levi	34	West, John T.	59
Wallace, Thomas	34	Woodrow, Stephen	59
Wirt, John T.	34	White, Clinton J.	59
Willerston, James	35	Williams, Green	59
Woods, Samuel	35	Walmsley, John K.	59
Winchester, John	35	Wilson, Alexander	59
Wilson, Edward	36	Wilson, Isaac	59
Wright, Samuel	37	Wroth, John	60
Wiley, John	37	Wood, Enos T.	60
Walmsley, John Y.	37	Walker, John	60
Wingate, Thomas	37	Wardell, Isaac	60
Willis, John	37	Walmsley, John	60
Warner, Francis A.	38	West, Thomas	61
Whitelock, Moses	39	Wilson, James	61
Wilson, George	39	White, Eli	61
Wallace, Charles	39	Watkins, Samuel	61
Whitaker, Abie	39	White, David	61
Wilson, John	39	Walmsley, Benjamin	62
Whitelock, Edward	39	Wherry, David	62
Wills, John	40	Walmsley, Robert	62
Warner, Francis A.	40	Wright, John	62
Woodrow, Benjamin	40	Whitelock, James	63
Wingate, Richard	40	Willard, James H.	63
Wright, Edward	40	Williams, William	63
Ward, William	40	Whitelock, James	63
Wiley, Nathaniel	41	Whitelock, Samuel	64
White, Eli	41	Williams, John	65
Wingate, John	41	Wilkins, John	65
Welch, Ebanizer	41	White, John	65
Wright, Daniel	41	White, Robert	66
Watson, Abraham	41	Wilson, John	66
Williams, Robert	41	Williams, Sylvester	67
Willy, Nathaniel	42	Wingate, Richard	67
White, Eli	42	Wood, Thomas	68
White, Eli	42	Ward, John	69

	Page		Page
Williams, John C.	50	Whitelock, Henry	54
Whitelock, Samuel	50	Wood, William Simmons	54
Williamson, James A.	50	Worth, Joseph	55
White, Jefferson W.	50	Walmsley, Benjamin	55
Were, Andrew	50	Wilson, William H.	55
Wingate, Thomas	51	Woodrow, Jeremiah	56
William, Samuel	51	Watson, William	57
Whitelock, Joseph	51	Wherry, John D.	57
Webb, Edward	51	Ware, Robert	70
Walmsley, Robert M.	52	Ward, William	70
Walton, James	52	White, John	70
Ward, Joshua	53	Wainick, William	70
Willey, Charles	53	Wilson, James	70
Wallen, Henry	53	White, James	70
Wooleyhan, Jacob	54	Wingate, Joseph S.	70
Wilson, Thomas	54		

Y

	Page		Page
Young, William	2	Young, Thomas	17
Young, Robert	4	Yoemans, Thomas	21
Young, James M.	28	Young, John	22
Young, George	28	Young, Robert	37
Young, William	28	Yoemans, John	52
Yoeman, Thomas	12		

Z

	Page
Zanes Jonathan	69

www.ingramcontent.com/pod-product-compliance
Lightning Source LLC
Chambersburg PA
CBHW071625170426
43195CB00038B/2134